The Reverend Albert Cleage Jr. and the Black Prophetic Tradition

Rhetoric, Race, and Religion

Series Editor: Andre E. Johnson, University of Memphis

This series will provide space for emerging, junior, or senior scholars engaged in research that studies rhetoric from a race or religion perspective. This will include studies contributing to our understanding of how rhetoric helps shape race and/or religion and how race and/or religion shapes rhetoric. In this series, scholars seek to examine phenomenon from either a historical or contemporary perspective. Moreover, we are interested in how race and religion discourse function rhetorically.

Recent Titles in This Series

Reverend Albert Cleage Jr. and the Black Prophetic Tradition: A Reintroduction of The Black Messiah
By Earle J. Fisher

Rhetorics of Race and Religion on the Christian Right: Barack Obama and the War on Terror
By Samuel P. Perry

Rhetoric, Race, Religion, and the Charleston Shootings: Was Blind but Now I See
By Sean Patrick O'Rourke and Melody Lehn

Rhetoric and the Responsibility to and for Language: Speaking of Evil
By Matthew Boedy

The Struggle over Black Lives Matter and All Lives Matter
By Amanda Nell Edgar and Andre E. Johnson

Desegregation and the Rhetorical Fight for African American Citizenship Rights
By Sally F. Paulson

Contemporary Christian Culture: Messages, Missions, and Dilemmas
Edited by Omotayo Banjo Adesagba and Kesha Morant Williams

The Motif of Hope in African American Preaching during Slavery and the Post-Civil War Era: There's a Bright Side Somewhere
By Wayne E. Croft

The Womanist Preacher: Proclaiming Womanist Rhetoric from the Pulpit
By Kimberly P. Johnson

Women Bishops and Rhetorics of Shalom: A Whole Peace
By Leland G. Spencer

What Movies Teach about Race: Exceptionalism, Erasure, and Entitlement
By Roslyn M. Satchel

Womanist Ethical Rhetoric: A Call for Liberation and Social Justice in Turbulent Times
Edited by Annette Madlock Gatison and Cerise L. Glenn

The Reverend Albert Cleage Jr. and the Black Prophetic Tradition

A Reintroduction of *The Black Messiah*

Earle J. Fisher

LEXINGTON BOOKS
Lanham • Boulder • New York • London

Published by Lexington Books
An imprint of The Rowman & Littlefield Publishing Group, Inc.
4501 Forbes Boulevard, Suite 200, Lanham, Maryland 20706
www.rowman.com

6 Tinworth Street, London SE11 5AL, United Kingdom

Copyright © 2022 The Rowman & Littlefield Publishing Group, Inc.

All rights reserved. No part of this book may be reproduced in any form or by any electronic or mechanical means, including information storage and retrieval systems, without written permission from the publisher, except by a reviewer who may quote passages in a review.

British Library Cataloguing in Publication Information Available

Library of Congress Cataloging-in-Publication Data

Names: Fisher, Earle J., 1978- author.
Title: The Reverend Albert Cleage Jr. and the Black prophetic tradition : a reintroduction of *The Black Messiah* / Earle J. Fisher.
Description: Lanham : Lexington Books, [2022] | Series: Rhetoric, race, and religion | Includes bibliographical references and index. | Summary: "Reverend Albert Cleage Jr. and the Black Prophetic Tradition probes the sermonic material in Albert Cleage Jr.'s groundbreaking book, The Black Messiah (1969) and explores how and what the book has contributed to the broader scope of Black Liberation Theology and Black religious rhetoric in the past and present"— Provided by publisher.
Identifiers: LCCN 2021038986 (print) | LCCN 2021038987 (ebook) | ISBN 9781793631053 (cloth) | ISBN 9781793631077 (paperback) | ISBN 9781793631060 (ebook)
Subjects: LCSH: Cleage, Albert B., Jr., 1911-2000. Black messiah. | Cleage, Albert B., Jr., 1911-2000. | African Americans—Race identity. | Jesus Christ—African American interpretations. | Black power—United States.
Classification: LCC E185.625 .C6224 2022 (print) | LCC E185.625 (ebook) | DDC 230.089/96073—dc23
LC record available at https://lccn.loc.gov/2021038986

To my mother Claudia, my wife Denise, my sister Teiryne, my son Jalen, all of my family, friends, colleagues in ministry and the academy, the Abyssinian Baptist Church (the Blackest Church in Memphis and Shelby County) and all who have helped shape my love of God, myself, Black people, and the Black Prophetic Tradition.

Contents

Preface		ix
1	Introduction	1
2	What *The Black Messiah* Offers Religious and Rhetorical Studies	27
3	A General Rhetorical Assessment of Albert Cleage's *The Black Messiah*	53
4	Albert Cleage's Epistle to Stokely (A Close Reading): The Rhetorical Relationship between Black Theology and Black Power	75
5	Brother Malcolm, Dr. King, and Black Power: A Close and Complimentary Reading	117
6	Conclusions: Building on and Beyond *The Black Messiah*	145
Bibliography		155
Index		161
About the Author		165

Preface

I accidentally stumbled upon Albert Cleage Jr. in 2012. I was preparing to develop a course called "Gangster Theology" while teaching in the Religious Studies Department at Rhodes College. I reached out to Dr. Randall C. Bailey and explained to him my concept for the class and asked for recommended resources. One of the books he suggested was the epic text, *Is God A White Racist*, by the late William Jones. Being a student of Black Liberation Theology and learning about James Cone and Dwight Hopkins while I was a M.Div. student at Memphis Theological Seminary, I thought I had a pretty good grasp on the development and determinism of Black religion, prophetic rhetoric, and the major personalities associated with them. I was wrong. I had been underexposed.

Jones's book unsettled me (in a good way). As I stared at his chapter entitled, "Black Christian Nationalism and Albert Cleage Jr.," what startled me the most was not the revolutionary theology and liberationist rhetoric by which Cleage was being presented and challenged) by Jones. It was that I had recalled making numerous statements that mirrored Cleage's convictions during my preaching and teaching sessions at Abyssinian Baptist Church in Memphis, TN. I began serving at Abyssinian in the spring of 2011. Finding Cleage's work in 2012 was a breath of fresh air and a wind of sacred fire. It was refreshing to know that I was not some isolated and marginalized voice within an echo chamber of hegemonic homilies and deradicalized religion.

I tabled my engagement with Cleage until I entered the Ph.D. program in Rhetoric and Communication at the University of Memphis in the fall of 2014. Having built an excellent relationship with my pastor and mentors—Drs. Frank Thomas, Valerie Bridgeman, Barbara Holmes, and Andre E. Johnson—I was able to build upon works that converged preaching, prophesy, and politics. Dr. Johnson would coin this convergence the intersection of Rhetoric, Race, and Religion. The academic advisement that Holmes gave me (even paying my Ph.D. program application fee out of her own pocket) coupled with her sagacious mysticism convinced me to study Black religion with *Unspeakable Joy*. The work Bridgeman and Thomas have done in homiletics helped shape my research interests in African American Religious and Prophetic Rhetoric. Johnson's groundbreaking work on Bishop Henry McNeal Turner would be a paradigmatic influence on my engagement with Cleage.

What affirmed me the most in my pursuit of learning more about Cleage's theology and rhetoric is the relationship I've built with his successors—Bishops Kimathi Nelson, Mbiyu Chui, and the foremost Cleagian scholar, Dr. Jawanza Eric Clark. Their direct encounters with Cleage and willingness to openly dialogue with me about those experiences, their thoughtful responses to my musings, their appreciation of my curiosity and concentration on Cleage's rhetoric, and their compassionate embrace of my pastoral and academic vocations have made me a better preacher, pastor, and scholar.

I was clear at the offset that I wouldn't be able to tackle Cleage's copious career—his decades of pastoral leadership, hundreds of sermons, game-changing politics, and personal life—in any reasonable amount of time. My first few semesters in the Ph.D. program proved that. I went from trying to assess Cleage's rhetoric and theology in general, to looking at his sermons between 1960 and 1970, to the sermonic material in *The Black Messiah*. I ultimately landed on a close reading of three of his most provocative sermons. This leaves much more terrain for me to cover throughout my academic career. I consider this book an introductory offering seeking to reclaim, recover, and reintroduce a forerunner of Black Theology, a fierce advocate for Black Liberation and cardinal figure in the Black Prophetic Tradition.

Chapter 1

Introduction

In 1967 race, uprisings broke out around the United States. Detroit, Michigan, was the epicenter of some of the most rigorous forms of this revolutionary expression. At the same time, a forerunner and father of what would come to be known as Black[1] Liberation Theology was transforming a religious community and Christian congregation through Black Power rhetoric and Afrocentric religion. Rev. Albert Cleage Jr. (who would later change his name to Jaramogi Abebe Agyeman) articulated a transformative, textured, multivalent, and revolutionary theology through his sermonic militancy[2] in response to this "rhetorical situation."[3] Cleage went on to publish some of the sermons preached at his church during and after the rebellion. Cleage would sermonically assess the rebellions of that period this way,

> Something has happened to black people in these United States. We are not as we were a few years ago, a few months ago, a few weeks ago. Something has happened to *us*: not to America, but to *us*, to the way we think, the way we fight, the way we work together. This is the most important thing that has ever happened to America.
> What is that something? It is that fear is gone.[4]

Labeled by PBS, in their series *This Far by Faith*, "By far the most vocal Christian minister advocating a more radical approach to obtaining civil rights," Albert Cleage, Jr. was born in Indianapolis, Indiana, in June 1911. Early on, Cleage's father, Dr. Albert Cleage Sr., would move the family from Kalamazoo, Michigan, to Detroit while helping to build the only hospital that would train African American residents and grant admitting privileges to Black doctors—Dunbar Hospital. Cleage graduated from Detroit Northwestern and obtained his BA in sociology at Wayne State University and his Bachelor of Divinity from Oberlin Graduate School of Theology, respectively.

Cleage was ordained in the Congregational Christian Churches and would have "a brief—and disappointing—term as pastor at an integrated church in San Francisco" before returning to Detroit in 1951. While back in Detroit, Cleage would form the Central Congregational Church in midtown. PBS goes on to state,

> Throughout the 1960s, Cleage was active in issues of education and black political leadership. By the late 1960s, his vision of Christianity had radicalized alongside the disappointments of the civil rights movement and rise of Black Power. He launched the Black Christian National Movement in 1967, which called for black churches to reinterpret Jesus' teaching to suit the social, economic, and political needs of black people. That Easter, Cleage unveiled an 18-foot painting of a Black Madonna, and renamed Central Congregational the Shrine of the Black Madonna.[5]

During that same time frame, Cleage compiled twenty sermons in his groundbreaking and provocative 1968 book *The Black Messiah*.[6] This publication sent shockwaves throughout religious, academic, and political communities around the globe. In fact, the conversation began to go global with Cleage being asked if his work could be translated into Italian.[7] Especially in many Black Church spaces, Cleage's book became a pivotal point in discussions about Black Faith and Black Power. From Cleage's vantage point, the 1960s represented a "present crisis, involving as it does the black man's struggle for survival in American" and demanded "the resurrection of a Black Church with its own Black Messiah."[8]

The physical and rhetorical presentations in *The Black Messiah* had an enormous impact on the theological and rhetorical landscape of the late 1960s and continue to echo into the early part of the twenty-first century. Cleage's rhetoric was disruptive to a white supremacist's religious consciousness that plagued the mainstream religious arena and general American public. *The Black Messiah* as a publication contributed substantially to the change in public conversation about Jesus, Christianity, Black Power, and what it meant to the Christian then (and now).

Cleage exemplifies an African American religious rhetor working through historical, philosophical, political, and practical forms and frames as he is reconstituting his congregation to redeem themselves from what Carter G. Woodson called *The Mis-education of the Negro*[9] and what Cleage himself would refer to as "the white man's *declaration of Black inferiority*."[10] *The Black Messiah* also became the platform for Cleage's second and final book in 1972 and new denominational creation *Black Christian Nationalism*[11] (which would also be identified as the Pan-African Orthodox Christian Church [PAOCC]).

Cleage opens his book stating,

> For nearly 500 years the illusion that Jesus was white dominated the world only because white Europeans dominated the world. Now, with the emergence of the nationalist movements of the world's colored majority, the historic truth is finally beginning to emerge—that Jesus was the non-white leader of a non-white people struggling for national liberation against the rule of a white nation, Rome.[12]

It is important to foreground that Cleage's claim that Jesus of Nazareth was literally a "black messiah" is a rhetorical strategy which sought to achieve political ends—Black Liberation and the creation and sustainment of a Black Nation. I will say more about this in detail later as it relates to the intellectual and rhetorical context of *The Black Messiah*. What is more pressing at the offset is to understand how Cleage would build on the social, political, and theological principles of Marcus Garvey (as described in Cardinal Aswad Walker's essay "Princes Shall Come Out of Egypt"[13]), Malcolm X (as laid out in Cleage's 1967 Speech entitled, "Myths About Malcolm X"[14]), and most recognizably Jesus (as portrayed in the New Testament Gospels). Cleage seeks to achieve the goal of social, political, and spiritual liberation through his rhetoric and theology which both undergird his political practices. In the introduction to *The Black Messiah*, Cleage writes:

> Black Americans need to know that the historic Jesus was a leader who went about among the people of Israel, seeking to root out the individualism and the identification with their oppressor which had corrupted them, and to give them faith in their own power to rebuild the Nation. (3-4)

He continues:

> We, as black Christians suffering oppression in a white man's land, do not need the individualistic and otherworldly doctrines of Paul and the white man. We need to recapture the faith in our power as a people and the concept of Nation, which are the foundation of the Old Testament and the prophets, and upon which Jesus built all of his teachings 2,000 years ago. (4)

Cleage is laying out his agenda for establishing Jesus as a historical figure that African Americans in the twentieth century can draw upon for inspiration to merge their theology and political practice. When Cleage claims a "need to recapture the faith" he is reaching back into the origins of a tradition that did not attempt to neatly separate faith and politics. And as we consider Cleage's words today, his merger of piety and the public echoes ancient religious discourse attributed to Old Testament prophets and can be thusly be categorized as prophetic (and Cleage himself, as I will display, as a prophet). Building on what Andre Johnson defines as "prophetic rhetoric,"[15] I understand such discourse as not only sacred (or religious) rhetoric "offering a critique of existing communities and traditions by challenging society to live up to [its] ideals," but also keenly focused on the power dynamics of the society and centering equitable responsibility on those in power while simultaneously seeking to empower those rendered powerless.

To that end, Cleage does not simply offer an idealized critique of America in the twentieth century. He goes further into offering marginalized people an opportunity to seize political power and independence through a revolutionary theology. Cleage's public works led to him being recognized by some as a modern-day prophet—one who speaks/acts on behalf of those disempowered addressing hard and necessary truths to and about those in power. This label, prophet, is recognizable in the title of the only biography written about Cleage, H. H. Ward's pertinent, *Prophet of the Black Nation (1969)*. Also, in a 1974 dissertation by Myran Elizabeth Lewis (now known as My Haley—wife of Alex Haley) entitled "Cleage: A Rhetorical Study of Black Religious Nationalism,"[16] the opening epigraph cites a statement made by arguably the most notable Black Liberation Theologian, James Hal Cone. The epigraph reads, "In my estimation, Cleage is a prophet. If you read the Old Testament, you will see good parallels. No, I find no problem with that notion at all. He is a prophet." Using this logic, *The Black Messiah* becomes a place for us to study Black prophetic rhetoric more intimately, as well as its relationship to African American Rhetoric more broadly and African American Religious Rhetoric in particular. These distinctions are necessary because, as I will describe more fully in the next chapter, conventional approaches to religious and prophetic rhetoric in communication studies are deeply Aristotelian and Eurocentric. For instance, James Darsey describes prophetic discourse within the context of prophetic *logos*, prophetic *pathos*, and prophetic *ethos*.[17] This derives directly from Aristotelian logic and strangles African American religious and prophetic rhetoric at the hands of Eurocentricity.

I contend there are potential remedies to these challenges and constraints found in Cleage's discourse in *The Black Messiah*. Cleage was not only a prophet, but as is the case with most prophetic figures (albeit to varying degrees), he was also a rhetorician. To be sure, as Cleage's successor at Shrine #1 in Detroit, Bishop Mbiyu Chui has described to me,[18] Cleage identified himself as more of a religious historian than a homiletician or rhetorician. At the same time, however, when we consider how Cleage constructed, invented, utilized, and appropriated images, symbols, and language as means of communication and potential persuasion the term "rhetorician" remains equally apropos. For example, on Easter/Resurrection Sunday of 1967 Cleage unveiled a sanctuary statue that would concretize a new commitment to Afrocentric Christianity in what was formerly known as Central United Church of Christ in Detroit. Cleage renamed the church after this monument—The Shrine of the Black Madonna. "The Shrine," as the church would affectionately become known, would be the place Cleage preached the sermons found in *The Black Messiah*. This social and spiritual location has significant rhetorical impact and must be considered as we reflect on the life and legacy of Cleage and the profound impact of his writings and speeches.

Rhetorical studies offer a potentially insightful path of engagement with *The Black Messiah* as well as with Cleage's prophetic persona and rhetorical strategies. *The Black Messiah* was published around the same time Molefi Asante (then known as Arthur Smith) was beginning to work on African American rhetoric as an academic discipline and the African American rhetorical tradition was beginning to become an academic field of study. Asante found an overlay of what he called "cultural imperialism" in the field of rhetoric and beyond. In similar vein, as Asante explicates in his groundbreaking essay, "Markings of an African Concept of Rhetoric,"[19] the scope and strands of African rhetoric, predating both African American and Classical Greek rhetorics, are laced throughout *The Black Messiah* in Cleage's bold, repetitious, and probing critiques of Eurocentricity and beckons for a more African-centered epistemology and theology. Therefore, *The Black Messiah* is an ideal site for interrogating the relationship between the matrices of power, democracy, rhetoric, race, and religion.

The Black Messiah celebrated its fifty-year publication anniversary in 2018. In recent years, scholars such as Drs. Jawanza Eric Clark, Kamasi Hill, Angela Dillard, Weldon McWilliams, and Kelly Brown Douglas have promoted a reengagement with Cleage's works and social/spiritual witness.[20] However, no substantial or significant rhetorical engagement with Cleage's writings/sermons have been offered since Lewis's dissertation in 1974.

To that end, this project intends to address a few critical and pertinent themes. In general, I will display how Cleage's rhetoric and theology offers insight into (and disrupt the boundaries of) the fields of rhetorical and religious studies. Methodologically, I'll build a case for the need for a more intentional and intimate engagement with religious rhetoric and how that quest compliments scholarship in both fields. For instance, a close reading of Cleage's work and the reception history of *The Black Messiah* can contribute to an important discussion relative to the intersections of rhetoric, race, and religion in public discourse. Close reading as a rhetorical method is described extensively by Michael Leff and Andrew Sachs as an attempt to avoid reductionist approaches to texts (and the personality/ies associated with it/them). Leff and Sachs caution rhetorical scholars against a "form/content dichotomy"[21] and toward a more balanced engagement with a product and the social, political, and personal realities that create the environment in which the product is produced. In remedy, Leff and Sachs propose, "there exists a kind of textual criticism that views the rhetorical work, not as a mirror of reality, but as a field of action unified into a functional and locally stable product."[22] Leff also offers more insight into close reading as a methodology in his 2009 lecture at the University of Windsor entitled, "What Is Rhetoric?" There Leff posited that rhetoric is not only a means of accommodating or capitulating to a particular audience but is equally about an ability to "reconfigure the rules of the game."[23] Therefore, close readings are employed with the hope of capturing the methods, strategies, content, and context of a text (written or otherwise) that offers us an opportunity to see not only what the rhetoric *is* but what the rhetoric *does*.

Simply put, I will consider how Cleage, in *The Black Messiah*, seeks to "reconfigure the rules of the game" as it relates to Christianity and the social-political realities of Black people in Detroit and across the country. To best understand Cleage's theology, and its alignment with the Black Prophetic Tradition, we must also think about Cleage's work rhetorically. Consequently, I will explore how and what *The Black Messiah* has contributed to the broader scope of Black Liberation Theology *and* Black religious rhetoric. I want to provide an opportunity for those who may not be as familiar with rhetoric as they are with religion to obtain some rhetorical tools that are useful in interpreting not only what Cleage's rhetoric *is* but what that type of rhetoric is *doing* in his book and in the audiences his book addressed (in the moment it was presented and into our contemporary culture).

Another one of the contributions this book will make is adding more layers and texture in understanding the relationship between African American rhetoric, the Black Prophetic Tradition, James Darsey's concept of *The Prophetic Tradition and Radical Rhetoric in America*,[24] what I call liberationist proclamations, rhetorical renderings of the Black Social Gospel, and what might simply amount to socially conscious articulations. Too often, these genres of rhetoric and religious expression are conflated. There are some subtle distinctions that can be observed that demarcates the variations.

While African American rhetoric and the Black Prophetic Tradition are broad themes and areas of rhetorical and religious discourse, they center a Black experience in ways that Darsey does not venture into in his work. His oversight is somewhat understandable because to do so would require an intimacy with the Black experience that cannot be replicated by non-Black people.

Further, in a highly digitized and media-driven age where so much content is available to so many, so easily, we must be careful not to homogenize those who make religious appeals that consider social and political realities (socially conscious preaching), and those who simultaneously center the Black experience (Black social gospel), but do not provide a necessary interrogation or exegesis of the social and political power dynamics that give unique voice and empowerment to underprivileged and underrepresented voices (liberationist proclamations). Cleage claims, "This church is dedicated to a Black Messiah. This church believes that the purpose of Christianity is to free black people, to rid black people of injustice. This is what we believe. This is why we are so important to the Black Revolution."[25] This is not the same claim as the Black social gospel,[26] or a preacher who merely lists and denounces contemporary social ills or suggests that "racism is a 'sin' problem and not a skin problem."[27]

In a vein similar to Kerry Pimblott's publication *Faith In Black Power: Religion, Race, and Resistance In Cairo, Illinois*,[28] this book reintroduces the relationships between Black Power and Black Liberation Theology within a situational context—Detroit, Michigan, in 1967–1968. It provides some real teeth to the intersection of rhetoric, race, and religion. Using some of Cleage's sermonic material (I can't adequately deal with all twenty sermons in this book), I will build upon the work of Mark Chapman's *Christianity on Trial*[29] and respond to the inquiry, "What has been the relationship between Black Faith (Christianity more specifically) and Black Power?" I'll also display how *The Black Messiah* leads us into uncharted spaces related to Black Power and Black Faith.

I am mindful that my research considerations are numerous, with each reflection worthy of lengthy engagement. Each section will not be allotted the same amount of attention. However, each of these themes and aims is interconnected and compliments the larger goal of this project. Again, my aim is to offer a substantive contribution to the broader areas of communication and religious studies. Nevertheless, my primary focus in this book is to deeply engage the rhetoric and force of *The Black Messiah*.

On a more aspirational note, I hope this book can spark a broader, interdisciplinary project of reclaiming and reconsidering Cleage's work (and others like Cleage) and be viewed in concert with existing scholarship in the areas of rhetoric, race, and religion.

OVERVIEW OF SECTIONS AND CHAPTERS

The Black Messiah is a cornerstone for the convergence of rhetoric, race, and religion. All of these areas are important to understanding the text. This will especially be displayed in the deep engagement with the selected sermons in the latter chapters. Having said that, rhetorical studies is the foundation or canvas for this project. History, religious studies, radical Black politics, and other areas of social science will help to add flavor to the specificity of this project and its unique contribution to rhetorical studies. In that vein, the remainder of this introduction will present a brief overview of the subsequent chapters, the historical, intellectual, and rhetorical context of *The Black Messiah,* and briefly discuss how the Black Power Movement impacted the academic landscape of the 1960s. I will also lay out how Cleage's role as a contemporary prophet contributed to the discussion of Black Faith, Black Theology, and Black Power during that era. Thereafter, I provide a review and engagement with previous scholarship and examine the gaps which make my primary research endeavors pertinent. Although Cleage has been understudied, his personality is not completely unknown to academicians (and even a few scholar-pastors). I wrap up the introduction by beginning to build upon the existing scholarship and paying homage to those who have already begun what I am describing as a reclamation project. Finally, I list a few contemporary implications and opportunities this book provides.

In the next chapter, chapter 2, I will make a case for the study of religious rhetoric in general and *The Black Messiah* more specifically. Even when rhetoric, race, and religion seem to explicitly overlap we must still wonder "why" and "how?" And although *The Black Messiah*, as I will display, is prime real estate to explore these inquires, unless sufficient ground and framework are presented in a proper sequence someone can easily miss or misinterpret the necessity of this academic and practical adventure. Accordingly, before we can dive more directly into the content of the book itself and analyze some of the sermons therein, I must present a more general discussion of communication studies engagement (or lack thereof) with Black religious rhetoric. We must know what Black religious rhetoric has to offer as a remedy to both traditional (Aristotelian) and contemporary rhetorical theory as a field. Again, Cleage is not a rhetorician, per se, but he is engaged in a direct and constructive rhetorical strategy with both theological and political impact when he sermonically suggests that his church, "as an independent Congregational Church" could "ordain workers in the Student Non-Violent Co-Ordinating Committee for the civil rights work which they are now doing" in order to "protect them against the conspiracy to either kill them in Vietnam or take them out of active work by putting them in the penitentiary."[30] These types of claims plant a flag in Black religious rhetoric and call forth a more intentional and nuanced level of research and reflection than conventional rhetorical studies seems to offer.

In chapter 3, I begin engagement with *The Black Messiah* as a rhetorical artifact. As mentioned before, Cleage's theology has been examined rhetorically. My Haley (Myran Lewis) offered an insightful engagement of Cleage's contribution to Black Theology overall. However, her dissertation was published almost fifty years ago. What has not been done is a deep dive into the specific sermonic content and sociopolitical context of *The Black Messiah* itself. It would be misguided to dive directly into the sermonic content of the book without providing an overarching assessment of the book and what it represented as a rhetorical production in the midst of the Black Power Movement. To that end, this chapter sets up an overview of the book, it's reception history, it's alignment (and disalignment) with traditional concepts of Black prophetic and protest rhetoric, and a rhetorical engagement of the book overall. This section situates the book squarely within the Black Prophetic Tradition as an artifact and simultaneously adds nuance to the ways in which communication studies scholars, theological scholars, and practitioners of public oratory can benefit from. My hope is that this section sets the stage for the close readings that will take place in the proceeding chapters when the specific sermonic content (in chapter 4) and (in chapter 5) is complemented by other writings in a similar genre focusing on a similar rhetorical time frame.

While all of the sermons in *The Black Messiah* have value, there are three sermons that situate themselves more directly within the tensions of the Black Faith and Black Freedom Movements in the 1960s. In chapter 4, I deal intimately and intentionally with Cleage's sermon, "An Epistle to Stokely" found in the third chapter of *The Black Messiah*. The sermons published in *The Black Messiah* were preached (in one version or another) at The Shrine between 1967 and 1968. This is at the heart of the Black Power Movement. This social-political timeframe places Cleage at a rhetorical disadvantage in trying to use Christianity as a tool of Black Liberation. There was a common sentiment among Black revolutionaries, militants, and agnostic contributors to the Black Power Movement that Christianity was "the white man's religion"[31] and offered no productive or prophetic path forward. The sermon centered in this chapter is Cleage's response to that. Using rhetorical strategies of disbarment, disruption, rhetorical hermeneutics, (re)constitutive rhetoric, parrhesia and nommo, Cleage seeks to embrace (and ordain) Black revolutionaries for their own political protection and for the church's social-political advancement. Cleage uses bold and frank speech (*parrhesia*) to deconstruct and condemn unjust theologies associated with the Black Church and Black Preaching. At the same time, Cleage will use language to create or bring into existence (*nommo*) a more authentic and liberatory understanding of Christianity. The close reading methodology is employed in this chapter as the primary function of engagement with the content of the sermon as printed in the book. I examine not only what Cleage was saying but what he was doing with what he was saying in the sermon.

The tensions of the Black Power, Civil Rights, Black Freedom, and Black Faith Movements are on full display in the 1960s. Tenacles of this tension extend beyond the congregational church into the hall of the academy as the Black consciousness movement required a reckoning of research institutions with their racial insensitivity and ignorance. Cleage's sermonic material impacts this discussion directly in the field of religious studies. Chapter 5 places Cleage in conversation and contradistinction with one of his contemporaries—Dr. James Hal Cone. Cone emerges in the late 1960s and early 1970s as a premier academic voice in Black Theology. As the current Jaramogi and holy patriarch of the PAOCC, Bishop Kimathi Nelson noted to me in conversation, "Dr. Cone was teaching at Albion College in Michigan as Cleage was teaching and preaching Black Theology at the Shine. Cone would attend the bible studies and take copious notes."[32] Cone and Cleage's collegiality is complicated. Yet, their works on Black Theology and Black Power complement each other when read in contrast. This chapter looks intently at excerpts from Cleage's sermons, "Brother Malcolm," and "Dr. King and Black Power" and puts them in conversation with excerpts from Cone's book *Martin and Malcolm in America*.[33] This chapter will show the variance in perspectives and theological convictions, as well as the rhetorical strategies employed by Cleage and Cone to make their case for the most faithful engagement to Malcolm and Martin's contributions to Civil Rights, Black Power, and Black Theology.

In the conclusion, chapter 6, I offer a brief review of the chapters and discuss the contemporary implications and offerings of this project. I also allude to further research aspirations and opportunities beyond the scope of this book.

WHAT IS *THE BLACK MESSIAH?*

The Black Messiah is much more than just a set of sermons. It is a publication of rhetorical expressions associated with a theoretical, theological, and political agenda. For Cleage, Jesus of Nazareth was (and is) *the* Black Messiah. Cleage's proclamation of Jesus as *the* Black Messiah is a claim of fact that seeks to rehabilitate Black Christians in particular, and the Black Faith community more broadly, away from the slavocracy's[34] distortions into a more authentic, African-centered understanding of the religious tradition.

It is important to note that the structure of *The Black Messiah* is such that it is near impossible to situate the text within the confines of conventional notions of audience. Cleage preaches to a congregation that varies in its makeup every week. It is not likely that the exact same people show up each Sunday. The structural demographics would suggest that Cleage's appeals are not necessarily dictated simply by who is physically in front of him. If we are to adequately engage the content and context of the sermonic materials and communicative strategies of Cleage in the book, we must select a methodology that is more applicable than neo-Aristotelian logic will allow. Also, these sermons take place over a broader span of time than one occasion in a week, month, or season. What I seek to draw out through close readings of Cleage's sermons is a communicative pattern. What are the ideological, rhetorical, theological, and cultural threads that exist throughout the sermons irrespective of sermonic titles, scriptural foundations, and liturgical occasions (Resurrection Sunday, Christmas, Pentecost Sunday, etc.)?

This is the type of textual criticism this offers. I will peer into the window of the Black Power period (and its implications for the here-and-now) using the form, content, and context of *The Black Messiah*. The text will be the foundation of my "interpretive understanding"[35] of how the intersections of rhetoric, race, and religion provide scholars, practitioners, and everyday people with a perspective on the past that offers us instructive insight into the present.

THE HISTORICAL CONTEXT OF *THE BLACK MESSIAH*

Without a doubt, the 1960s were a tense time in the United States politically (and otherwise). During that period, many figures emerged into the social spotlight espousing different theories and ideologies that would have a significant effect on the trajectory of America in general and Black America more specifically. There was not a more controversial, complex, and compelling figure than the Rev. Albert Cleage, Jr. In the 1969 memoir/biography *Prophet of the Black Nation*,[36] Ward introduces readers to a militant and meek, brash and beloved, thoughtful and trivial pastor. Ward describes Cleage as "probably the most hated man in Detroit, by all reckoning, including his own."[37] Despite the disdain that Cleage garnered (or maybe even because of it) his persona, philosophies, and rhetorical projections are quite compelling. Ward goes on to say, "For political analysts, sociologist, and economists, this practical prophet who talks of a revision of society, the economy, and a process, if not dialectic, that does not exclude revolution, must hold some fascination."[38] These "talks" are captured in *The Black Messiah*.

Ward also offers a significant snapshot into the cultural, political, and social environment of Detroit in the 1960s. She writes,

> The rebellion of 1967 itself continued to dominate discussion in Detroit and localized the black movement in such a way that the attention of the country and of the world was focused on Detroit. And the forming of the Detroit-based National Black Economic Development Conference took attention.

Still, Albert Cleage continued to maintain a vision of new black nationalism [*sic*], peculiarly centered in the church, which would match the nationalistic movements of the past and possibly go far beyond them in actually facing needs and giving blacks an esprit de corps.[39]

In a narrow sense, the historical context of *The Black Messiah* is the Detroit rebellion of 1967. But this time frame also invites us to consider a broader historical context that Cleage and *The Black Messiah* speaks to—the theological and cultural tensions between the Civil Rights and Black Power Movements. More will be said about Black Power later. The point here is to note that *The Black Messiah* as a rhetorical artifact does not speak only to the rhetorical situation of political unrest in Detroit; it also speaks to theological combustion between religious conservatives, moderates, liberals, progressives, radicals, and most of all prophets like Cleage.

One looming question of Black Faith in the 1960s was, "What is role of the Black Church in the freedom struggle?" While Black Theology intended to provide some direction academically and intellectually, *The Black Messiah* is a documented treatise on how to respond to the question practically. In other words, Cleage not only pontificated on ways to make Black Theology a field of study, *The Black Messiah* is evidence of him putting this theology into practice at a time when many presumed the Black Church was ineffective or irrelevant. Cleage writes:

> The Black Church has not always been revolutionary, but it has always been relevant to the everyday needs of black people. The old down-home black preacher who "shouted" his congregation on Sunday morning was realistically ministering to the needs of a black people who could not yet conceive of changing the conditions which oppressed them. . . . The Church was performing a valuable and real function. However uneducated the old-time preacher was, he was relevant and significant.[40]

But in a rhetorical pivot and embracing a revolutionary posture, Cleage retorts,

> But today the Church must reinterpret its message in terms of the needs of a Black Revolution. We no longer feel helpless as black people. We do not feel we must sit and wait for God to intervene and settle our problems for us. We waited for four hundred years and he didn't do much of anything, so for the next for hundred years we're going to be fighting to change the conditions for ourselves. This is merely a new theological position.[41]

Mainstream Christianity in the 1960s was considered by many radicals as overtly pacifist. This political strategy was met with stark and unforgiving criticism from personalities like Malcolm X and others who viewed Christianity as "the White Man's religion" and a tool of oppression for Black people. And with all due respect to the canonized forefathers of Black Theology, even when they are contesting the contours of conventional Christianity (or what William Jones refers to as "Whiteanity"), they remain more moderate in comparison to Cleage's Christian and sermonic militancy.

Black Theology as a field emerges in the 1960s as a by-product of the Civil Rights and Black Power Movements.[42] The primary aim of Black Theology was to describe and define an understanding of God that centers the Black experience. While many Black preachers and professors had done sermonic, pastoral, and academic work for centuries, it was not until the 1960s, with the rise of the Black consciousness movements, that Black Theology was confirmed as both a phraseology and praxis. Cleage has been included in the litany of the forefathers of Black Theology along with James Hal Cone, J. Deotis Roberts, and Dwight Hopkins. However, Cleage does stand apart from the others in unique ways. In William Jones's work entitled, *Is God A White Racist? A Preamble to Black Theology*, Jones finds Cleage's contribution (along with other more recognizable theologians) incomplete, but still too significant to be ignored. Jones writes,

> Each of the current black theologians—Albert Cleage, James Cone, Major Jones, J. Deotis Roberts, and Joseph Washington—has answered in his own way Du Bois' perplexing question, What meaneth black suffering? However, their answers, individually and collectively, compound the confusion of an already inscrutable mystery. They have painstakingly drawn a theological road map to guide the black faithful from distorted conceptions to prophetic enlightenment. But the road is full of logical potholes, theological washouts, and elaborate but unsound detours. Consequently the theological terrain they have scouted must be surveyed again.[43]

The above quote exemplifies how Cleage has been synthesized with other Black theologians of his day. However, Jones does not offer the nuances that I believe are necessary. I find Jones's critique aggressive, but still acute. I contend that Cleage must be included in the litany of necessary personalities of interest and investigation, but not because I believe Cleage's rhetoric and theology is flawless. Like Jones, I do not find Cleage's contribution infallible, but I do find it irreplaceable. Later, I will describe in more detail what separates Cleage from the other founding forefathers of Black Theology, especially with regards to his rhetoric and theology—his more aggressive sermonic militancy, his Afrocentric theology, and what Raphael Warnock calls Cleage's "radical pastoral praxis."[44]

Building on those distinctions, Cleage's credence extends beyond the theoretical and conceptual. Cleage was a pastor for over fifty years. Cleage's rhetoric and theology are reflective of his pastoral, ministerial, and political praxis. How Cleage understands and articulates who God is and what God is requiring of God's people is not simply shaped by his intellectual engagement with ideas. It is polished in the crucible of his concrete experience as a pastor during one of the most crucial periods in American history (and the history of the Black Church) while in one of the most controversial cities in the country. Many of the more notable Black theologians have served only minimal stints in the parish as pastors (if at all) or have come to be far more associated with their professional relationship with the academy than their personal relationship with the Black Church. As a result, their theology can ofttimes be rather abstract and primarily academic. But not so with Rev. Cleage. Cleage speaks as a reporter from the front lines of the Black Church.

In light of this, we cannot begin to profess to know about the broadness of Black religious thought (especially Black Christianity) without a sincere and sufficient engagement with *The Black Messiah* which argues that Christianity—a religious and political movement founded by a Black Hebrew, Jesus of Nazareth—was not only important to the Black Freedom struggle but also, historically and theologically, most significant. In that vein, this book details how the frameworks of American Christianity and the Civil Rights and Black Power Movements have come into conflict with the American political landscape. The democratic project which quite often (and even constitutionally) excludes Black people from full participation and privilege—often does so explicitly in the name of religion. Within the pages *The Black Messiah* we observe the quest for Black Liberation in America coalesce rhetorically, religiously, and racially. And they coalesce quite radically.

THE INTELLECTUAL AND RHETORICAL CONTEXT OF *THE BLACK MESSIAH*

As stated earlier, Cleage's claim that Jesus of Nazareth was literally *the* Black Messiah is a rhetorical strategy which sought to achieve political ends—Black Liberation and the creation and sustainment of a Black nation. This claim was also disruptive to the conventions of Black Theology itself. Jawanza Eric Clark in his anthology *Albert Cleage Jr. and the Black Madonna and Child*[45] argues,

Albert Cleage Jr. performed a theological paradigm shift away from Jesus as the White or ontologically black Christ to Jesus as the black messiah. This shift is much more than a mere pigmentation change or difference in terminology, but a distinction that actually helps Cleage avoid the reification problem of more orthodox black theologians. In fact, in calling Jesus the black Messiah, Cleage is establishing that his Christology is entirely distinct from his doctrine of God, that Jesus was a human being and God is something else entirely.[46]

Clark goes on to describe the Black Messiah as "Cleage's symbol of black liberation."[47] This defines Cleage's claim as ultimately theological, political, *and* rhetorical. In other words, not only did a Black Messiah—a divinely inspired, political revolutionary—previously exist as a model or template for a revolutionary struggle for liberation, but, moreover, this template is righteously applicable and, for Cleage, *must* be replicated in the current struggle for Black Liberation for people across the diaspora. Cleage's claim is an attempt to reconstitute Christianity and reclaim it as an authentically African, politically Black, and essentially revolutionary religion that meets the relevant and contemporary needs of its adherents. Cleage is seeking to persuade his audience to relinquish its allegiance to the vestiges of white supremacy which masquerades as (among other things) a universally upright and spiritually sincere faith tradition. However, what Cleage's claim makes clear is if our religion does not take into account our social and political realities, if the faith tradition is not constructed (or reconstructed) into what Clark refers to as "particular, political, and culturally specific,"[48] then it is ultimately irrelevant in addressing the human needs and always subject to becoming a tool of oppression, manipulation, exploitation, conformity, and enslavement. Nevertheless, for Cleage, as stated above, even though the church hasn't always embraced a revolutionary posture, he believed it had become essential to the longevity of Black people and the efficacy of the Black Church. This posture is most evident in his preaching.

The sermonic substance of Cleage's attempts at this reinterpretation and reconstitution, this construction and symbolism of a more African-centered Christianity is fundamentally rhetorical. Cleage uses words, images, metaphors, and other linguistic tools at his disposal to challenge and attempt to change the dominant cultural paradigm of Black religion. In that vein, Cleage's evoking of a Black Messiah is making clear a claim fundamental to my argument in this book—all theology is experiential (culturally), contextual, and rhetorical. And if we are to understand the type of Christianity that Cleage is professing and practicing in *The Black Messiah*, and how it differs or diverts from other religious presentations, we have to understand more about his experience, his cultural context, and his rhetorical purposes and strategies. Cleage's theology is found within the pages of his book within the substance of his sermons.

Theology, simply put, is the study of God, the divine, or the supernatural. Theology is what some theologians refer to as "God-Talk."[49] Theology is rooted in human experience. As the experiences deviate and/or evolve, the understanding of how, who, and what God is corresponds. These human experiences take place in a distinct context. Human beings experience the world in a particular geographical location, in a particular time frame, and a specific cultural environment. This is what makes theology innately political. These experiences must also be communicated if they are ever going to be corroborated. This means theology is eternally bound by and subject to rhetorical claims.

Again, Cleage's Black Messiah is a rhetorical construction which addresses the historical realties of Christianity but, moreover, responds to the social, political, and cultural particularities of Black people in America in the mid-twentieth century. Clark describes it this way,

> Cleage's Christological reconstruction, therefore, is not simply an inversion of the racial hierarchy grounded in essentialist rhetoric, but ultimately an attempt to move beyond racial constructs altogether. This Christological paradigm shift is more specifically a movement away from traditional European (primarily Greek) theological formulations to Hebrew/African thought forms. Cleage is intentional about this philosophical/theological reframing. He indicates that his goal is to "build a Black Liberation movement which derives its basic religious insights from African spirituality, its character from African communalism, and its revolutionary direction from Jesus, the black messiah."[50]

More simply put, the white Christ is a rhetorical symbol, socially constructed, that is ahistorical and primarily concerned with individual morality, prosperity, and salvation. Even as scholars like Stephen Prothero discuss (white) Jesus as a social construction,[51] he still doesn't go as far as to claim Jesus's ontological Blackness. Meanwhile, Cleage's Black Messiah is a rhetorical device, divinely inspired, and representative of a historical reality—a Black, religious-political-revolutionary who is primarily concerned with collective liberation of oppressed peoples (especially the Black Hebrew-Israelites). This rhetorical distinction is important because the white Christ symbol is a diversion away from the historical reality of who Jesus was/is. At the same time, Cleage's Black Messiah is a rhetorical device that is true to the historical reality but still being employed as a tool to reach for a transformative shift in the matrices of social and political power.

My Haley situates Cleage's Black Messiah within a rhetorical framework of constitutive rhetoric. Haley argues, "In spite of the demands and constraints of his position [Cleage] is a man who is involved in an authentic commitment to prompt and urge his people to accept the responsibility for their liberation."[52] Building on Haley's analysis, but centering more on Cleage's sermonic material in *The Black Messiah*, this project will consider how Cleage is utilizing and applying what James Boyd White describes as "constitutive rhetoric."[53] According to Maurice Charland, this is the type of rhetoric that is deployed to shape a group's identity. Charland posits that these identities are rhetorical insofar as they "induce human cooperation."[54] Constitutive rhetoric, then, is the process by which a speaker/rhetor/preacher develops an audience's convictions and practices and gives uniqueness and stability to a culture, organization, or a people. Just like the U.S. Constitution is intended to establish a particular governing order, reaching into religious themes and stitching them into the fabric of the social and political landscape, Cleage intends to establish (or reclaim) a new, revolutionary governing order grounded in an Afrocentric interpretation of the Christian and Hebrew faith traditions. Constitutive rhetoric establishes a set of values that influence our interpretation of current (and past) realties. But in the context of Black folks in America seeing liberation and political agency, this process would have to be redone, reconstituted, because the constitution of the country was not intended to include Black people as fully human. And if Cleage intends to reshape the future of Black Faith and reconstitute the ways religion has been used to "induce human cooperation" with enslavement and second-class citizenship, Cleage has to design and deploy a rhetoric that honors Black life but condemns and rejects mainstream (white) interpretations of Christianity and its political ineptitude toward Black Liberation.

Cleage does this sermonically; rhetorically. This is the fundamental substance of *The Black Messiah*—a set of sermons Cleage offers to reconstitute his audience to reinterpret Christianity and reclaim its revolutionary nature as a tool of inspiration in the fight for Black Liberation. This project will detail how the content in *The Black Messiah* exhibits how Cleage produces what Leff called "hermeneutical rhetoric" as Cleage proposes new means of interpretation; a new adaptation of sacred texts (most often the Christian bible) and sociopolitical-historical contexts (Black oppression in the United States in general but in Detroit in particular).

Leff describes hermeneutical rhetoric as a project whereby the focal interest "centers on rhetorical practice as manifested in texts that directly and overtly engage political circumstances."[55] An example of Cleage engaging in rhetorical hermeneutics is his claim that what he is proposing is a different way to interpret the role and function of Christianity:

> This is merely a new theological position. We have come to understand how God works in the world. Now we know that God is going to give us strength

for our struggle. As black preachers we must tell our people that we are God's chosen people and that God is fighting with us as we fight. When we march, when we take it to the streets in open conflict, we must understand that in the stamping feet and the thunder of violence we can hear the voice of God. When the Black Church accepts its role in the Black Revolution, it is able to understand and interpret revolutionary Christianity, and the revolution becomes a part of our Christian faith.[56]

Cleage's rhetorical strategy is an amalgamation of White's conceptuality of the constitutive rhetoric, Asante's work on Black Rhetoric (especially Black Religious Rhetoric), and a theological hermeneutic centered on Black (social and political) Liberation. Centering on all of these areas is necessary for both interrogating systematic notions of what constitutive rhetoric is, how it works when the rhetor is an African American religious leader, and assessing the impact of Black Power and Black prophetic rhetoric on Black Theology. I will show how Cleage is promoting Black Liberation as a foundational premise. This premise informs his discursive proclamations and practices.

Cleage's rhetoric and theology as presented in *The Black Messiah* functions in both a constitutive and hermeneutical fashion simultaneously. As Frank Thomas has rightly asserted, "African American preaching is fundamentally both a rhetorical and theological enterprise."[57] Both rhetoric and theology are essential to the understanding of the complexities of Black Preaching. As such, they are equally necessary for making the textures of *The Black Messiah* more tangible. To that end, this project argues that *The Black Messiah* is the personification and tangible production of Black prophetic rhetoric seeking to advance a radical Black politics rooted in Black Power theology.

REVIEW OF PREVIOUS SCHOLARSHIP AND SCHOLASTIC OPPORTUNITIES

Albert Cleage Jr. and his theological offerings have by no means been unstudied, but in my estimation have been understudied. Similar to how Rev. Dr. Jeremiah Wright, Jr. has been marginalized and demonized within the framework of the mainstream religious (especially Christian) imagination, Cleage has also slipped through the scholastic grasp of so many rhetoricians, theologians, and historians.

For example, although, as stated previously, James Cone comes to recognize Cleage as a prophetic figure, in Cone's well known and groundbreaking book, *Black Theology and Black Power,* Cone contends that "if, as I believe, Black Power is the most important development in American life in this century, there is a need to begin to analyze it from a theological perspective."[58] Nevertheless, in over 150 pages of spectacular and sufficient critiques of white supremacy as well as creative constructions of Black Power philosophy and theology, Cone offers only one sentence with regards to Cleage. Cone states, "The Rev. Albert Cleage of Detroit is one of the few Black ministers who has embraced Black Power as a religious concept and has sought to reorient the church-community on the basis of it."[59] Cone then proceeds to provide a treatment of the influence and contributions of the Black Muslims and Islam on Black Power and religious thought. No mention of Cleage's conspicuous and creative theology nor is there any reference to *The Black Messiah* at all. Part of what this project will do is fill in this gap and also (in chapter 5) put Cone in direct conversation and rhetorical comparison with Cleage. Cone's numerous works on Black Theology, Black Power, and Black Liberation have been hallmarks of academic analysis of race and religion in America. To know that a book that bears the name of the precise theology Cleage personified only casually drives by Cleage's address is disconcerting. I will drive home Cleage's impact more aggressively.

Most of the contemporary scholarship engages Cleage's theological tenets and how Black Christian Nationalism laid a foundational plank for Black Liberation Theology as an extension of a broader Black Freedom project. William Jones's chapter on Cleage's theology in his aforementioned *Is God A White Racist* interrogates Cleage's claims of the blackness of Jesus in association with religious frameworks of liberation. Jones's work was my initial introduction to Cleage as a historical figure—I did not hear about Cleage in seminary. As such, I want to make sure more people hear about Cleage. And although Jones groups Cleage with other forefathers of Black Theology, he does not, as I will, specify the nuances in rhetorical strategies that differentiate Cleage's substance, sermonic militancy, and pastoral praxis from the others.

Kelly Brown Douglas's *The Black Christ*[60] offers a theological assessment of Cleage's claims in a few sections. Douglas analyzes Cleage's claims of Jesus's blackness, but she also conflates those claims with what Clark disaggregates as the difference between the Black Christ and the Black Messiah. Although in religious study circles, this distinction might seem minute, in rhetorical studies, these word choices matter significantly. This rhetorical oversight is understandable because a rhetorical analysis was not the intent of Douglas's work. I will dig into the distinctions between *a* Black *Christ* and *the* Black *Messiah*. The former is evoked in a much more apolitical way than the latter—defending Jesus's ontological Blackness but diminishing his revolutionary politics. I will dive more deeply into Cleage's unapologetically aggressive and revolutionary political theology.

Weldon McWilliams's work *The Kingdom at Hand: Black Theology, The Pan African Orthodox Christian Church and their Implications on the Black*

Church,⁶¹ follows a similar vein as Douglas's. Even while considering the impact Cleage has on his audience through appeals to Afrocentric thought, McWilliams is interested in how Cleage constructs his theology and utilizes it to form a new denomination. He also analyses what that denomination offers to Black Liberation Theology in practice and not simply principle. This is important, for me, because it verifies the institutional and organization impact Cleage's ministry has. He is not some religious zealot disconnected from a broader political, theological, and institutional movement. Cleage is able, through his rhetorical prowess and radical pastoral praxis, to construct an entire denomination that spans across the country and still exists with thousands of members over fifty years after its inception.

Angela Dillard's work *Faith in the City: Preaching Radical Social Change in Detroit*⁶² engages thirty years of political development in the Motor City and the role faith and Black Preaching played in its trajectory. The book is organized around Cleage and Rev. Charles A. Hill. Dillard discusses the fusion of faith and politics and its contribution to the Black Freedom struggle in Detroit. Her aim is not to provide an assessment of what Black Preaching is, how Cleage engages in it, or how that fits in the milieu of Detroit's faith communities (that's where I hope to come in). Dillard is more focused on what ways the Black Faith Movement in Detroit helped to construct or (re)constitute a framework for political participation. Dillard continues to advance the argument of how past analyses reduce religiously rooted social movements to the South while misunderstanding and mislabeling similar movements up North. Dillard's focus is more sociological than rhetorical even though she looks at the impact of Black Faith leadership and its rhetorical appeals. I'll gladly add some rhetorical flavor to her righteous analysis.

Clark's aforementioned anthology *The Shrine of the Black Madonna and Child* analyzes the impact of the statue Cleage unveiled in the sanctuary of (then) Central United Church of Christ in 1967 and reflects on theological developments associated with Cleagian ideals and their impact fifty years later. While Clark's work centers on an event with significant rhetorical appeal, only Lewis's 1974 dissertation addresses Cleage rhetorically. But neither Clark nor Lewis deal directly with the substance of the sermons that shaped the theological and political psychology of The Shrine membership or the Black Theology Movement more broadly. I intended to deal with that in ways they have not.

What stands as a scholastic opportunity is a direct, robust, rhetorical engagement with his seminal text *The Black Messiah*, specifically. This project will not concentrate very much on Cleage's prophetic persona other than its association to the cultivation and development of his rhetorical stature and strategies. The bulk of this book will hone in on *The Black Messiah* itself and how the text speaks to the realities of its time and helps us understand contemporary realities in rhetoric, theology, and politics. I am not simply interested in what *The Black Messiah* is (form/subject), or merely what it says (content), but also how the text *works* in terms of reconstituting an audience to embrace or reclaim a radically different existential and ontological reality.

To contextualize Cleage as a personality is one thing. That project is already being done in meaningful ways by the aforementioned scholars. What Cleage's rhetoric does and what is exemplified in *The Black Messiah* and is personified in Cleage's rhetoric more expansively offer us an interpretive window into the intersections of contemporary rhetorical theory, African American Religious (and Prophetic) Rhetoric, and Black Power Studies. *The Black Messiah* will serve as a test-case for what it means to produce a text that lives at the intersections of rhetoric, race, and religion at a critical moment in American history.

CONCLUSION AND CONTEMPORARY IMPLICATIONS

As stated earlier, the sermons that make up *The Black Messiah* were orated during the heart of the Black Power period and during the race riots in Detroit, Michigan, in 1967. Consequently, *The Black Messiah* is a by-product of the Black Power Movement and is part and parcel of what Black Power studies must include in its catalogue. Whereby most other religious reflections of the Black Power period are analyzed by those who are on the outside looking in, *The Black Messiah* is a rhetorical artifact containing the declarations of an insider—an active participant with a bird's eye view into the Black Power Movement and undeniable leader in the Black Church. There were a few other notable Black Church leaders involved in the Black Power Movement. Wilmore and Cone write,

> A few theological professors participated in the movement from the beginning, but it was men like Albert B. Cleage, Jr, Lawrence Lucas (a Harlem Roman Catholic Priest) and Calvin Marshall (an AME Zion minister in Brooklyn) who were preaching every Sunday in the ghettos of the nation and hammering out the first tenets of Black Theology on the anvil of their experience.[63]

Of those listed with Cleage above, Cleage was the first to chronicle his experiences, ecclesiology, and theology. And while Lucas wrote a memoir of sorts, Cleage is the only one to publish the sermons he was preaching during that time. This further substantiates the importance of this project.

My primary aim in this project is not to answer every rhetorical or theological question about Cleage's sermonic presentations. This project is intended to bring religious studies and rhetorical studies scholars and practitioners into a more intimate discussion about their complementarity. I expect some religious studies scholars to readily identify with theological interventions Cleage is making. I also anticipate rhetorical studies scholars will recognize some of Cleage's rhetorical strategies and devices. Some will view *The Black Messiah* as a theological document that uses rhetoric. Others will engage the book as a rhetorical document/artifact with an embedded theology. I believe both understandings are plausible, necessary, and beneficial to the overall understanding of the mastery of *The Black Messiah* and its contribution to the fields of contemporary rhetorical theory, African American Religious/ Prophetic Rhetoric, and Black Power studies. My hope is that what these fields do not understand about their relationship with one another will be more adequately affirmed and that inquiries about their relationship will be further researched.

Again, this book will be part of a larger reclamation project regarding the life, legacy, and works of Rev. Albert Cleage Jr. (Jaramogi Abebe Agyeman) from a rhetorical studies vantage point. The primary purposes of this project will be to (a) offer a detailed engagement with a document that epitomizes the relationship between rhetoric, race, and religion, (b) advance the conversation of rhetoric's rehabilitation in a contemporary context, (c) fill in some of the scholastic gaps in Black Power studies, Black Theology, and Black rhetoric.

Lastly, Albert Cleage's *The Black Messiah* is a premier artifact that allows rhetoricians, theologians, and others in the humanities an opportunity to delve more deeply into the contours and nuances associated with the intersections of rhetoric, race, and religion. More directly, the areas of contemporary rhetorical theory, African American (Religious and Prophetic) rhetoric, and Black Power studies can both inform and be informed by *The Black Messiah*. As the contemporary landscape continues to exemplify the ways social movements, cultural sensibilities, and matrices of social and political and religious power collide, a book of sermons that articulates an uncompromising commitment to Black Liberation and the Black experience is ripe for scholastic and social engagement. That said, before we can dive more deeply into the content of *The Black Messiah*, we must take time to discuss the current landscape of rhetoric and what a fuller engagement with and appreciate of Black religious rhetoric can offer.

NOTES

1. The term "Black" will be capitalized throughout this book. I do so echoing Lori L. Tharps who argues that lowercase black is merely a color. Uppercase Black refers to people of the African diaspora. As such, I use Black and African American

interchangeably. I also will capitalize the Black in Black Liberation, Black Theology, and Black Prophetic Tradition as they refer to experiences, political ideologies, and religious/spiritual understandings of people of African descent that have been codified into fields of study that should be honored and affirmed. See, https://www.nytimes.com/2014/11/19/opinion/the-case-for-black-with-a-capital-b.html#:~:text=When%20speaking%20of%20a%20culture%2C%20ethnicity%20or%20group,African%20diaspora.%20Lowercase%20black%20is%20simply%20a%20color.

2. I explain this concept further in a forthcoming essay Introducing Sermonic Militancy—A Call Towards More Revolutionary Homiletics and Hermeneutics. *The Journal of Communication & Religion* 44, no. 3 (Fall 2021).

3. Lloyd F. Bitzer, "The Rhetorical Situation," *Contemporary Rhetorical Theory: A Reader* (1999): 217–225.

4. Albert B. Cleage, *The Black Messiah* (New York: Sheed and Ward), 11. (Also note, remaining references to *The Black Messiah* will be listed by in-text page number citations and not footnotes).

5. "This Far By Faith—Albert Cleage," *PBS*. Accessed May 7, 2015—http://www.pbs.org/thisfarbyfaith/people/albert_cleage.html.

6. Albert B. Cleage, *The Black Messiah* (New York: Sheed and Ward, 1968).

7. Sheed & Ward Publishers to Albert Cleage, July 18, 1968, Box 1, Albert Cleage, Jr., Papers.

8. Cleage, *The Black Messiah*, 9.

9. Carter G. Woodson, *The Mis-Education of the Negro* (Book Tree, 2006).

10. Albert B. Cleage Jr., *Black Christian Nationalism: New Directions for the Black Church* (Luxor Publishers of the Pan-African Orthodox Christian Church, 1987), xxv.

11. Cleage, *Black Christian Nationalism*.

12. Cleage, *The Black Messiah*, 3.

13. Aswad Walker, "Princes Shall Come Out of Egypt: A Theological Comparison of Marcus Garvey and Reverend Albert B. Cleage Jr.," *Journal of Black Studies* 39, no. 2 (2008): 194–251.

14. Albert Cleage Jr., "Myths About Malcolm X," February 24, 1967, https://www.marxists.org/history/etol/newspape/isr/vol28/no05/cleage.htm.

15. Andre E. Johnson, *The Forgotten Prophet: Bishop Henry McNeal Turner and the African American Prophetic Tradition*, 2012, 7.

16. Myran E. Lewis, "Cleage: A Rhetorical Study of Black Religious Nationalism" (PhD diss., The Ohio State University, 1974), vii.

17. James Darsey, *The Prophetic Tradition and Radical Rhetoric in America* (New York: NYU Press, 1999), 10.

18. Bishop Mbiyu Chui (currently, pastor at Shrine #1, Detroit, Michigan) in discussion with the author, March 2016).

19. Arthur L. Smith, "Markings of an African Concept of Rhetoric," *Communication Quarterly* 19, no. 2 (1971): 13–18.

20. See Jawanza Eric Clark, ed. *Albert Cleage Jr. and the Black Madonna and Child* (Palgrave Macmillan, 2016); Angela D. Dillard, *Faith in the City: Preaching Radical Social Change in Detroit* (Ann Arbor, MI: University of Michigan Press,

2007); Weldon McWilliams IV, *The Kingdom At Hand: Black Theology, The Pan African Orthodox Christian Church and their Implications on the Black Church* (Denver, CO: Outskrits Press, 2016); Kelly Brown Douglas, *The Black Christ* (Maryknoll, NY: Orbis Books, 1994).

21. Michael Leff, "Words the Most Like Things: Iconicity and the Rhetorical Text," *Western Journal of Communication (includes Communication Reports)* 54, no. 3 (1990): 255.

22. Ibid., 255.

23. Antonio de Velasco et al., eds., *Rethinking Rhetorical Theory, Criticism, and Pedagogy: The Living Art of Michael C. Leff* (Lansing: Michigan State University Press, 2016), 472.

24. Darsey, *The Prophetic Tradition and Radical Rhetoric in America*.

25. Cleage, *The Black Messiah*, 20.

26. See Gary J. Dorrien, *The New Abolition: WEB Du Bois and the Black Social Gospel* (Yale University Press, 2015).

27. This statement has been popularized by Black evangelical pastors such as Tony Evans, see https://tonyevans.org/not-a-skin-problem-but-a-sin-problem/.

28. Kerry Pimblott, *Faith in Black Power: Religion, Race, and Resistance in Cairo, Illinois* (Lexington: University Press of Kentucky, 2016).

29. Mark L. Chapman, *Christianity on Trial: African-American Religious Thought Before and After Black Power* (Eugene, OR: Wipf and Stock Publishers, 2006).

30. Cleage, *The Black Messiah*, 35.

31. See, Chapman, *Christianity on Trial*.

32. Bishop Kimathi Nelson (currently, Holy Patriarch of the PAOCC) in discussion with the author, February 2018.

33. James H. Cone, *Martin & Malcolm & America: A Dream or a Nightmare* (Orbis Books, 1991).

34. Merriam-Webster defines "slavocracy" as "a faction of slaveholders and advocates of slavery in the South before the American Civil War. By "slavocracy" I mean the relationship between the Transatlantic Slave Trade and its relationship to and influence on the democratic project in America. Of particular interest here is the way the slave trade and the democratic project engaged with Christianity as a religious tradition.

35. Michael Leff and Andrew Sachs, "Words the Most like Things: Iconicity and the Rhetorical Text," *Western Journal of Communication (includes Communication Reports)* 54, no. 3 (1990): 256.

36. Hiley H. Ward, *Prophet of the Black Nation* (Philadelphia, PA: Pilgrim Press, 1969).

37. Ibid, ix.

38. Ibid, xv.

39. Ibid, 16–17.

40. Cleage, *The Black Messiah*, 5–6.

41. Ibid, 6.

42. See, James H. Cone and Gayraud S. Wilmore, eds., *Black Theology: A Documentary History: Volume One: 1966–1979* (1993).

43. William Jones, *Is God A White Racist?: A Preamble to Black Theology* (Boston, MA: Beacon Press, 1998), Kindle Locations 126–130.

44. Raphael G. Warnock, *Divided Mind of the Black Church: Theology, Piety, and Public Witness*. Vol. 9 (NYU Press, 2013).

45. Clark, *Albert Cleage Jr. and the Black Madonna and Child*.

46. Ibid, 4.

47. Ibid, 6.

48. Ibid, 6.

49. Gustavo Gutierrez, *On Job: God-Talk and the Suffering of the Innocent* (Maryknoll, NY: Orbis Books, 1987).

50. Clark, *Albert Cleage Jr. and the Black Madonna and Child*, 8.

51. See Stephen Prothero, *American Jesus: How the Son of God Became a National Icon* (Macmillan, 2003).

52. Lewis, "Cleage: A Rhetorical Study of Black Religious Nationalism," 98–99.

53. James Boyd White, *When Words Lose Their Meaning: Constitutions and Reconstitutions of Language, Character, and Community* (Chicago: University of Chicago Press, 2012).

54. Maurice Charland, "Constitutive Rhetoric: The Case of the Peuple Quebecois," *Quarterly Journal of Speech* 73, no. 2 (1987): 133.

55. Michael Leff, "Hermeneutical Rhetoric," in *Rhetoric and Hermeneutics in Our Time: A Reader*, edited by Walter Jost and Michael Hyde (New Haven, CT: Yale University Press, 1997), 196–214.

56. Cleage, *The Black Messiah*, 6–7.

57. Frank A. Thomas, *Introduction to the Practice of African American Preaching* (Nashville, TN: Abingdon Press, 2016), Kindle Location 1204.

58. James Cone, *Black Theology and Black Power* (Maryknoll, NY: Orbis Books, 1997), Kindle Locations, 151–152.

59. Ibid, Kindle Locations, 1847–1848.

60. Douglas, *The Black Christ*.

61. McWilliams IV, *The Kingdom At Hand*.

62. Dillard, *Faith in the City*.

63. Cone and Wilmore, *Black Theology*, 67.

Chapter 2

What *The Black Messiah* Offers Religious and Rhetorical Studies

As I stated in the introduction, traditional rhetorical theory and systematic theology are both far too white.[1] Both fields were established without any significant engagement with contributions from black and brown people (and in most instances dismissive of the contributions of women). Even though the most ancient associations of oratory and religion are African, the foundations of traditional (or classical) rhetorical theory and systematic theology are still Eurocentric. Albert Cleage's claims in *The Black Messiah* explicitly attempt to tackle the whiteness of religion and theology. Those claims also, more subversively, can help us deal with the whiteness of rhetorical studies. While this chapter will not leap directly into the sermonic content in Cleage's book, it will look at the landscape of traditional rhetorical theory—its shortcomings and blind spots (especially in relation to race and religion)—and consider what contributions religious and sacred rhetoric might offer to contemporary rhetorical theory and religious studies.

There's a part of me that wishes to ask those disinterested in rhetoric to skim past this chapter and rush to the next one. However, this impulse is part of the problem this chapter (and this book) seeks to address. Rhetoric has a direct relationship with religion (and vice versa). And although some readers may be unfamiliar with some of the terms and names I am about to present, I encourage everyone to look a little closer into what they are unfamiliar with. Also, ask why rhetoric and religion has been seen as so dichotomous? When the relationship between rhetoric and religion are brought into focus, it helps us see the problems and promises in both fields and how a more robust engagement with material *The Black Messiah* can respond to the problems and realize the promises. So while this section may lean more heavily into the rhetorical studies side of this discussion, it should be helpful in introducing those who are unfamiliar with the rhetorical tradition to some of the foundational arguments and personalities. It also will thread together some of the innate connections between Black Preaching (or Black religious rhetoric more broadly) and how it helps us see the field of communication more clearly. So when Cleage states, "The present crisis, involving as it does the black man's struggle for survival in America, demands the resurrection of a Black Church with its own Black Messiah,"[2] he is describing a rhetorical situation and a theological response to it. And when it describes how "the sermons included in this volume were preached to black people" and "white people who read these pages are permitted to listen to a black man talking to black people"[3] this is the epitome of a rhetor constructing their audience. This cannot be analyzed or appreciated properly with the conventional landscape of rhetorical studies unbothered.

Recognizing a problem or dis-ease embedded within traditional rhetorical theory is not a new claim. Maurice Charland establishes a provocative platform in his 1990s essay "Rehabilitating Rhetoric."[4] By providing a methodical engagement with this essay, both religious studies and rhetorical scholars alike can benefit from their reciprocal relationship and serve rhetoric's rehabilitation more astutely. Charland's essay helps establish the need for rhetoric to be rehabilitated. I will offer something Charland does not; an engagement with Molefi Asante's work on Afrocentric rhetoric as well as Leff's work on contemporary rhetorical theory. After that, I will introduce some of Frank Thomas and Vorris Nunley's work on African American religious rhetoric and embed some Cleage quotes throughout to try to keep the overall aim of the book in focus. Asante charts a path forward for us to take more seriously the Afrocentric nature of rhetoric at its foundations—foundations that precede the Greco-Roman classical periods. Frank Thomas highlights a framework of religious rhetoric that is fundamentally theological and rhetorical guiding us into deeper engagement with material that helps to rehabilitate rhetoric from its cultural and ideological exclusions. And Nunley offers us a more Afrocentric view of parrhesia—frank speech. This sequence will help us better understand the relationship between rhetoric, race, and religion. Proceeding in this order will also aid us in interpreting the material in *The Black Messiah* in the latter chapters.

CHARLAND SENDS RHETORIC TO REHAB

Charland's essay title dictates a flaw or insufficiency in traditional rhetorical study and criticism with relationship to contemporary/postmodernist/poststructuralist realities. Charland seeks to introduce us to a background of rhetorical studies that had ignored a "link between discourse and praxis" and thereby compartmentalized the "literary" aspects of rhetoric "within the realm of psychological effects and personalized or romantic conceptions of aesthetics."[5]

Charland highlights the ways in which rhetoric has been misinterpreted and reinterpreted over time. He also grounds his analysis early on in the words and theories of Terry Eagleton who roots rhetoric in both the "practical and political."[6] Charland applauds the Marxist literary theorist for "rediscover[ing] rhetoric."[7] This means that rhetoric had been descending into the shadows, or at least veering far from its original course, but, because of the work of Eagleton and others, had begun to be revived, rerouted, and reconsidered with respect to its functions and being.

As far as Charland is concerned, Eagleton's assessments of the contours of rhetorical studies are left wanting. Simply put, the gulf between cultural theory and rhetorical theory had not been sufficiently bridged or minimized. Charland expresses how "Eagleton writes seemingly unaware of the American discipline of rhetorical studies within communication studies."[8] Therefore, at the offset, Charland pivots toward a more robust analysis of not only how rhetoric is considered academically but, moreover, where rhetoric is placed within the academy and what rhetoric is ontologically.

Charland grapples with how recent theoretical and practical developments have impacted rhetoric as a field of study and practice. Charland sees rhetoric as having been dismissed, a stepchild of other (more important) disciplines. He cites how deconstructionist thought has "cast a blind eye to rhetoric" and poststructuralist conceptions of cinema, mass communication, and culture have all engaged various forms of rhetorical criticism but "have not engaged the harlot of the arts."[9] This disengagement has created a chasm between "rhetoricians" and "cultural theorists." Charland attempts to build a bridge over this divide and shorten the distance between the relationship of rhetoric, politics, and society.

RHETORIC AND CULTURE

Charland assesses a working relationship between rhetoric and culture that has been reduced to theories about persuasion and power that neglect rhetorical strategies and practices that produce social change. Understanding how rhetoric, and especially the rhetoric of "progressive" social movements, requires a rhetor developing a problematic dynamic between and the matrices of social and political power, Charland intends to address the quandary by expanding the reach and broadening the functions of rhetoric. In light of the unavoidable challenges rhetoric faces, Charland aims, first, to (re)situate rhetoric. He calls for "the forging of a broader and more inclusive discursive field" hoping to achieve "a theoretical engagement and alliance informed by an appreciation for and a confrontation with theoretical difference."[10]

Rhetoric, for Charland, must provide much more than the substance for cosmetic analysis, but, moreover, "a basis for a fundamental analysis of the relationships of discourse, communication, power, and culture."[11] Charland is not suggesting that rhetoric provides the totality of research options when we attempt to understand social constructions, values, and communicative methods. But, he does argue that rhetoric provides "primary insight" and is so essential to the understanding of how social constructions emerge, how cultural values are institutionalized, and communicative methods become normalized, that any analysis that does not center on rhetorical criticism, theory, and functions will be insufficient.

Demanding that rhetoric be understood as a primary and foundational academic pursuit and not merely an academic addendum to more centralized subject matters, Charland calls for rhetoric's rehabilitation.

> Rhetorical study needs to be rehabilitated in a double sense: its proper place within the human sciences and contemporary cultural theory should be recognized; also, however, those working within the rhetorical tradition need to shed their insularity, enter into the grand debates within the human sciences, and critically reexamine the assumptions of their own practice. Rhetoric's contribution to cultural theory will only be realized if those within the rhetorical tradition understand and situate the significance of their own work.[12]

Charland begins his quest for rhetoric's rehabilitation by concentrating, first, on rhetoric's situation—both as a field and as a form of engagement with discourse in general. While the terms "rhetoric" and "situation" evoke associations with Lloyd Bitzer's essay, "The Rhetorical Situation,"[13] Charland and Bitzer have two different agendas.[14] Bitzer aims to analyze the social contexts and happenings that create "exigencies" and give human communication its unction, uniqueness, and meanings. Bitzer is considering rhetoric primarily as an expression to be studied but not as a subject to be situated in its proper place within a broader scope of scholastic material.

Charland contends that "rhetorical theory anticipated by over a millennium the recent "linguistic turn" of the human sciences"[15] This statement essentializes rhetorical theory with respect to how language and communicatory methods (the techniques humans use to communicate) relate to who we are, how we think, and what we (think we) know. This statement also lays the foundation for where Charland sees rhetoric as a field of study in relation to other fields.

THE HABITATION OF RHETORIC

Charland examines what Michael Charles Leff refers to as "The Habitation of Rhetoric"[16] and aims to consider where the field should be placed and why. The placement of rhetoric as a field is significant because where rhetoric is situated—its habitat, if you will—determines the field's trajectory, impact, and the values placed within and upon it. There is a quote some attribute to Albert Einstein that states, "If you judge a fish by its ability to climb a tree, it will live its whole life believing that it is stupid." Advancing that analogy further, the same fish, if it is conditioned to use those misaligned metrics, will develop a dis-appreciation for the water in which it has been designed to exist in.

In other words, the conceptual or theoretical placement of rhetoric will either strain or liberate the potential fruit bore from the tree of our academic pursuits. If rhetoric is rooted appropriately, the fruit flourishes and other fields of study can enjoy its array of flavors. If rooted inappropriately, the fruit becomes contaminated with poisons that seep into the realm of historical, sociological, literary, and cultural studies by proxy.

Leff warns of this danger using metaphor. Leff interprets two traditional takes on rhetoric, neo-Aristotelian and neo-Sophist, which he gleans from concepts within Cicero's *De inventione*. Leff sees neo-Aristotelian perspectives of rhetoric as placing rhetoric in a container. Meanwhile, he sees neo-Sophist perspectives as seeking to liberate rhetoric from the container but compartmentalizing rhetoric nonetheless. Leff argues, "The neo-Aristotelians regard rhetoric as a thing contained; it is an art domiciled within the territory of politics and domesticated by its political confinement . . . the neo-sophists [sic] attempt to liberate rhetoric by conceiving it as a container, or more properly, as a containing force."[17] Leff is extremely helpful. However, Leff, even in his attempts to liberate rhetoric, is still conditioned and contained by a Eurocentric framework.

I had the pleasure of taking a class from Leff while in seminary. We discussed, over the course of several weeks, some of the nuances that Black religious rhetoric offers. He was open-minded and intrigued. He would ask me, as he had asked his former students like Frank Thomas and Andre Johnson, and his colleague Barbara Holmes, questions about how to make sense of Dr. King's sermonic materials, speeches, and writings. Leff seemed to be raising his consciousness about how Eurocentric and white-centered approaches to rhetoric were excluding necessary and provocative approaches to materials that shed light on not just Black life in America but life in general across continents and chronologies. I neglect I never got the opportunity to discuss Cleage and *The Black Messiah* with him. But I still chuckle every time I think about him referring to Molefi Asante as "Arthur Smith."

RHETORIC'S FOUNDATION, FUNCTION, AND THE ROLE OF RELIGIOUS RHETORIC

If Leff, Charland, or any other rhetorical scholar, is going to be successful in liberating or "rehabilitating rhetoric" they must reclaim the balance between rhetoric's foundations and functions. What rhetoric *does* and what rhetoric *is* are of equal importance—two sides of the same coin. Since rhetorical studies scholars tend to neglect the role and function of religion in general and religious rhetoric in particular, the field itself remains in need of even more rehabilitation that Leff, Charland, and most of their academic offspring have been willing to offer. But, luckily, as mentioned earlier in my reference to Leff, there are some who are charting a path forward and must be taken more seriously.

To establish this point, I must offer a prelude to what I intend to discuss more thoroughly later in this chapter (and exemplify in the book methodologically). There is a theoretical framework that seeks to balance the foundation and functions of rhetoric. This aspect of scholarship has been understudied because of the misconceptions about both rhetoric and religion. However, Frank Thomas's recent study on the role and function of African American preaching offers insight into this relationship and provides another potential method of rehabilitating rhetoric as Charland intends.

Thomas contends that African American preaching, which is a primary form of religious rhetoric, is equally and essentially theological *and* rhetorical. Aligned with my earlier contention that any engagement with rhetorical theory that privileges Eurocentric thought inevitability remains insufficient, Thomas examines how Western approaches to religious rhetoric have prohibited scholars (and nonacademics who are interested in and impacted by religious rhetoric) from understanding and embracing the equality of importance between what this type of rhetoric *is* and what it *does*.

Thomas argues,

> African American preaching [and religious rhetoric] is fundamentally both a rhetorical and theological enterprise. African American preachers utilized the oral traditions of West Africa and the slave experience of America to shape verbal and nonverbal expressions (sounds and gestures) that were inherently and necessarily rhetorical and theological. Within the African American preaching tradition, there has not been a hard and fast debate distinguishing rhetoric and theology, that is, a total separation of the art of persuasion from theological reasoning in the preaching process. In contradistinction, in the history of Western preaching, there has been an ongoing discussion of whether or not preaching is a theological or rhetorical act.[18]

In this regard, theology is the philosophy and ideology that undergirds whatever may become a religious rhetors strategy and/or pedagogy. Religious rhetoric is often undervalued for its pedagogical functions. Religious rhetoric has been valued for its theological content but understudied because of how theology is formed. Theology is a rhetorical construction that develops out of preexisting social and political structures (that, ironically, were established through rhetorical processes). As Charland points out,

> Rhetorical studies consider the terms of the policies, practices, values, and ideologies . . . speeches or writings articulate, the forms in which these prescriptions are thereby cast, and the manner in which these articulate *with* existent discourses and the at least attributed logics and understandings of their audience.[19]

In other words, I am proposing a more intentional engagement of religious rhetoric, not merely for its theological purposes, but, also, as far as rhetoric as a field of study is concerned, for its pedagogical purposes. Religious rhetoric assists us in seeing (among other things) the interconnectedness of rhetorical pedagogy and rhetorical philosophy. Theology is, to some degree, a philosophy of religion. And if the function of religion is to instruct, inform, inspire, or even indoctrinate, then there is an intricate element of religious rhetoric that is primarily pedagogical. This type of pedagogy is also helpful in examining rhetorics relationship with power, ethics, and truth. I will say much more about this in the latter portion of this chapter.

The broader point here is this, rhetoric has a responsibility to address the relationship between existing policies, practices, values, and ideologies because it can offer a window into how these entities were constituted in public. The challenge is, as Charland seeks to resolve, what should our fundamental understanding of rhetoric's purpose(s) be and where should rhetoric be placed in relationship to the other social sciences?

RHETORIC'S RELATIONSHIP TO POWER

It is important to understand rhetoric as a tool for building and obtaining power. It is also a tool for usurping power. I think about this frame precisely when I think of the Black Prophetic and Rhetorical positions and how Black preachers, like Cleage, in sermons (like those found in The Black Messiah) organize thoughts and distribute them to cultivate power among people often rendered powerless by public policy, political exploitation, and theological malnutrition. When Cleage preaches sermons like "Brother Malcolm" and reflects on the role Malcolm X played in the Black

Power Movement as a religious icon and "Dr. King and Black Power" when he complicates the role of nonviolent resistance in the revolutionary struggle for Black Freedom, he is using rhetoric as a power building tool (see chapter 5). Cleage exemplifies what I mean when I say that (Black) prophetic and liberationist rhetoric is not just "speaking truth to power." It is also speaking truth with power, seeking to empower those who have been rendered powerless. Conventional rhetorical analyses tend to miss (or undervalue) rhetoric's relationship to power.

What I want to do with much of the remainder of my engagement of Charland's essay is hone in on the relationship between rhetoric, power, society, and the social sciences.

Charland helps us to reconsider the shortcomings of traditional rhetorical theory. Although he does not state this explicitly, Charland understands rhetoric to be in need of reconsideration and rehabilitation from its seemingly irrevocable roots in ancient Greek classical literature. What we find is that whenever rhetorical studies that root itself too deeply in Aristotelian or Gorgianic (Sophistic) logic, or any other Eurocentric epistemologies for that matter, it tends to forsake the conventions and structures that inevitably contribute to the dynamics of power, speech, cultural formation, pedagogy, and politics. Leff articulates this problematic by stating,

> While neo-Aristotelians seek to constrain the range of the rhetorical process and the neo-sophists [sic] seek to expand it, both alike center attention in process. Rhetoric is either process confined within some larger domain from which it draws substance, or it is the unbounded action of process itself. In either case, rhetoric per se is not substantive, since it is a form of action that generates or manages material without ever resting in a material embodiment.[20]

Under this rubric rhetoric is damned if it does and condemned if it doesn't. However, Leff and Charland both propose rhetoric as independent of classical claims of associations and boundaries. Rhetoric is not to be placed as a limb of the body but, moreover, as the life blood that activates the body and must be studied through independent methods. Blood can exist independent of a body, but the force and activity of blood are best understood in relation to the body it has helped to activate.

To that end, Charland's suggestion that social theory is a necessary partner to rhetorical theory and criticism because it brings "an adequate theorization of the place of discourse, the forces that put it in place, the ideological and affective grounds from which it proceeds, and the silences that it imposes"[21] is most helpful. This idea contends that rhetorical studies, while independent of other academic fields, is best understood in its relationship to the social structures that it has helped to make a reality.

RECONSIDERING RHETORIC'S HISTORICAL PLACEMENT

The primary shortfall of traditional rhetorical theory is its historical placement. Classical rhetorical theory ignores the fact that rhetorical study and criticism shows up in a movie in the middle of it, even as rhetoric itself was involved in the creation of the movie at the offset. As a result, much of the necessary tools of engagement have been lost or even dismissed by traditional rhetorical scholarship. Leff argues that the loss of necessary tools of engagement achieved "a nearly total, a revolutionary, disjunction between the study of the rhetorical process and a serious interest in any particular rhetorical product . . . the placement of rhetoric at the abstract level of process has become a largely unconscious but well-established orthodoxy."[22] Leff sources this analytical flaw in "the Enlightenment's anti-rhetorical presuppositions."[23]

Irrespective of where the orthodoxy is sourced, both Charland and Leff recognize its insufficiency when dealing with what the processes and the products of rhetoric. Nevertheless, due to its inherent problems Charland calls for an inward critique of rhetoric. Charland is contending that rhetoric has been addicted to and dis-eased by its own insularity.

What, then, does Charland propose as the means and methods of rehabilitation? True to form, Charland evokes an idea of confession or admittance of the issues as a starting point for rehabilitation. Throughout the essay, Charland cites the deficiencies of traditional rhetorical theory. His strongest concession is related to how rhetoric had been situated in and sheltered by its historical conservatism. He reveals,

> Rhetorical theory has a blindspot [sic]. It's apparent "conservatism," or at least absence of radicalism, is not merely the product of a theoretically derived political realism. It results as well from its own history as an institutionalized discourse and from an ideological commitment that tends to inhibit a reflection upon its own presuppositions.[24]

In other words, rhetorical theory, criticism, and scholarship have suffered from what sociologist Thorstein Veblen called "trained incapacity."[25] Burke, who also associated the term with Veblen, offers a treatment of this idea in *Permanence and Change*.[26] Burke argues, "By trained incapacity [Veblen] meant that state of affairs whereby one's very abilities" and orientations "can function as blindness."[27] Burke goes on to utilize the concept this way:

> The concept of trained incapacity has the great advantage of avoiding the contemporary tendency to discuss matters of orientation by reference to "avoidance" and "escape." Properly used, the idea of escape should present

no difficulties. It is quite normal and natural that people should desire to avoid an unsatisfactory situation and should try any means at their disposal to do so. But the term "escape" has had a more restricted usage. Whereas it properly applies to *all* men, there was an attempt to restrict its application to *some* men. As so restricted, it suggested that the people to whom it was applied tended to orientate themselves in a totally different way from the people whom it was not applied, the former always trying to escape from life or avoid realities, while the latter faced realities. . . . In the end the term came to be applied loosely, in literary criticism especially, to designate any writer or reader whose interests and aims did not closely coincide with those of the critic.[28]

If we engage the section above and replace the term "men" with "rhetor" and "people" with "field of study," we can see more clearly what Burke highlights and how it applies to the conceptuality of traditional rhetorical theory. Classical rhetoric orientated itself too closely with local texts and circumstances. This inward focus created a blindness which prohibited the field from seeing how communicative methods are inextricably tied to broader historical, contextual, cultural, symbolic, and material "forces" that shape local texts and situations the critic studies.

Charland continues his confession stating,

Contemporary rhetorical theory is naïve when it presumes that the culture of good reasons can be attained simply through study and practice of public speaking. In rhetorical theory we rarely find an adequate account of social and political forces and determinations. Rhetorical theory usually does not render problematic the categories of the rhetorical situation. It tells us neither why certain occasions, speakers, and topics and privileged, nor what unspoken interests are served, nor what audiences are excluded. Indeed, rhetorical criticism has far too often focuses on "official" discourses in the less-than-open public sphere, and thus has failed to bring to light the rhetoric of those hegemony would silence.[29]

Charland sufficiently addresses rhetoric's inability to be integrous in-and-of-itself. Rhetoric is not innately virtuous—no field of study is. What Charland compels us to do is reconsider the ethics of rhetoric and where rhetoric has been most commonly situated. What could or does rhetoric offer when hegemonic forces are evil and unjust? What are the ethical and moral impetuses of rhetoric, if any? How could rhetoric serve Quintilian's "good man speaking well"[30] and how would it make said man "good" if the DNA of the rhetorical situation is political oppression and social subjugation? And does it even matter?

Charland does, mildly, address the issue of morality and ethics through his references to constitutive and "radical" rhetoric. This deserves a significant amount of attention. My understanding of rhetoric, radicalism, and ethics is inconsistent with Charland's. Therefore, I'll reserve a deeper engagement with the material for the end of this section.

REHABILITATING RHETORIC THROUGH RELATIONSHIP

Meanwhile, Charland offers what he perceives to be a more radical path forward (whether or not what he proposes is indeed "radical" will be discussed later). Charland offers confession as a form of rehabilitation and proposes to couple the confession with a complimentary relationship with the social sciences. Charland sees a reciprocal relationship between rhetorical theory, critical theory, and cultural theory. In other words, not only should rhetoric "confess" but, for Charland, it must also "repent." He posits, "While my claim is that a theory of discourse concerned with practical politics cannot ignore rhetoric, I see in the 'posts-' both points of complementarity with and significant challenges to the rhetorical tradition."[31]

Charland recommends that rhetoric open itself up not only to the validity of its own reluctant associations and machinations but also through "an increased attention to political and cultural theory by rhetorical theorists."[32] Charland's remedy is for rhetorical scholars to "theorize properly the position of their project within the human sciences as well as within the social formation."[33] This is a wonderful proposition. But I believe there needs to be a broader road of rehabilitation than the one Charland offers in his essay. A major necessity in rehabbing rhetoric is reconsidering the efficacy of researching religious rhetoric, especially from a Afrocentric and Black liberationist perspective.

RHETORIC AS CONSTITUTIVE AND NECESSARY RADICALITY (PARRHESIA PERSONIFIED)

Charland's notion of necessary rehabilitation is beneficial but also incomplete. In the same manner in which he observes the inadequacies of classical and American versions of rhetorical studies, as well as his notification of Eagleton's unawareness of how his attempt to help redeem rhetoric still misappropriates the field, Charland confesses blind spots with respect to insularity and the need to build bridges between rhetoric and other social sciences. At the same time, Charland neglects the blind spots of racial, gendered, abled, and classed theoretical frameworks that are part and parcel of any considerations that privilege Western, Eurocentric epistemologies. Charland has not given sufficient attention to the relationship between rhetorical productions and cultural realities (at least not from a Black or Afrocentric perspective). Molefi Asante has consistently sounded the trumpet with respect to our need to not only interrogate the rhetorical products (texts, speeches, etc.) but equally investigate the existing matrices of social power and how they impact rhetorical processes. This necessary investigation is intensified whenever the aim of the rhetorical project is social change and social movement.

Although this investigative proposal might be seen by some as radical and unorthodox it is nonetheless a necessity if rhetoric ever intends to be something other than a coopted entity used to maintain unjust and unequal status quos. In his essay, "An Afrocentric Communication Theory,"[34] Asante caught wind of this need and offered a different angle of engagement that I believe is more fruitful in our attempts to rehabilitate rhetoric. Asante states,

> It is my intention to address in a systematic way the pragmatics of communication, particularly with respect to the way we are affected by our environment. Such a task undertakes a reorientation of the enterprise of social science, a reformulation of assumptions, and a more thorough response to the diversity of human experiences in communication.[35]

Asante is not simply offering a nuanced form of deconstructionism. He is proposing a revolutionary way of revisiting the origins of our rhetorical norms and assumptions. He is asking explicitly for "a new world voice."[36] And the means of obtaining this voice is discursive and disruptive if we are accustomed to ignoring the relationship between rhetoric and social-political power.

Asante goes on to detail his plan for renewing rhetoric by proposing "a comprehensive plan for analysis rather than the legitimization of any political, economic, or social system."[37] He continues, "This is in line with the Afrocentric philosophy which views the communication person as the center of all systems, receiving information from all equally, and stimulating all with the power of his or her personality."[38] Also, there are ways where Black liberationist theology and rhetoric spotlight this Afrocentric philosophy. *The Black Messiah* is full of this type of material. Cleage repeatedly sets at odds a religious conceptuality of Jesus of Nazareth, a Black revolutionary freedom fighter rooted in an Afrocentric worldview, against Paul of Tarsus, who Cleage sees as an accommodationist contaminated by a Eurocentric epistemology. Consider when Cleage writes,

Jesus was distorted by the institution that was set up in his name. Jesus didn't organize anything except a few people who believed in him, some revolutionaries who followed him in a nationalistic movement. Jesus didn't organize any kind of Church He brought together people who believed in doing what was necessary to create change. That's what Jesus did. But after Jesus was killed they organized a Church in his name. The Apostle Paul, who was really a great organizer, set up Churches everywhere and said, "This is Christianity. All of you who follow after Jesus, come right on in here." And then he changed the whole thing around. No longer was it building a Nation, it was tearing down a Nation. It was leading people right back to the same old individualistic kind of thing which Jesus had fought against all of his life. In the name of Jesus, they created a new kind of individualism. "Come into the Church, be washed in the blood of the lamb and you will become white as snow."[39]

These types of nuggets, a playground for rhetorical analyses, will be ignored when we platform a rhetorical studies landscape centered on a "demos" that highlights people like Aristotle, Plato, and Socrates but devoid of any deep interest in Afrocentric or Black liberationist rhetoric that includes personalities such as Ptah-hotep, Maat/Mayet, the Hebrew prophets, or (again) Jesus of Nazareth.[40]

Using this line of reasoning, we can see more clearly that a system comes into being because a person or set of persons have engaged in a communicative method and obtained a sufficient amount of rhetorical cache which normalizes certain modes of thought, actions, practices, policies, and power dynamics. This is the foundation of constitutive rhetoric. Asante articulates it this way, "Social science cannot be separated from political science, but neither can it be separated from communication. While politics may regulate how and where people will live, communication provides the substance of their living together within certain territorial boundaries."[41]

In other words, while most rhetorical studies have been rooted in a Eurocentric vision that romanticizes and fetishizes conceptualities of the state/society, an Afrocentric vision centers more firmly on the affirmation of the person. This person is connected to a broader social and political structure, but the social and political structures do not exist without persons. These persons must communicate a unique vision of existing for the society and state to move into being. It is not until rhetoric affirms the preeminence of the person that we will develop a more faithful relationship with the social sciences and adequately situate rhetoric where it ought to be.

This is, partly, what I am contending is offered through the study of religious rhetoric in general and *The Black Messiah* in particular. The case I am building here is that generic (or Eurocentric) and conventional methods of rhetorical studies are not neatly compatible with Black religious rhetoric.

And religious and (Black) prophetic rhetoric has been historically viewed as efficacious to building social movements, institutions, and political power for disenfranchised, marginalized, and oppressed people of color. If rhetoric is going to be rehabilitated it must take more seriously products like *The Black Messiah* and religious figures like Albert Cleage Jr. *The Black Messiah* is a wonderful tool to explore rhetorical offerings, strategies, and production, but will not be understood or appreciated if religious rhetoric is continually demonized and ostracized because of its conventional associations. We must reconsider not only rhetoric's relationship with religious studies as a social science but also Afrocentricity writ large as an irreplaceable piece of the puzzle of rhetoric's potential to understand and change society.

THE AFROCENTRIC VISION OF RHETORIC

When the Afrocentric vision of the communicative person is centered in our discussion of rhetoric, its placement, and its potential, then we are more readily available to reconsider the relationship is between power, politics, language, and social systems are. We also can more effectively consider the ways in which social movements emerge and what types of rhetorics have been and must be utilized to respond to an unjust and inequitable social order.

In other words, where do ideas of radical rhetorics, prophetic rhetoric, and parrhesia fit into the rehabilitation and placement of rhetoric today? Although Charland is noted as a premier scholar in constitutive rhetoric, he does not make much room in his essay on rehabilitation for us to delve into this necessary question. Therefore, echoing some of my earlier commentary with relationship to religious rhetoric, I will attempt to offer some perspective into how rhetoric can function as constitutive and necessary radicality.

Charland's essay leaves us with an open-ended inquiry. Charland suggests,

> Rhetorical theory is pertinent only if what Farrell has termed "rhetorical culture" is possible. Should public spaces, always threatened, finally disappear, or should a culture reach the point where consistency or reason-giving are no longer valued or recognized, rhetoric would be irrelevant. Such a world is to be resisted however, for the absence of reasons and judgement are the mark of a reign of terror.[42]

Although the statement reads rather righteously, there is a need to challenge its truthfulness. Rhetoric can only be irrelevant if we accept a close-minded or narrow conceptuality of its functions and abilities. The threat of terror is legitimate. Rhetorical cultures are real things. Nevertheless, Charland's call for resistance needs to be parsed further. I concede that the fleshing out may not have been his intention. Therefore, I want to offer some ideas that may advance Charland's cause.

Terror has reigned for centuries if we affirm the realities of white supremacy, patriarchy, and colonialism. These ideologies and their militaristic ventures have created social, political, and institutional structures that have terrorized those who Frantz Fanon referred to as *The Wretched of the Earth*.[43] Fanon also describes how the marginalized have, in a countercultural fashion, shaped and invented rhetorics that served to radicalize the oppressed and empower them to organize social movements that contest the inhumane structures (and individuals) that have a grip on social and political power.

Considering this reality, a necessary inquiry associated with Charland's proposal for rhetoric's rehabilitation is "What is rhetoric's radical potential and how can we obtain it?" The answer to this depends on what one considers to be radical and what rhetorical means are available toward achieving the radical ends.

RHETORIC'S RADICAL AND TRANSFORMATIVE POTENTIAL

I define radicalism as a contextual ideology and maladjusted response to social norms that are accompanied by a set of expressions which reveal more about the social, political, and cultural norms than it does about the person(s) or organization(s) expressing the radical ideals and utilizing radical rhetorics. Under the auspices of this definition, rhetoric and rhetorical studies are blessed with a burden. We must delve deeper into the rhetorical development of the social structures; we must muse through the constitutive rhetorics that give life, shape, and spirit to a culture and society before we can understand both the potential and pragmatic necessity of radicalism and radical rhetorics.

Rhetorical studies have offered some significant contributions to the area of radical rhetoric and the prophetic tradition. James Darsey felt compelled to redress misconceptions about radical rhetorics of the 1960s. He developed a constructive response to his "professional dissatisfaction as a student of rhetoric with attempts to explain the behavior of the radicals" in his seminal work, *The Prophetic Tradition and Radical Rhetoric in America*.[44] Darsey observes, "It was widely held [during the 1960s] that the strident, often violent discourse of blacks, students, feminists, and other disaffected groups would not only hinder their various causes, but threatened to rend the very fabric of society."[45] Darsey also sees radicalism in direct association with the Old Testament prophets. Yet his interpretation of the prophetic tradition and radical rhetoric is still wrought with Eurocentricity. Thus, Darsey confesses, "I have no idea how [prophetic and radicalized] principles are created except through the most calculated and strategic of Platonic or Machiavellian means, and I am not at all certain that now moribund ideas that have sustained us in the past can be revived."[46] Darsey's appeals to Plato and Machiavelli are examples of a white epistemology that ignores the cultural, geographical, and lived experiences of Black Hebrew prophets in the Old Testament.

Darsey is echoing the pitfall of other endeavors associated with rhetorical analyses—the same ones both Leff and Asante have addressed. Rhetoric cannot be hyper-politicized, Americanized, or pigeonholed into a Eurocentric paradigm. This pitfall is dug deeper as we engage the traditional associations with rhetoric, radicalism, and parrhesia. Interestingly, Darsey does work on rhetoric and radicalism but only mentions parrhesia once in his book (and there it is in association with Robert Welch's artistic works with no substantial engagement whatsoever). This is peculiar. But, given Darsey's perspective of its origins, it becomes more enlightening. I see a direct connection between parrhesia, radicalism, and prophetic rhetoric. And all these quantifiers (and more) are prevalent in *The Black Messiah*.

PARRHESIA AND RHETORICAL POTENTIAL

Whereby rhetorical scholars center the origins of parrhesia in the fifth century, Darsey and others who associate radicalism and bold speech with the eighth-century Hebrew prophets propel us into a quandary. How is parrhesia adequately defined and where/when can it be found?

A reputable perspective on parrhesia comes from Arthur Walzer's essay, "*Parrēsia*,[47] Foucault, and the Classical Rhetorical Tradition."[48] Attempting to delve into the particulars of parrhesia through the works of Foucault in year leading up to his death (1981–1984), Walzer observes two primary public manifestations of parrhesia, "(1) an orator criticizing the demos in a democratic political context and (2) a counselor offering frank criticism of a prince in a monarchical context."[49] Walzer also recognizes the problematics of Foucault's historicity regarding parrhesia. Consequently, Walzer intended to "offer an alternative analysis of *parrēsia* as well as a critique of Foucault's description of classical rhetoric . . . by re-reading from a rhetorical perspective many of the [classical] texts that Foucault analyzes, as well as attending to the treatment of *parrēsia* within rhetoric that Foucault neglects."[50] Charland's attempt at rehabilitating rhetoric also neglected an appropriate treatment of parrhesia.

But Walzer's engagement with parrhesia is still deeply politicized. What Walzer seeks to do is to expand the political considerations beyond the scope of democratized spaces and more inclusive of monarchies (more specifically imperial Rome and Early Modern England). Walzer is seeking to intensify the dynamics of power and establish the counselor to the monarch as "the normative idea of the rhetor, since there is little opportunity under the principate or Renaissance monarchies for a speaker to empower a people or senate."[51] Walzer is closing the gap of separation among power, parrhesia, and prophetic rhetoric. It's necessary to mention prophetic rhetoric here because this monarch/counselor relationship exists very vividly in the relationship between King David and the prophet Nathan who uses a masterful rhetorical presentation to indict King David for the brutal murder of an Israelite soldier—Uriah the Hittite.[52] As mentioned earlier, religious rhetoric becomes vital in our attempts to understand and contextualize prophetic rhetoric and, in this and other cases, parrhesia.

To be fair, Foucault would not connect parrhesia to the prophet, sage, or teacher because of what he sees as a disconnection between the truth being told and its source. Foucault perceives prophets as acting out convictions that are ultimately not their own. I and others disagree with this premise. Pat J. Gehrke, Susan C. Jarratt, Bradford Vivian, held a forum and offered three responses to Walzer's essay.[53] In the forum, they hone in on some of Foucault's misunderstandings of rhetoric and Walzer's engagement with Foucault's concepts. I would add that Foucault misunderstood rhetoric, religion, and the (biblical) prophetic tradition. Gehrke recognizes how religion and rhetoric disrupted the philosophical understanding of parrhesia Foucault embraced. He writes,

> Walzer is certainly correct that Foucault is not writing a history of rhetorical *parrēsia* (or even civic *parrēsia*) but instead a history of the one who can claim to be the philosopher who cares for the soul, the teacher and friend to whom one confesses. Foucault offers us a history of one sense of *parrēsia*, the one that comes to dominate the philosophical tradition, tracing a set of practices and discourses about who holds a relationship to truth and on what conditions. In the Christian era this sense of *parrēsia* transitions (in rather bloody fashion) from the philosopher to the priest.[54]

Furthermore, Gehrke continues to press the claim for a reconsideration of the relationship between power, truth, risk, and parrhesia that Walzer offers via Foucault by highlighting the rise of Christian resistance to Roman power. Gehrke contends,

> Note the importance of the preservation of a *parrēsia* distinct from rhetoric in Christian doctrine. The term, in Greek, retains the Latin, all the way up to present Church usage, and becomes almost inseparable from the Apostle Paul. *Parrēsia* in the Christian world becomes the statement of God's truth in the full care of one's own soul and the care for the soul of others, righteous not for the

discipline and practices of the philosopher but by obedience to divine authority. Declaring oneself Christian and preaching was done not only without concern for the punishment that might be inflicted, but was all the more pressing right in the face of the authority that might kill one for doing so.[55]

I contend that these rhetorical presentations were not done "without concern for the punishment that might be inflicted" but, moreover, despite the concern. These rhetorical presentations offer us a more robust example of parrhesia personified.

Nevertheless, what Gehrke, Jarratt, and Vivian do is provide the necessary pushback to the proposals about parrhesia that Walzer presents, especially with respect to the historical understanding of rhetoric. For me, the primary problem with Walzer's shift from the democratic to the (more) imperial and monarchic is the subversive nature of privilege. For instance, a counselor to a monarch has already attained a level of social and political privilege that empowers them. A counselor to the monarch is not a marginalized person but a privileged person (usually male). This relationship would, in fact, lessen the risk or penalty of speaking truth to power because, in some instances, it would be expected and possibly even welcomed. The counselor would be more concerned with the rhetorical strategy or communicative method than the substance of a critique of a king.

PARRHESIA'S DEMOCRATIC RADICALISM

To be sure, there are elements within the scope of democratic societies (both idealized and actualized democracies) that afford certain people privileges while other people accumulate oppressions. The record of people on the margins—especially people of color, especially women—who have been subject to the American democratic project who have been brutalized, incarcerated, and killed for speaking truth to politicians would far outnumber that of counselors who spoke truth to monarchs. Consequently, what Walzer is doing is not necessarily personifying parrhesia but deradicalizing it. But it is Walzer's commitment to centering the truth or the moral conscience of parrhesia that is most helpful. Walzer embraces Foucault's understanding of parrhesia as a truth act—it is the personification of truth in action.

There are more productive ways to engage parrhesia as a concept and practice. Vorris Nunley offers a perspective on parrhesia that centers on the African American rhetorical tradition. Analyzing African American rhetoric through the lens of the hush harbors, Nunley contends that hush harbor rhetorics, rhetorics that are discursive from more epidictic and formalized rhetorics, "are deemed *parrhesiatically* dangerous."[56] This perspective on parrhesia highlights the relationship between rhetoric, radicalism, and the matrices of social and political power. Most Eurocentric scholars underestimate the amount of courage and faith that contribute to parrhesiatic expressions. Nunley also refers to Foucauldian perspectives on parrhesia. He argues,

> Parrhesia alludes to fearless, dangerous speech. Influenced by the courage of Socrates and the boldness of Black folks such as Dr. Julia Hare attempting to dismantle the disciplinary gaze of a White audience, Cornel West and Michel Foucault address the centrality of *parrhesia* and the parrhesiastes (the rhetor/speaker willing to engage in parrhesia). Parrhesia is important to any substantial notion of democracy that pushes beyond the procedural (e.g., electoral politics, reduced to voting) to fundamental questions of the good, justice, and power as they relate to the soul of the body politic that seriously pivots around knowledge, life, culture, and suffering.[57]

Nunley is not merely inserting Black perspectives on parrhesia into a Eurocentric conversation about cultural and communicative method. Nunley is helpful here, in large part, because he is decentering Eurocentrism, privileging a communicative method that necessitates radicalism, and reconstituting the landscape of rhetoric in general. This is parrhesia personified. And this is exactly the rhetorical method that Cleage employs in *The Black Messiah*. Nunley continues,

> Parrhesia requires the rhetoric to put herself at risk in speaking truth to power, to the dominant political rationality, or to a hegemony that could result in the loss of status, influence, resources, legitimacy, or life. African American parrhesia, then, embodies the aforementioned, but the African American parrhesiastes deploys African American truths and knowledges through African American terministic screens. Parrhesia is endemic to [African American Hush Harbor Rhetorics], as not only are African American knowledges and ways of knowing privileged, but also as Black notions of civility, decorum, and permissible speech are dominant.[58]

Nunley concludes his engagement with parrhesia connecting the dots between rhetoric, radicalism, and the necessity of parrhesiatic projections. He writes, "African American parrhesia is often constructed as angry, militant, distorted, irrational, unreasonable, unpatriotic, divisive, and, of course, dangerous. However, the African American parrhesiastes who is willing to wedge African American knowledges and standpoints into the public sphere is highly valued."[59]

In other words, we cannot underestimate the importance of parrhesia when researching the relationship between rhetoric, power, and social justice movements. If rhetoric is concerned about power, then this relationship has to take priority. Charland's rehabilitation of rhetoric ought to be more considerate of this positioning. Parrhesia is an attempt to reconstitute the public with relationship to power and representation.

THE BLACK PROPHETIC TRADITION

Regarding matters of reconstituting the public with relationship to power and representation is where the Black Prophetic Tradition has excelled. Cornel West connects parrhesia directly with the excellence of the Black Prophetic Tradition in his conversation with Christa Buschendorf through their publication *Black Prophetic Fire*.[60] West argues, "Malcom X is the great figure of revolutionary parrhesia in the Black prophetic tradition."[61] At the same time West engages in sins similar to Walzer. West contends,

> The term parrhesia goes back to line 24A of Plato's Apology, where Socrates says, the cause of my unpopularity was my parrhesia, my fearless speech, my frank speech, my plain speech, my unintimidated speech. Malcolm is unique among the figures in the prophetic tradition to the degree to which he was willing to engage in unintimidated speech in public about white supremacy.[62]

Not only has West mis-historicized the foundation of parrhesia, but he also has rooted the Black Prophetic Tradition in the streams of Eurocentricity. As Robert Terrill points out in his book, *Malcolm X: Inventing Radical Judgement*, Malcolm is a unique personality, but he is rhetorically building from a landscape of African American prophetic discourse that ended up "interwoven in Malcolm X's public address."[63] Terrill situates Malcolm on the shoulders of Frederick Douglass speech, "What to the Slave Is the Fourth of July?," W. E. B. Du Bois's "The Conservation of Races," David Walker's *Appeal to the Coloured Citizens of the World*, and *The Confessions of Nat Turner*.[64]

Furthermore, if we understand the eighth-century Hebrew prophets as ethnically African peoples, then the biblical prophetic tradition is also part of the foundation of the Black Prophetic Tradition and parrhesia is akin to what Sinfree Makoni, Geneva Smitherman, Arnetha F. Ball, and Arthur K. Spears refer to as *Black Linguistics*.[65] Makoni, Smitherman, Ball, and Spears describe "Black Linguistics" as

> a postcolonial scholarship that seeks to celebrate and create room for insurgent knowledge about Black languages. Black Linguistics is committed to studies of Black languages by Black speakers and to analyses of the sociopolitical

consequences of varying conceptualizations of and research on Black languages. The overall goal of Black Linguistics is to expunge and reorder elitist and colonial elements within language studies.[66]

This description is vital to our engagement of Black rhetorics, radicalism, and parrhesia. Within a colonial context, as Nunley articulates, anyone who is black and communicates discursively in public is to some degree personifying parrhesia. However, if Black people are fully human, this boldness in being and in communicating must be valued.

CHARLAND AND THE BLACK PROPHETIC TRADITION

Returning this discussion to Charland's essay, there can be no legitimate rehabilitation of rhetoric that is dismissive or negligent of the periodic necessities of radicalism and the personification of parrhesia. We must construct a communicative research method that centers parrhesiatic expressions as a means of obtaining the necessary understandings of social and political constitutions. The Black Prophetic Tradition, African American (Religious) Rhetoric, and the personalities that fit within those frameworks must become primary figures in understanding the rhetorical situation of what Darsey calls radical rhetoric in America. West and Buschendorf are attempting to do this. However, this cannot be achieved through prioritizing Eurocentric epistemologies of traditional rhetorical theory. Those ways of knowing rhetoric and interpreting rhetoric's being have to be modified if rhetoric is concerned with its relationship to truth, ethics, morality, and social justice movements. And if rhetoric is to become more intentional about its contribution to necessary and progressive social change, it must reconsider the importance and necessity of parrhesia in particular and religious and prophetic rhetoric in general. To that end, Cleage's *The Black Messiah* is a rhetorical artifact that centers on parrhesiatic expressions. The book illuminates rhetorical methods and material exemplifying the best of contemporary rhetorical theory through African American religious and prophetic rhetoric.

CONCLUSION

Charland's essay provides rhetorical scholars and other interested parties with an excellent foundation for a contemporary discussion on what rhetoric is, where rhetoric ought to be situated and understood in relation to the social sciences, and what method ought to be undertaken to rehabilitate rhetoric from its conservative, insular, hyperpoliticized, and exclusive history. This is the Charland's theoretical platform. Classical rhetorical theory has suffered from shortsightedness and compartmentalization within a broader field of communication and cultural studies. It is incumbent upon students and scholars of rhetoric to rehabilitate and/or reclaim rhetoric's rightful place as a pillar of how we conceptualize power, identity (being), politics, and culture.

Simultaneously, however, Charland's theoretical platform and revolutionary potential must undergo a necessary expansion. Rehabilitating rhetoric requires more than a deeper appreciation of the relationship between rhetoric and the social sciences. It requires a reconsideration of rhetorics relationship to power, white supremacy, sexism, classism, colonialism, and other Eurocentric epistemologies that privilege the rhetorical traditions in Greece and Rome over the rhetorical traditions in Northeastern Africa. For this restructuring to take place, we need a revolutionary turn toward what Asante proposes as Afrocentric Communication Theories. We must value people at least as much as we value processes, humanity as much as we value hubris, materialism, and power.

Charland's essay also offers us an invitation to reconsider the role and function of radicalism and the peculiar relationship rhetoric must have with social structures in their constitutive formation and the sociological contestation. In other words, there is far too much rhetorical scholarship that erases the contributions and cultural-critical implications of radicalism, prophetic rhetoric, African American religious rhetoric, the Black Prophetic Tradition, and other marginalized rhetorics. There's an inordinate amount of rhetorical scholarship that continually embraces reductionist receptions of parrhesia. To be clear, there is no need to dismiss the totality of scholarship and imagination that has been given to traditional notions of radical rhetoric, prophetic rhetoric, or parrhesia. What I am suggesting is that those traditionalized notions associated with those terms are far too Eurocentric, much too arrogant and ignorant of the social and political structures that gave rise to their understandings, and ultimately incapable of providing rhetorical scholars with the materials and textures they need to more faithfully understand the relationships between rhetoric, power, and society.

What I am proposing is a necessary reconsideration of those areas through an engagement with *The Black Messiah* and other religious and sermonic material akin to it. Significant and substantial research must be done to reclaim, renew, revive, and uncover the ways in which radical rhetorics (including parrhesia) have been personified. I'm recommending a shift in perspective that echoes Andre Johnson's work in African American Religious and Prophetic Rhetoric. I am convinced that there is no sufficient understanding of the rhetorical climate and culture of the twenty-first century that is devoid of a sufficient understanding of the seemingly unrecognizable overlap of secular and sacred rhetorics. Therefore, while contemporary rhetorical theory is seeking redress and reformulation, it must become more interested in and inclusive of religious rhetorics.

Deep engagements with contributions of African American religious rhetors are not merely ventures for theologians, ministers, and bible scholars. Those who sincerely seek to understand the rhetoric of social movements, communicative strategies on the margins, and seeking to maximize its social and political impact, must take more seriously the intersections of rhetoric, race, and religion.

NOTES

1. See Wanzer-Serrano, Darrel, "Rhetoric's Rac (e/ist) Problems," (2019): 465–476.
2. Cleage, *The Black Messiah*, 9.
3. Ibid., 9.
4. Maruice Charland, "Rehabilitating Rhetoric," in *Contemporary Rhetorical Theory: A Reader*, edited by John Louis Lucaites, Celeste Michelle Condit, and Sally Caudill (1999), 464–73.
5. Ibid., 464.
6. Ibid., 464.
7. Ibid., 464.
8. Ibid., 464.
9. Ibid., 464.
10. Ibid., 464.
11. Ibid., 465.
12. Ibid., 465.
13. Lloyd F. Bitzer, "The Rhetorical Situation," in *Contemporary Rhetorical Theory: A Reader* (1999), 217–225.
14. Scholars continue to take Bitzer to task on his conceptuality. Richard Vatz and Barbara Biesecker albeit helpful, Bitzer's position deserves interrogation and further development.
15. Charland, "Rehabilitating Rhetoric," 465.
16. Michael Leff, "The Habitation of Rhetoric," in *Contemporary Rhetorical Theory: A Reader* (1999), 52–64.
17. Ibid., 53.
18. Frank A. Thomas, *Introduction to the Practice of African American Preaching* (Nashville, TN: Abingdon Press, 2016), Kindle Locations 1204–1209.
19. Charland, "Rehabilitating Rhetoric," 465.
20. Leff, "The Habitation of Rhetoric," 53.
21. Charland, "Rehabilitating Rhetoric," 472.
22. Leff, "The Habitation of Rhetoric," 56.
23. Ibid., 56.

24. Charland, "Rehabilitating Rhetoric," 471.
25. There has been discussion regarding the origins of the term. See http://kbjournal.org/wais.
26. Kenneth Burke, *Permanence and Change: An Anatomy of Purpose* (Univ of California Press, 1984).
27. Ibid., 7.
28. Ibid., 8.
29. Charland, "Rehabilitating Rhetoric," 471.
30. Quintilian (12.1.1).
31. Charland, "Rehabilitating Rhetoric," 469.
32. Ibid., 471.
33. Ibid., 471.
34. Molefi Kete Asante, "An Afrocentric Communication Theory," in *Contemporary Rhetorical Theory: A Reader* (1999), 552–562.
35. Ibid., 552.
36. Ibid., 552.
37. Ibid., 522.
38. Ibid., 552.
39. Cleage, *The Black Messiah*, 192.
40. See, Cecil Blake, *The African Origins of Rhetoric* (Routledge, 2010).
41. Asante, "An Afrocentric Communication Theory," 553.
42. Charland, "Rehabilitating Rhetoric," 472.
43. Frantz Fanon, *The Wretched of the Earth* (Grove/Atlantic, Inc., 2007).
44. James Francis Darsey, *The Prophetic Tradition and Radical Rhetoric in America* (New York: NYU Press, 1997), ix.
45. Ibid., ix.
46. Ibid., x.
47. This spelling of the term "parrhesia" intends to communicate its enunciation. I will be using the terms/spellings interchangeably.
48. Arthur E. Walzer, "Parrēsia, Foucault, and the Classical Rhetorical Tradition," *Rhetoric Society Quarterly* 43, no. 1 (2013): 1–21. DOI: 10.1080/02773945.2012.740130.
49. Ibid., 1.
50. Ibid., 2.
51. Ibid., 3.
52. Cross Reference 2 Samuel 11–12.
53. Pat J. Gehrke, Susan C. Jarratt, Bradford Vivian and Arthur E. Walzer, "Forum on Arthur Walzer's 'Parrēsia,' Foucault, and the Classical Rhetorical Tradition," *Rhetoric Society Quarterly* 43, no. 4 (2013): 355–381. DOI: 10.1080/02773945.2013.846180
54. Ibid., 359.
55. Ibid., 359–360.
56. Vorris L. Nunley, *Keepin' It Hushed (African American Life Series)* (Wayne State University Press), 46.
57. Ibid., 46.
58. Ibid., 46.
59. Ibid., 46.

60. Cornel West and Christa Buschendorf, *Black Prophetic Fire* (Beacon Press, 2015).
61. Ibid., Kindle Location 1692.
62. Ibid., Kindle Location 1692.
63. Robert Terrill, *Malcolm X: Inventing Radical Judgment* (MSU Press, 2004), 27.
64. Ibid., 28–29.
65. Sinfree Makoni, *Black Linguistics: Language, Society, and Politics in Africa and the Americas* (Psychology Press, 2003).
66. Ibid., 1.

Chapter 3

A General Rhetorical Assessment of Albert Cleage's *The Black Messiah*

In 1968, Albert Cleage, Jr., Pastor of what was originally known as Central Congregational United Church of Christ published a book of sermons entitled, *The Black Messiah*.[1] This theological and rhetorical treatise, drawing from figures such as David Walker, Martin Delany, and Bishop Henry McNeal Turner, of Cleage would help shape what would come to be known as Black Christian Nationalism, and what was provocative and controversial. Not long prior to the publication of the book, Cleage had changed the name of the church he was serving to the Shrine of the Black Madonna. The name is reflective of a mural Cleage had erected as a symbolic and rhetorical expression of his theological sentiment. The mural was unveiled on Resurrection (Easter) Sunday in 1967. H. H. Ward describes the mural, "At the center of the chancel in the sanctuary is a thirty-foot high portrait of a plump, sad-faced Black Madonna in the whites and blues of Africa with a black baby in arm."[2] This symbolic change would also be part of the contribution to the psychological, theological, and political reconstitution that Cleage was presenting to the country and more specifically Detroit, Michigan. Allan Boesak would say of Cleage,

> His theological program is an instrument through which Cleage tries to rally black people around a nationalistic ideal. . . . His theology begins and ends "with the historic fact that Jesus was a black man." . . . Cleage not only wants a separate political program for black people—black controlled economic, social, and political institutions; he wants a completer separation from white America.[3]

Boesak situates Cleage's rhetoric within the context of Cleage's broader theological and political project—Black Christian Nationalism.[4] Cleage's seminal text would bear the imprint of his assessment of the relationship between rhetoric, theology, society, and politics.

CLEAGE'S "PREACHING-IN-ACTION"

On December 3, 1967, Rev. Albert Cleage Jr. wrote a letter addressed to Rev. Charles Cobb, Executive Coordinator for the Committee for Racial Justice Now of the United Church of Christ. The letter was intended to express the gratitude, acknowledgment of, and update regarding the "receipt of $2000.00 from the Racial Justice Now Committee of the United Church of Christ."[5] The UCC Church had seeded Cleage and the Central United Church of Christ of Detroit these funds in order to assist with the "development of an experimental ministry involving the establishment of satellite preaching-in-action centers related to Central Church and located in various parts of metropolitan Detroit and surrounding areas."[6] "Preaching-in-action" is a phrase which rhetorically captures what Cleage attempts to provide as a ministerial leader in an urban area wrought with friction between the Black Church, the Black Power Movement, Black revolutionaries, and a white supremacist power structure. Cleage is focused on much more than Sunday morning oratory which renders his audience momentarily inspired but keeps them socially and politically impotent. Cleage describes the function of these centers as an attempt to "increase the influence of Central Church in the Detroit community" and "strengthen the movement of the black church toward a more meaningful involvement in the black community and the black revolution." To suggest that a "more meaningful involvement" was necessary eludes to an underlying problem or dilemma regarding the Black Church's efficacy related to the "black revolution" that had begun to take shape around the country in the late 1960s. This "revolution" was intense in Detroit, Michigan, and the subsequent quandary was front and center for Cleage and his ministerial colleagues.

What could, or should, the Black Church offer to the Black Revolution, Black Freedom, Black Power, and the Civil Rights Movement? From Cleage's perspective, the Black Church had been constituted in ways that were not meaningful enough, in ways that actually worked against those willing to engage in the revolutionary struggle from Black political and theological power. Nevertheless, Cleage turns this disadvantage on its head with some rhetorical maneuvers that would captivate a generation. Cleage sought to contrast his preaching with the pacifist inaction of far too many Black Christians. Cleage wanted to recreate his church into a preaching-in-action center and establish sites of training and instruction toward a more engaging and empowering form of faith for Black people.

According to Mark Chapman, the emergence of the Black Power Movement posed a significant challenge for the Black Church in general and Black preachers and pastors in particular. Chapman writes,

> Whereas pre-Black Power religious leaders attempted to make Christianity relevant for a generation of young people fighting racial segregation in the South, post-Black Power ministers and theologians in the 1960s and 1970s faced the challenge of making the gospel speak to the frustrations of black youth fighting institutional racism, joblessness, and police brutality in the urban north. In this latter period, African-Americans were more conscious of the fact that racism was supported by deep structural and economic roots; consequently, the younger generation changed its focus form integration and civil rights to a new emphasis on black nationalism and self-determination. If the black church and its theology could not answer Elijah Muhammad's claim that "Christianity is the white man's religion," then they wanted no part of it.[7]

The common form of homiletical and pastoral discourse was viewed by many Black community members as too passive and otherworldly to be of any use to the current struggle for freedom, justice, and equality in the 1960s.

Even as Kerry Pimblott poignantly cites spaces like Cairo, Illinois as a site where Black Power found its home in Black Christian spaces, these were exceptions not the rule.[8] The negotiation of sacred space and rhetorical strategies with respect to how to use Black Power as a tool of religious empowerment was an uphill battle for most congregations. Central United Church of Christ, which Cleage would later rename the Shrine of the Black Madonna, was no exception. While Cleage had done a great deal to promote and practice principles of Black Liberation (both symbolically and sermonically), there was still a dilemma facing him. How could Cleage get those emerging leaders of the Black Power Movement who were seen as radical and revolutionary to understand the Black Church as an institution and, more specifically, the Shrine itself was an ally and not an enemy of the Black Power Movement? In other words, the generic understanding of an association with Christianity in America had been lacking an enduring and necessary racial, historical, and rhetorical critique. To that end, the Christianity most Black people encountered was akin to what Carl F. Ellis calls a colonial, mercantile, evolutionist, materialist, racist, imperialist, and cultish "White Christianity-ism."[9]

> By and large, the Bible-believing community had been blinded to the institutional evils of American society. This blindness is somewhat understandable. For example, how can one understand institutional sin, like racism, when the scope of sin has been limited to personal issues, such as drinking, smoking or "chewing"? Furthermore, most members of the Bible-believing community

belong to t the middle class and middle-class life is highly individualistic. How can you see evil in a system which delivered the good so efficiently?[10]

Ellis would conclude, "It is White Christianity-ism which was bitterly denounced in the militant movement of the '60s, and rightfully so."[11] And with this version of the religious tradition being the mainstream and most dominant expression, Cleage's version of a religion that honors the Black origins of the Christian faith and embraces and calls forth the type of "preaching-in-action" he sought to produce would be countercultural. Ellis describes this as "A Black Dilemma" stating that Black militants in the 1960s had been contaminated with a secular humanism he calls "a little 'white' lie in the name of Black truth. And the Black movement degenerated from there into various do-your-own-thing-isms."[12] While Ellis's assessment is quite pejorative, it does articulate a major anchor in Cleage's ecclesiastical challenge. If Cleage's conviction is that Christianity is the most meaningful way to warehouse the Black Liberation Movement and shift Black militants and revolutionaries away from Eurocentric individualism (in the name of secular humanism) toward a more Afrocentric and liberating communalism, he would have to rhetorically reconstitute the framework of both Black revolutionaries and the Black Church.

One strategy Cleage employs in response to this dilemma is to concentrate his attention and rhetorical inventions on figures who are notable in the Black community and represents the ideals of a (Black?) secular humanism (i.e., Stokely Carmichael), Islam (i.e., Malcolm X), and mainstream Christianity (i.e., Martin Luther King, Jr.). All of these figures are revolutionaries in their own right. Cleage would use the sermons in *The Black Messiah* to engage these figures on Cleage's terms in hopes he could leverage them all to advance Black liberationists causes with the Black Church (especially The Shrine) as an institutional hub. Again, while all of the sermons in *The Black Messiah* have value, there are three sermons that situate themselves more directly within the tensions of the Black Faith and Black Freedom Movements in the 1960s. These three sermons, *An Epistle to Stokely* (chapter 4), *Brother Malcom* (chapter 5), and *Dr. King and Black Power* (chapter 5) all represent prima facia cases for Cleage's "preaching-in-action" set to the backdrop of notable figures engaged in the Black Freedom struggle from different vantage points. These figures (and these sermons) spotlight how close readings of Cleage's sermonic content enlighten us about the how the intersections of rhetoric, race, and religion manifest in real-time within a provocative and pertinent sociopolitical reality.

Let's consider, momentarily, Stokely Carmichael as a rhetorical stand-in for the Black Power Movement (more will be said about Cleage's rhetorical and theological engagement with Stokely in chapter 4). Peniel Joseph describes how "throughout the second half of 1966, politicians and bureaucrats urged military officials to draft Carmichael and send him to Vietnam even as he vowed to go to jail rather than fight."[13] And while Cleage might want to buffer this threat for Stokely individually, he is also aware of what Stokely represents for the broader Black Power Movement. Carmichael had begun to detangle himself from the Student Nonviolent Coordinating Committee (SNCC) in ways similar to Cleage's divergence from more mainstreamed, traditional, white evangelical theology (whose substances were embraced and espoused by many if not most Black Christians at that time). Echoing some of Cleage's criticisms of how Black Christianity served as a pacifier for Black Revolution, Carmichael "blamed SNCC for serving as an unwitting buffer between white society and the Black masses, as racial interpreters who helped to maintain the illusion that American democracy required little more than reform."[14] Carmichael presumed, "blacks, disabused of blind faith in whites, could now embark on a political mission to transform the nation on their own terms."[15] However, from Cleage's vantage point, that mission would be futile without an institutional base to build political power. The only institutional base worth Black folk's consideration would be the Black Church. But the Black Church generally did not appeal to revolutionaries like Stokely. Cleage sought to challenge and potentially change that.

Cleage and Carmichael would share sacred space on Tuesday, October 4, 1966. Stokely gave a speech at Central Congregational Church in Detroit (before it was renamed the Shrine of the Black Madonna six months later) to "a packed audience of Black Power militants."[16] Joseph describes the impact of the event in a way that lays a foundation for Cleage's sermon in The Black Messiah bearing Carmichael's name. According to Joseph,

> Carmichael's electrifying appearance at Central Congregation brought together two generations of Civil Rights and Black Power activists, offering a new genealogy of both movements. The presence of [Rosa] Parks, lauded as the spark of the Montgomery Bus Boycott and symbolic progenitor of the Civil Rights Movement's heroic period, elegantly reflected the era's ideological and organizational diversity. Cleage and [Milton] Henry illustrated the often-times hidden passions and spectacular ambitions of a northern black freedom struggle that, in instances such as Detroit's Walk for Freedom, converged with more-conventional civil rights demonstrations. Carmichael . . . represented the most unique political activist of his generation . . . Stokely now served as a living bridge between civil rights and Black Power activists.[17]

Likely motivated by this encounter, Cleage would utilize Carmichael's controversial notoriety, but he would go a step further. Cleage would use Stokely not only as a bridge, indeed but also as a synecdoche to bind together Black

Power and Black Theology. In a sermon addressed to Stokely, written in Epistle form akin to Paul writing to Timothy, Cleage seeks to address the tensions between Black Christianity, the Black Messiah—Jesus of Nazareth, White Christianity, and the Black Power Movement head on. While preaching/writing An Epistle to Stokely, we see Cleage employing what Mike Leff calls "hermeneutical rhetoric"[18] in strategic ways in efforts to reconstitute his congregation toward a more Afrocentric and revolutionary engagement with Christianity. In doing so, Cleage is reconstituting the relationship between Black Power and the Black Church in ways both powerful and, at times, problematic.

Cleage has one primary goal in mind—reorienting Christianity as a religion of resistance against white supremacy. Cleage saw Christianity at its origins as a movement for Black Liberation. Jesus is the model revolutionary. If Cleage can get Black revolutionaries to see and embrace a revolutionary Jesus and the Black Church as an institutional home for the Black Power Movement, the possibilities for Black radical politics and progression would be multiplied. Cleage's epistle is a fascinating case study in Black prophetic and religious rhetoric and exemplifies what "preaching-in-action" looks, sounds, reads, and feels like. As stated in the introduction, Cleage uses bold and frank speech (*parrhesia*) to deconstruct and condemn unjust theologies associated with the Black Church and Black Preaching. At the same time, Cleage will use language to create or bring into existence (*nommo*) a more authentic and liberatory understanding of Christianity.

What was going on with Cleage and The Shrine was indicative of a broader thrust toward Black Power present throughout the country. Individuals were advocating more aggressively for Civil Rights, Human Rights, and Black Liberation than had been the case a few years prior when Martin Luther King Jr. offered his "I Have a Dream" speech at the March on Washington for Jobs and Justice in 1963. This more militant advocacy had begun to interrogate and infiltrate traditional civil rights organizations demanding they become more radical. A young fiery Stokely Carmichael had helped to birth the original Black Panther Party in Lowndes County, Alabama, in 1965. This was only one year after becoming a field organizer for the SNCC. Stokely's emergence as chair of SNCC in 1966, subverting the chairmanship of John Lewis, signified the Black Power trend that Cleage's mural and ministry represented. (Again, I'll say much more about Stokely in chapter 4.)

THE RHETORICAL SITUATION FOR *THE BLACK MESSIAH*

In the introduction of *The Black Messiah,* Cleage sets his own rhetorical situation by contrasting the role and impact the Black Church had historically—not just in the South but also in the North. "In the North, where the black man's problems at one time seemed less pressing, the Black Church has failed miserably to relate itself to the seething ghetto rebellions and therefore has practically cut itself off from vast segments of the black community."[19] As he continues to lay the foundation for his treatise on Black Theology, Black Power, and Black Political Activism, Cleage sought to situate the ills and impotence of the Black Church, at the time, on its insufficient and immobilizing theology—namely the "whiteness" of Jesus of Nazareth. Detailing the impact such theology had on the infrastructure of the Black Church, Cleage argued: "The Northern Church has been black on the outside only, borrowing its theology, its orientation and its social ideology largely from the white Church and the white power structure."[20] In efforts to revive and revitalize the Black Church and thrust the once "invisible institution"[21] into a deeper realm of relevance and revolutionary practice, Cleage employed a rhetorical approach to preaching as a means of persuading his audience to reconsider the role and function of faith in the struggle for Black Liberation.

For Cleage, the relationship between faith and action, theology and praxis was clear. The only way to obtain freedom from white supremacist oppression was to use faith as the vehicle to reimagine a sense of being and behavior in the world. The contextual reality that Cleage found himself, his parishioners, and Black people (in general) in leads to his inspiration for the book. He writes,

> The present crisis, involving as it does the black man's struggle for survival in America, demands the *resurrection* of a Black Church with its own Black Messiah. Only this kind of Black Christian Church can force each individual black man to decide where he will stand—united with his own people and laboring and sacrificing in the spirit of the Black Messiah, or individualistically seeking his own advancement and maintain his slave identification with the white oppressor.[22] (Emphasis mine)

The use of the term "resurrection" in Cleage's rhetoric is imperative. One can only resurrect something that had once been alive. In that case, Cleage is not suggesting a new brand of theology, per se. Cleage's theology is rooted in his understanding of history and biblical literature. Therefore, Cleage's rhetoric seeks to reclaim what he perceives to be a truer and more faithful theology and representation of the Christian faith tradition.

Cleage offers theologians and rhetoricians a window into what we can call rhetorical theology—the association with and appropriation of religious rhetoric as a means of theological, political, and/or social affirmation, association, and persuasion. Cleage's *The Black Messiah* offers an opportunity to see the direct correlation between preaching (homiletics and rhetorical strategy) and theology. Although Cleage, in academic circles of his day, was seen more as a ministerial leader and pastor than a theologian, what remains pertinent is the use of his pulpit platform to produce rhetoric and language (along with the symbolic nature of The Black Madonna) to do what Walter Brueggemann calls, "[criticizing] the dominant consciousness while energizing communities to move towards an alternative vision of existing."[23]

In his own right, Cleage was an academician *and* a practitioner—a priest, professor, and prophet. Cleage's prophetic persona is captured in the only biography written about him entitled *Prophet of the Black Nation*.[24] Cleage used his rhetorical platform(s) to produce language that called unjust power into accountability while also enlightening and empowering those who were negatively impacted by injustice to fight for their own freedom and liberation. Cleage prophetically raised the social and spiritual consciousness of his audience (through print, pulpit, and public address) in order to move people into social and political action.

Edward Blum and Paul Harvey describe the correlation between Cleage's theology and the people's social and political activism this way:

> [Cleage's] movement went beyond ideas and preaching; it hit the streets. After the city's riots of 1967, black Detroiters painted the hands, feet, and face of a white Sacred Heart Christ with black and brown paint. Local whites then repainted the statue white, only to have it painted black again, a racial swapping signifying another contest over the body of Christ now set within the context of urban strife.[25]

Cleage's consciousness raising and challenging of white supremacist normality was a significant contribution to the social, spiritual, and political movement in Detroit and around the country in the late 1960s. The events and movements of the late 1960s also helped to shape (or in some ways simply concretize) Cleage's theology and ultimately made the phrase *Black Messiah* both a reference to Cleage's book and an entire theological disposition. The book, born out of the Black Power Movement and the need to advance a theology that fit the time period, was not simply the reclaiming of Jesus's ethnic and political blackness. The book also provided concrete and tangible material for people on the ground, in the city, and in Cleage's congregation to think through Black Theology before the term was ever accepted in academic and theological circles writ large.

Cleage does not explicitly state how he felt about the book overall. The closest thing to an expression on the book's efficacy speaks more to the rhetorical situation than the book as a rhetorical production. Mindful of his audience and his intent, Cleage states,

> The sermons included in this volume were preached to black people. They are published in the hope that they may help other black people find their way back to the historic Black Messiah, and at the request of many black preachers who are earnestly seeking ways to make their preaching relevant to the complex and urgent needs of the black community. White people who read these pages are permitted to listen to a black man talking to black people.[26]

This introductory clause confirms who Cleage sees as his primary audience—Black people. His concession to "permit" white people to eavesdrop and engage with the material is important to understanding the content within its pages and Cleage's commitment to the Black Prophetic Tradition. He refuses to allow white gazes to dictate his delivery and censor his content.

For Cleage, the historicity and factuality of Jesus's blackness is indisputable and irrevocable if one is to appropriately shape a Christian theology. Two years after the publication of the book, Cleage was asked if his claims were ever disputed to which he replied, "It is amazing. I've spoken at every major white seminary and I have yet to be challenged on the thesis of the Black Messiah. The audience will listen and ask questions but never dispute my argument. They know that essentially what I'm saying is true, although it shows that a lot of their ideas are historical distortions."[27] This concession by white academicians and seminary students is quite telling. It suggests that they understand the historic and cultural legitimacy of Cleage's claim. They may have even understood its efficacy for the Black Freedom struggle in the United States. Nevertheless, they do not seem to have moved beyond the abstract, academic considerations into a transformative theology or public proclamation that would denounce the heresy of what Cleage called the "historical distortions." In fact, both the book and Cleage's theology would be challenged from both within and without the Black community.

A RECEPTION HISTORY OF *THE BLACK MESSIAH*

Cleage's book (and the theological underpinnings associated with it) was often mentioned in tandem (and sometimes in conflict) with other books that began to develop Black (Liberation) Theology as a field of study. While the impact of Cleage's theology has gained traction in the twenty-first century, it became the pivot point for mainstream Christianity's cognitive dissonance both academically and ecclesiastically. Twenty-five years after *The Black Messiah* was published, Jon M. Temme argued, "It is not likely that the name of Albert B. Cleage, Jr. will be recorded alongside Augustine, Aquinas, Luther, Barth, or Cone in the annals of theological history. Yet for a few years in the late 1960s . . . Cleage was a theologian of impact."[28] One must ask, "Why not? Why wouldn't Cleage's name be recorded alongside them?" I contend, it is his unwavering commitment to the theological centering of the Black experience, coupled with his foregrounding of a Black audience that removes him from the litany. Cleage doesn't speak Greek like Augustine or Aquinas. Cleage does not quote nor directly engage European theologians like Luther or Barth as James Cone does. This is one of the distinctions that continue to explain Cleage's marginalization within the ministerial and academic mainstream. While Cleage's impact, years later, seems indisputable and distinct, initially it was subject of much critique and consternation.

More immediately after its publication, *The Black Messiah* was often grouped with James Cone's *Black Theology and Black Power* (notice how Temme mentions Cone in the litany where he perceives Cleage being left out—more will be said to this later). Several reviewers put Cleage and Cone's work in conversation and sprinkled in other works such as C. Freeman Sleeper's *Black Power and Christian Responsibility*[29] and Joseph Washington's *The Politics of God*,[30] both published within the same year, as well as other books that articulated and theorized Black Theology's intervention into academic dialogue on the Christian faith. This highlights one of the challenges Cleage (and other militant ministers, writers, and practitioners) face. There is a danger of a kneejerk homogeneity when it comes to Black religious identity. It doesn't do justice to Cleage or his contemporaries to simply group them together without describing the particular distinctions in their philosophies and presentations. Only one of these writings is a book of sermons (public speeches) produced by someone grounded in a congregation to which they are accountable. Even on its face, Cleage's work is different and deserves the necessary distinction in a thoughtful, affirming, and responsible way. But, too often, these types of comparisons and groupings are used to dilute the force of those who are more militant or radical and present them as outliers or outcasts.

John J. Carey sought to expound upon the intraracial-theological discourse of Cone, Cleage, and other contributors to the emergence of Black Theology in his essay "Black Theology: An Appraisal of the Internal and External Issues."[31] Therein, Carey includes Major Jones's *Black Awareness: A Theology of Hope*,[32] J. DeOtis Roberts's *Liberation and Reconciliation: A Black Theology*,[33] and an edited volume by Roberts and James J. Gardiner, S.A., entitled *Quest for a Black Theology* to the dialogue of Black Theology, Black Power, and Black political praxis. For Carey, these works "provide the basic framework for a radically different interpretation of the Christian faith that has prevailed for centuries in Western Christendom."[34] This dialogue is male-centered, lacking any substantive embrace of feminist or womanist perspectives. It soon became academically elitist and dismissive of unconventional methods of Black radicalism. Carey would express a peculiar affinity for Cone and a subtle indifference to Cleage's contribution to the academy as well as the church. Carey writes,

> Cone has been the most relentless exponent of the view that the concern of true Christianity is the liberation of the oppressed, and with blacks in particular . . . Cleage likewise emphasizes liberation of blacks but relates it more specifically to black nationalism [sic] under a Black Messiah and a Black Church. Cleage, properly speaking, is not a theologian but a pastor. . . . One can detect in Cleage some of the elements of black rage and the emotionalism of black folk religion. Yet on the primacy of liberation as a goal for blacks he stands with Cone.[35]

Carey makes Cone the standard bearer for Black Theology (well before his emergence into the national spotlight as such a towering figure and contributor) while simultaneously reducing Cleage's theology to "black rage" and "emotionalism." Carey fails to see the significance of Cleage's theology and rhetoric in an academic sense and, sadly, does not stand alone in that regard. Carey's early critique offers a window into an explanation as to why Cleage is left out of too many mainstream(ed) conversations regarding Black Theology as the years rolled on. Coupled with Cleage's militancy and radicalism is academia's and mainstream religion's subconscious disdain for Black religion in general. This disdain is associated with a demonization of Black Faith and Black life. This disdain is intensified when the Black Church and its constituents (academic and otherwise) operate with the type of autonomy that disconnects it from white men's academic musings about religion, faith, or church in general. All of this contributes to a continued lack of political empowerment. Nevertheless, Cleage's commitment to the Black Church (as an institution) and the people most directly impacted by its theologies and practices must also be viewed as part of his rhetorical and political strategies. In the *Essence* interview, Cleage posited,

> I did not get into ministry to go to heaven. I joined because I could best serve black people that way. . . . My main concern is to make the Black Church more effective as a power base . . . you don't put together a revolution without some institutional base. . . . What we must do is to restructure the Black Church so that the liberation struggle can have some institutional foundation. We cannot restructure our army or our economic system because we have neither. Thus, our Church must serve as our power base.[36]

In other words, Cleage's commitment to the Black Church as his primary platform did not make him any less academic, it simply made him more of a theological and political tactician. It made him more aware of and directly impacted by the realities that happen on the ground. Many of the early church theologians of high regard, such as Augustine of Hippo (North Africa), served as parish pastors. Bishop Henry McNeal Turner also comes to mind. Cleage is standing in the same tradition. The academy would not (and in many ways still does not) allow for the type of autonomy needed for a militant minister to express his/her deepest convictions (especially without tenure), even when those convictions are rooted in historical, literary, theological, and sociological research.

With respect to *The Black Messiah*'s collective embrace or rejection, the record is ambiguous. Cone clearly knew of Cleage's work prior to publishing *Black Theology and Black Power*. He was influenced by it, by his own (much later) admission.[37] However, as mentioned in the introduction, Cone does not present any significant treatment of Cleage's theology, political practice, or ministerial posture in the book. He mentioned Cleage in one sentence and immediately thereafter proceeds to provide a treatment of the influence and contributions of the Black Muslims and Islam on the Black Power Movement and Black religious thought.

In a similar spirit of modest (if not blatant) dismissal is the assessment reviewers like J. William Aldridge, who sought to "validly question [Cleage's] forceful and dynamic attempt at a reconstruction of both theology and the historical Jesus."[38] Aldridge would go on to refute Cleage's interpretation of Pauline Christianity, Jesus's connection with the Zealot revolutionary rebellion and conclude by stating, "It is unfortunate that there is no word of reconciliation to balance the account."[39] What I see as unfortunate is such a superficial treatment of such a complex work. Scholars like Reza Aslan have described Jesus's connection with zealotry with profound insight.[40] As is the case with so many of the responses to Cleage's work, I cannot comprehend Aldridge's conclusion because his premises seem so preconceived and contrived. What Cleage deserved then and deserves now is a fair hearing, a responsible review, and when necessary an honest critique. Those seem to come few and far between over the last several decades.

One reviewer (whose name is not listed in the archival documents) sought a fair and balanced approach to the book positing, "Cleage in his sermons reason, argues, quotes, derides, inspires; is in turn realistic, sarcastic, exulting, scathing, loving."[41] The same reviewer concludes, "There is no point in white Christians responding to [Cleage's] sermons by saying 'it wasn't like that,' 'that's not the whole story,' or something equally beside the point. On the contrary, it would be wise for every white Christian in the country to read the sermons, say nothing about them, simply keeping them in his heart—even if he has to change the shape of his heart considerably to manage that."[42] Maybe the reviewer left their name off the archival material because they wanted the type of anonymity that provided for an honest assessment of Cleage's work. The acknowledgment of his work as sermonic, the recognition of his rhetorical strategies of argument, quotation, sarcasm, realism, and so on, is the type of mining and reflection Cleage's work deserves. More often than not, that's not the case. That's not the case for Black religious rhetoric in general nor for Cleage's work in particular. Both of those realities need to change.

Responses to Cleage's book and Black Theology were not always modest or middle-of-the-road. Affirmation and wholesale acceptance came from Charles E. Cobb, Executive Coordinator for the Committee for Racial Justice Now of the United Church of Christ who wrote Cleage a few months after *The Black Messiah* was published and stated, "Your book was great and I looked hard but could not find disagreement anywhere."[43] Another correspondent named Stephen C. De Pass wrote Cleage an inspiring letter of affirmation less than two weeks after *The Black Messiah* was published. De Pass elated,

> I recently finished your current book "The Black Messiah" and it was truly a remarkable piece of work. I am 100% for a Black Nation and at present I am currently wandering for a religion. . . . After reading what you said about Apostle Paul and The Black Messiah I had to find myself. . . . Although I live in Queens, I would like to become an active member of the Shrine of the Black Madonna.[44]

One anonymous commentator was so drawn to the book that he/she provided an elaborate and rather detailed "examination of Cleague's [sic] true contribution to black thought."[45] Before offering a clear and concise reflection on every chapter of the book (with the exception of Chapter 6 entitled "He Stirs Up the People" and Chapter 11 entitled "But God Hardened Pharaoh's Heart," whereby the commentator simply states in both instances, "no comments on this chapter"), the writer contextualizes his/her angle into Cleage's work arguing,

> For the most part [Cleage's] message does not stray very far from the path so ably paved by any number of outspoken black men in America today or over the past several years. He belabors white injustice, black confusion, revolutionary rhetoric and repeated calls for black unity under the attractive phrase of Black Nation.
>
> But every thing [sic] offered by Rev. Cleage to his immediate congregation and more remote reading public is not just old hat, over used dialogue or hopelessly outdated clichés. In some of what Reverend Cleage preaches and teaches one finds a new and refreshing sense of determination of hope, and of pointed insight.[46]

While situating Cleage within the tradition of Black prophetic and protest rhetorics, the commentator grants Cleage residential placement among the exact people prophets must seek to represent. Cleage's contributions come "from within the church rather than his conscious efforts to continue a tired tradition of black verbiage, churchly passivity, and otherworldly dreams."[47] This claim is pivotal because, again, it draws a line of demarcation between Cleage and many of his academic contemporaries who offer profound academic theory from the periphery of the Black Church, even as children or offspring of the beloved institution, but lack the substantive, residential, and immediate practices and proximity to undergird their perspectives.

Continuing the theme of affirmation is Marvin T. Judy, a white professor of sociology of religion at Perkins School of Theology who referred to Cleage as "one of the most prominent black clergymen in America" and contextualized Cleage's sermons as vehicles which "lead the reader through the pathos of the ill-treated."[48] To be sure, it is not the agreement that is more riveting here (or in the previous reviews). It is how the particularity of what Cleage offers is brought to the forefront. This can be done in objection or disagreement as well, but, heretofore in the reviews, has not.

However, others expressed an overt skepticism and disdain for Cleage's bold and brash rhetorical posture and theological assertiveness. An editorial in *The Christian News* published less than two weeks after *The Black Messiah* was released headlined, "Christianity Is False Says UCC Pastor: Claims Apostle Paul Distorted Religion of Jesus; Denies Christian Doctrine of Salvation and Resurrection; Backs Violence, Looters, Rap Brown, Malcolm X and Carmichael."[49] This editorial is important because it speaks to the convoluted way some publications tried to demonize Cleage but still had to deal with the impact of his work. To say that Cleage claims Christianity is false is to ignore that Cleage's brand of theology is in direct opposition to white Christianity, specifically. However, the editorial is wrought with coded language, dog whistles, and framing that sought to discredit Cleage and dismiss the significance of his claims. Headlining the names of H. Rap Brown, Malcolm X, and Stokely Carmichael is intended to evoke fear and dismissal in the reader, to color Cleage as a radical militant and to signify a cultish and theological lunacy. The fact is, however, Cleage is not saying Christianity proper is false. He is saying white Christianity is a God-damned-lie, rooted in anti-Black hatred. This is a claim that needed to be made then and still must be made today.

The editorial also acknowledges that Cleage received support and notoriety from influential publications like the *United Church Herald Journal* where Cleage was featured in February 1968. It cites, "The HERALD [sic] believes Al Cleage's voice needs to be heard across the church." The implication here is that to do so would be at the detriment to the church writ large.

The editorial goes on to list January 15, 1968, edition of *Newsweek* which noted "Cleage is the most influential Negro clergyman in Detroit today." Nevertheless, the editorial provides conspicuous presentations intended to marginalize the militant minister and make him anti-Christian(ity). It reads, "Detroit congregation would experiment with some forms of Jewish worship," which was intended to appeal to the Jewish/Christian tensions at the time. The article also sought to provide a rhetorical read of the content and cover of the book. The writer states, "The jacket of THE BLACK MESSIAH [sic] says that Dr. Cleage is "America's most influential and controversial black religious leader." It further claims:

> THE BLACK MESSIAH, in short, represents not a rhetorical device but a theological statement. He is the founder of the Black nation and He gives strength and revolutionary ardor to his followers. No one interested in the future of either the United States or Christianity can afford to overlook Albert Cleage's strong and compelling rethinking of the Christian message.[50]

This assessment is partially accurate. *The Black Messiah* is an unapologetic theological statement, but it is also a subversive rhetorical device. The physical and rhetorical presentation of *The Black Messiah* had undeniable rhetorical impact. The phraseology was intentionally disruptive to a white supremacist religious consciousness that plagued the mainstream and American public—especially the Black community. To suggest Cleage is "the founder of the Black nation" is to seek to isolate him. To set him at odds and contention with other Black religious leaders who were either secular, integrationist, or of another religious tradition other than Christianity. The book literally changed the conversation regarding who Jesus was, what Christianity is, their relationship to Black Liberation and political empowerment, and what those terms could mean to the Christian Church in America specifically and the world more broadly. In fact, the conversation began to go global with Cleage being asked if his work could be translated into Italian.[51]

While Jon M. Temme's essay "The Black Messiah and Albert B. Cleage, Jr.: A Retrospective at 25 Years,"[52] establishes the responses to Cleage's Black Messiah (his theology not the book) between the boundaries of "A Necessary First Step" and "Critical Rejection," neither of those seem to encapsulate the essence of what Cleage had to offer, or what people had to say about Cleage and *The Black Messiah*, then and now. The essence of the offering can only be obtained through a close reading of the text itself. No amount of reviews or reflections could replace the direct engagement and entanglement with the primary source. At best, those musings can only be a compliment. As Cleage advocates for Black political and theological agency, we must trust that Cleage can speak for himself. We must let his text speak.

A BRIEF RHETORICAL ENGAGEMENT WITH *THE BLACK MESSIAH*

An insightful angle to engage and interpret the contents and context of *The Black Messiah* is through the lenses of African American preaching and the Black Prophetic Tradition. Generally, when engaging Black religious rhetoric (preaching and otherwise), there is a temptation to limit the frames of analysis to either the African American preaching or the African American Prophetic Tradition (which often contains the former). Andre Johnson describes the latter as having been "the primary vehicle that has comforted and given voice to many African Americans."[53] Johnson goes on to interpret the tradition as expressing "[B]lack people's call for unity and cooperation, as well as the community's anger and frustrations. It has been both hopeful and pessimistic."[54] Further, he articulates a necessary distinction to the tradition that creates space for alternative, radical, and more revolutionary rhetorics. He writes, "It is, also, a tradition that does not exclusively reside in either the apocalyptic forms of prophetic discourse, the contextual restraints of rhetorical exigencies have not always allowed for an apocalyptic or jeremiadic appeal."[55] Building on that, I want to contend that there is a uniqueness to the Black Prophetic Tradition that intentionally seeks to include, affirm, and center those Black theorhetorical expressions that reside beyond the boundaries of the African American experience. To be sure, the African American Prophetic Tradition is a part, but not the sum total of, the Black Prophetic Tradition. Even the African American Prophetic Tradition itself leans into prophetic rhetoric and material that predates African people's experience in the America's by way of the European slave trade. Appeals to biblical material such as Jeremiah, Ezekiel, or Daniel confirm that there is a tradition of rhetorical expression that describe a people's hope and pessimism in ways that cannot be confined to what Christopher Hobson's "Mount of Vision" which situates the African American Prophetic Tradition (and it's biblical foundations) within the time frame of 1800–1950.[56]

When Cleage introduces the sermonic material in *The Black Messiah* by describing "The Nation Israel" as "a mixture of Chaldeans, Egyptians, Midianites, Ethiopians, Kushites, Babylonians and other dark peoples, all of whom were already mixed with the black people of Central Africa"[57] he is intentionally including people whose religious rhetoric and experience extend beyond the borders of North and South America. He is also drawing on a Pan-African or more Afrocentric tradition that appeals to Black people's experience as presented in (but not limited to or by) the Hebrew Bible or white theologians interpretations of it. The Black Prophetic Tradition includes Black people who grappled with conceptions of God, government, destiny, liberation, redemption, exile, hope, and despair. People who preached and "prophesied" with courage and conviction. But, most of all, people who had an experience with God prior to their experience with Europe or white supremacist theology.

With regards to Black or African American preaching, *The Black Messiah* is a literary reservoir of Cleage's alignment with what Martha Simmons and Frank Thomas refer to as, "*Preaching for black identity,* [which] is preaching to construct and reconstruct humanity and dignity, and to enhance the self-esteem of blacks."[58] Countless times throughout the book Cleage speaks of his desire and aim to uplift the bowed down head of Black peoples thereby reconstructing their dignity. It is within this conviction that Cleage so emphatically champions the claim of the Black Messiah—Jesus of Nazareth. Throughout the book, Cleage continues to affirm the physical blackness of Jesus as not only an appeal to a historical fact but also an opportunity for self-identification for oppressed blacks in America.

Each of Cleage's twenty sermons, as well as his introduction, states firmly and forcefully his desire to reclaim the Black Church as a place of empowerment. Each sermon is prefaced by a reference to a biblical passage and concluded with a formalized (and possibly corporate) prayer. Cleage's rhetorical strategy is more philosophical than it is homiletic. Simmons and Thomas describe the first principle of the Black preaching tradition as "the centrality of the Bible."[59] Customarily, this means that the biblical text is used as the platform for which the preaching moment is built. Similarly, the content of the text is presumed to be the focal point of the preaching message. With regards to the most classic style of homiletics, Cleage is unorthodox. Cleage's sermons use scripture and its sociopolitical-historical context as a pretext to provide a theological perspective on contemporary political reality. This is not to suggest that Cleage is rhetorically deceptive. He is more interested in substance than style. In his sermon "New Time Religion" Cleage argues,

> The Church has come a long way in thirty years. I don't mean the whole Church. I know a lot of preachers who are preaching just like they were thirty years ago in some little country church in West Virginia. But we have come a long way in what we expect of a Church because we have come a long way in the kind of problems we face and the kind of questions we are trying to grapple with. . . . We have come a long way, and these changes which are taking place in our thinking impose strange new demands upon the Black Church.[60]

In other words, Cleage's rhetorical strategy is a response to what he presumes to be a more informed and educated audience whereby the stylistic tropes and traditions of simple biblical exposition no longer resonate with the Black congregation in an informative and inspiring way. To that end, Cleage is intent on using the biblical text as a springboard but not as a lifejacket. For

Cleage, embracing and affirming one's blackness (seen through the experiences of Jesus of Nazareth as portrayed in the New Testament gospels) is the lifejacket, while the Bible itself is the point of common departure for the preacher and the audience. Cleage's sermons lift off from scriptural foundations. He situates his sermons within a biblical text. But he is not so wed to theories of biblical inerrancy or infallibility that he cannot contest the portrayals and interpretations of those texts when they do not function in liberating ways for Black people.

Cleage identifies himself and his work as militant and in the vein of Marcus Garvey whom Cleage argues was "the only leader in this country to meet this problem [of self-exclusion of most Black militants from any religious affiliations whatsoever] head-on."[61] Throughout the book, Cleage contrasts his own militancy with what he perceives to be the more dominant Black apathy and the prevailing "Uncle Tom" and "Aunt Jemima" syndrome. The lines of demarcation are drawn well in his sermon entitled, "He Who Is Not With Me." Therein, Cleage contends,

> The Black Nation of Israel had degenerated into total corruption and hopelessness. Black people no longer believed in themselves and black people no longer loved each other. Their lives were molded by what they thought they could get out of the Romans. They loved their oppressors and hated their brothers because their oppressors had power and their brothers were powerless.[62]

Drawing the contrast even more sharply, Cleage expresses how revolutions (which he posits Jesus was engaged in) are thwarted by those within more than those without. Cleage states,

> That's the way it is. When the man gets ready to hang us, he gets some Aunt Jemima or Uncle Tom to do it. What this whole situation means is that when people don't realize that they belong to anything, when they don't see any power that is theirs or can be theirs, they start looking for individual benefits. That's all [Uncle Tom's and Aunt Jemima's do . . . they look] at the world and [say], "This white man has everything. I'm going to work with him."[63]

Although some are prone to presume Cleage to be insensitive and bombastic, when read and interpreted contextually (with specific attention to the relationship between rhetoric and theology) Cleage's rhetoric is akin to *parrhesia* and becomes what James Darsey calls "meaningful incivility," "radical engagement," and what Matthew Arnold called, "fire and strength."[64]

The Black Messiah tackles more content than the capacity of this project allows. Cleage shares perceptive views on religion, faith, spirituality, power, riots, violence, Dr. King, Malcolm X, Stokely Carmichael, Black politics, white supremacy, and more. The book serves its purpose of expressing the experiences and sentiment of Black Theology in a way that weds militancy with ministerial acumen and thus planted sufficient seeds for the development of Black Christian Nationalism.

While this book cannot dive into every angle of *The Black Messiah* sermonically, rhetorically, theologically, and politically, what I will do is provide a deeper engagement with the content and context of a few sermons in particular. So this brief rhetorical engagement will now give way to a more detailed rhetorical engagement with Cleage's sermons "An Epistle to Stokely," "Brother Malcolm," and "Dr. King and Black Power," as well as the contextual realities and complementary readings associated with them. These sermons are vintage for Cleage in that they clearly address a concrete and controversial issue facing his congregation. They also display Cleage's affinity for discursive rhetorical hermeneutics. He stands in the Black Prophetic Tradition using sacred texts and rhetorical strategies to reconstitute his audience with hopes they would embrace and employ radical Black politics.

NOTES

1. Cleage, *The Black Messiah*.
2. Ward, *Prophet of the Black Nation*, 6.
3. Allan Aubrery Boesak, *Farewell to Innocence: A Socio-Ethical Study on Black Theology and Black Power* (1977), 116–117.
4. See, Albert B. Cleage, *Black Christian Nationalism: New Directions for the Black Church* (1972).
5. Cobb Charles, *Letter to Rev. Albert Cleage*. December 3, 1967. Albert Cleage Papers, Box 1. University of Michigan, Bentley Historical Library, Ann Arbor.
6. Ibid., Box 1.
7. Mark Chapman, *Christianity on Trial: African American Religious Thought Before and After Black Power* (New York, 1996), 5.
8. See Pimblott, *Faith in Black Power*.
9. Carl F. Ellis, *Beyond Liberation: The Gospel in the Black American Experience*, 133–135.
10. Ibid., 135–136.
11. Ibid., 136.
12. Ibid., 136.
13. Joseph E. Peniel, *Stokely: A Life* (Civitas Books, 2014), 149.
14. Ibid., 149.
15. Ibid., 150.
16. Ibid. 152.
17. Ibid. 152–153.
18. Michael Leff, "9 Hermeneutical Rhetoric" (2017).
19. Cleage, *Black Messiah*, 8.

20. Ibid., 8.

21. Albert J. Raboteau, *Slave Religion: The "Invisible Institution" in the Antebellum South* (Oxford University Press, 2004).

22. Cleage, *Black Messiah*, 9.

23. Walter Brueggemann, *Prophetic Imagination: Revised Edition* (2001), 3.

24. Ward, *Prophet of the Black Nation*.

25. Edward J. Blum and Paul Harvey, *The Color of Christ: The Son of God and the Saga of Race in America* (2012), 221.

26. Cleage, *The Black Messiah*, 9.

27. Ida Lewis (1970, December 1). Conversation: The Rev. Albert B. Cleage, Jr. *Essence*, 22–25, 27.

28. John M. Temme, "The Black Messiah and Albert B. Cleage, Jr.: A Retrospective at 25 Years," *Trinity Seminary Review* 17 (Spring 1995): 23–31.

29. Charles Freeman Sleeper, *Black Power and Christian Responsibility: Some Biblical Foundations for Social Ethics* (Abingdon Press, 1968).

30. Joseph R. Washington, *The Politics of God*. Vol. 326 (1969).

31. John J. Carey, "Black Theology: An Appraisal of the Internal and External Issues." *Theological Studies* 33, no. 4 (1972): 684–697.

32. Major J. Jones, *Black Awareness: A Theology of Hope*, 1971.

33. James Deotis Roberts, *Liberation and Reconciliation: A Black Theology* (2005).

34. Carey, "Black Theology," 685.

35. Ibid., 689–690.

36. Lewis, "Conversation: The Rev," 24.

37. See, James H. Cone, *Said I Wasn't Gonna Tell Nobody: The Making of a Black Theologian* (Orbis Books, 2018), 9, 14.

38. John Aldridge, "The Black Messiah (Review)," *The Princeton Seminary Bulletin*, 61, no. 1 Winter (1969): 95.

39. Ibid., 95.

40. See, Reza Aslan, *Zealot: The Life and Times of Jesus of Nazareth* (Random House Trade Paperbacks, 2014).

41. Black Messiah Reviews, December 1968, Box 5, p. 5a, Albert Cleage, Jr. Papers.

42. Ibid., 5a.

43. Charles E. Cobb to Albert Cleage, Jr., January 27, 1969. Box 1, Albert Cleage, Jr. Papers.

44. Stephen C. De Pass to Albert Cleage, Jr., November 22, 1969. Box 1, Albert Cleage, Jr. Papers.

45. Black Messiah Reviews, February 17, 1969, Volume 4 Number 35, Box 5, p. 6, Albert Cleage, Jr. Papers.

46. Ibid., 6.

47. Ibid., 6.

48. Marvin Judy, "The Black Messiah (Review)," *Religion for Life* 38, no. 3 Autumn (1969): 447.

49. *The Christian News*, November 25, 1969, editorial. Box 1, Albert Cleage, Jr., Papers.

50. Ibid., Box 1.

51. Sheed & Ward Publishers to Albert Cleage, July 18, 1968, Box 1, Albert Cleage, Jr., Papers.

52. John M. Temme, "The Black Messiah and Albert B. Cleage, Jr.," 23–31.

53. Andre E. Johnson, "To Make the World So Damn Uncomfortable': WEB Du Bois and the African American Prophetic Tradition," *Carolinas Communication Annual* 32 (2016): 22.

54. Ibid., 22.

55. Ibid., 22.

56. See Christopher Z. Hobson, *The Mount of Vision: African American Prophetic Tradition, 1800–1950* (Oxford University Press, 2012).

57. Cleage, *The Black Messiah*, 3.

58. Martha Simmons and Frank Thomas, *Preaching with Sacred Fire: An Anthology of African American Sermons, 1750 to the Present* (2010), 10.

59. Ibid., 7.

60. Cleage, *Black Messiah*, 101.

61. Simmons and Thomas, *Preaching with Sacred Fire*, 8.

62. Ibid., 60.

63. Ibid., 65.

64. James Darsey, *The Prophetic Tradition and Radical Rhetoric in America* (1999), x.

Chapter 4

Albert Cleage's Epistle to Stokely (A Close Reading)

The Rhetorical Relationship between Black Theology and Black Power

The sermons preached in *The Black Messiah* were preached (in one version or another) at The Shrine between 1967 and 1968. This is during the heart of the Black Power Movement. This social-political timeframe places Cleage at a rhetorical disadvantage in trying to use Christianity as a tool of Black Liberation.

There was a common sentiment among Black revolutionaries, militants, and agnostic contributors to the Black Power Movement that Christianity was "the white man's religion" and offered no productive or prophetic path forward. The sermon centered in this chapter, *An Epistle to Stokely*, is Cleage's response to that. Using rhetorical strategies of disruption, rhetorical hermeneutics, (re)constitutive rhetoric, parrhesia, and nommo, Cleage seeks to embrace (and ordain) Black revolutionaries for their own political protection and for the church's social-political advancement. Cleage uses bold and frank speech (*parrhesia*) to deconstruct and condemn unjust theologies associated with the Black Church and Black Preaching. At the same time, Cleage will use language to create or bring into existence (*nommo*) a more authentic and liberatory understanding of Christianity.

The close reading methodology is employed in this chapter as the primary function of engagement with the content of the sermon as printed in the book. I examine not only what Cleage was saying but what he was doing with what he was saying in the sermon.

CLEAGE'S RHETORICAL STRATEGY OF DISRUPTION

The subtext of *An Epistle to Stokely*, the scriptural foundation for the sermonic presentation, reads, "But no one can enter a strong man's house and plunder his goods, unless he first binds the strong man; then indeed he may plunder his house" (Mark 3:27). This is an obscure text and is rather difficult for preachers and religious enthusiasts to interpret. Nevertheless, Cleage, seeking to address the tensions between young Black radicals and the Black Church in America opens his third sermon in *The Black Messiah* with this passage.

Cleage's introductory remarks in the sermon are left-handed, unorthodox, and rhetorically poignant. He opens, "I'd like to call your attention to the hymn we often sing."[1] It is common for Black preachers to highlight hymns in their sermons. Scholars like Paula A. Minifee would likely call it rather "womanist,"[2] tracing the use of hymns in religious rhetorical presentation back to the likes of Rev. Jarena Lee.[3] However, the attention Cleage is calling forth in his congregation is not merely one of a celebratory or harmonic tone but instead one of critical engagement. Cleage cites the opening stanza of the Christian melody, "Fairest Lord Jesus."[4] How many times had his congregation or Black Churches all over the country sung these lyrics? The hymn is not quite as popular in late twentieth- and twenty-first-century hymnology. It is not listed in the litany of the African American Heritage Hymnal.[5] This is with good reason. Cleage will explicate this in his early sermonic commentary. The song is intended to evoke an audience's identification of the persona of Jesus, and the substance of the song is a rhetorical tool Cleage uses to highlight a conceptual and liturgical problem in the Black Church.

Cleage quotes the lyrics, "Jesus is fairer, Jesus is purer, He makes the willful heart sing!" The stage is set, and the runway is clear for Cleage to disrupt the sacred and theological Eurocentric epistemology. He remarks, "I only mention [these lyrics] to point out the very simple, but obvious fact that Black Christians have a whole lot to do to rewrite much of the ritual and songs that are used by Christian churches."[6] Drawing these connections between ritual, song, and theology is part of Cleage's rhetorical strategy of disruption. We might even call this the prelude to a rhetorical disassembly. Cleage is using familiar and sacred material to call his audiences attention to material he seeks to take apart now and reconstruct in a more progressive and prophetic way later.

A PROPHETIC RESPONSE TO WHITE THEOLOGY

There is an inextricable tie among music, worship, theology, and Black Identity in our communities of faith. These elements are often synthesized in Black Preaching. At the start of the sermon, Cleage has already sought to disarm the audience. Rhetorical disarmament, using familiar and palatable references before introducing a discursive idea, is a recognizable strategy in prophetic rhetoric.[7] Direct dismissal of the "fair Jesus" without providing the congregation with a point of identification could prove to be too abrupt or jarring. Cleage calculates that his congregants are aware of the substance of the song but have not quite recognized how the symbolism in the lyrics reinforce a white supremacist theology,[8] and, for Cleage, Black Theology demands a prophetic response to any manifestation of white supremacy.

Cleage continues, "It's kind of ridiculous for us to be sitting here singing about 'Fairest Lord Jesus.' We might sing about 'Darkest Lord Jesus' or something else. We might rewrite the song. I'd just like you to bear this in mind as we go through the sermon."[9] This statement forecasts the primary substance of the sermon and one of Cleage's rhetorical methods—reconstitutive rhetoric.[10] Cleage is seeking to reconstitute his parishioners (and the readers of his sermons) toward a different understanding of Christianity, one which Cleage sees as more authentically aligned with its origins. The depth of courage and creativity needed to move Black people within and outside of the Black Church to engage in the Black nationalist and liberatory project would require a willingness to forfeit misconceptions about the personality of Jesus—the Black Messiah. It would also call for a revisioning of what the Black Church was (in the 1960s) and what the community—especially the most radical among them—would need the Black Church to be or at least consider becoming.

Cleage observed how some songs sung in Black sacred spaces articulated messages that were incompatible with a Black Power ideology many young people, in Detroit and beyond, had begun to embrace. Kelly Brown Douglas suggests that Cleage's message continues to resonate with young people in the twenty-first century. According to Douglas, "After hearing about Cleage's interpretation of Christ's Blackness, [young adults] typically ask where they can get more information on Jesus's ancestry and possible African connections."[11] Cleage would provide the young people in his vocal and literary audience similar information in this sermon.

CLEAGE'S DILEMMA

After his opening comments, Cleage moves from forecasting to laying the groundwork for the fundamental premise of the sermon. What must the Black Church do to embrace Black political radicalism? Also, how can Black radicals be convinced of the Black Church's efficacy (and necessity) in the endeavor of Black empowerment? To respond to this rhetorical situation,[12] Cleage invites the reader into an ongoing conversation with his congregation. He highlights,

I have suggested that it would be possible for us as an independent Congregational Church to ordain workers in the Student Non-Violent Co-Ordinating Committee for the civil rights work which they are now doing and, in that way, protect them against the conspiracy to either kill them in Vietnam or take them out of active work by putting them in a penitentiary.[13]

Cleage views religious ordination as a tactic to protect Black radicals from what would become known as J. Edgar Hoover's infamous counterintelligence program—COINTELPRO.[14] This program actually targeted Black revolutionaries from Fred Hampton to Angela Davis and sought to neutralize any potential for a mass uprising against the U.S. government. According to Finkelman and Williams, "Few who study the history of black activism in the United States discount the role played by COINTELPRO in inhibiting black liberation movements."[15] COINTELPRO, in fact, is quite relevant to a reading of the sermonic material in *The Black Messiah*. Finkelman and Williams cite the COINTELPRO Papers which describe one of the goals of the program as being the prevention of "the rise of a "messiah" who could unify, and electrify, the militant black nationalist movement" and to "prevent militant black nationalist groups and leaders from gaining respectability, by discrediting them."[16] COINTELPRO's code term for a personality who could cause the masses of Black people to rise in rebellion against the United States was exactly how Cleage framed his understanding of who Jesus is—the Black Messiah.

This phraseology actually draws some direct parallels between religion and politics and sets the stage for a rhetorical inversion of sorts. By that I mean, Cleage will be able to use the same term that Hoover uses in a negative way to empower the same people Hoover seeks to exploit. To be able to describe Jesus as the Black Messiah, one whom (based upon biblical tradition) the Roman government sought to neutralize because of his capacity to inspire and electrify Black peasants in Jerusalem, Nazareth, and Galilee, gives Cleage some rhetorical leverage. It positions those who organize against the American imperialism a religious fervor (maybe even zealotry) that they can appeal to for inspiration and motivation despite the structural and institutional forces at work against them. Unbeknownst to Hoover, he would give Cleage and others a religious angle to play in support of the Black Power and Civil Rights Movements.

Cleage was concerned that without the covering of religious freedom, many of the Black radicals in Detroit (and elsewhere) who were anti-religious, sacrilegious, agnostic, or even self-proclaimed atheists subjected themselves to governmental usurpation of their constitutional rights. Cleage observes Black radicals being drafted into wars and carted off to prison as by-products of illegal, political surveillance and concludes that unless something is done to protect these strong men (and women) "certainly the Movement would be rendered virtually helpless."[17] For Cleage, "The suggestion was practical" and "It could be done and there is no real reason why it should not be done."[18]

Indeed, there was a reason. However, Cleage does not dignify the reason as "real." From Cleage's vantage point, the reason was illegitimate because it did not recognize and affirm the origins and essence of Black Faith or the parallels between the work Black radicals were involved in and the revolutionary origins of Christianity as evidenced through the Black Messiah—Jesus of Nazareth. This perspective becomes the centerpiece for Cleage's dilemma. He must persuade the civil rights workers and other Black activists who are disconnected from institutionalized religion that the work they are doing is not only, according to Cleage, religious but also synonymous with the spiritual and liberating work of Jesus. They are targeted, as Jesus was targeted. They are subject to a crooked court system—so was Jesus. They are Black radicals and revolutionaries—and so was Jesus!

One of Cleage's approaches is self-preservation through a type of custodial opportunism. This means that the church can offer cover to preserve the civil liberties and constitutional rights of the activists, thus making their affiliation with the church not much more than opportunistic. Yet, this opportunity cannot be taken advantage of if Black activists see the Black Church as the problem and not a source of solution. Cleage describes, "The contention has been advanced for many years that civil rights workers should be exempted from the draft because of the significance of the work they are doing."[19] Then he pivots, "Actually, new legislation is not necessary because they are already exempt in terms of the religious nature of what they are doing."[20] At the same time, Cleage affirms the challenges highlighting "one very simple inescapable fact,"[21] and that is, "Most of them do not realize that what they are doing is religious, and most of them, like most young people in the 20th Century, have rejected the Christian Church, as they know it."[22] The addendum, "as they know it," is essential to understanding the philosophy that undergirds the psychology of the sermon. Cleage does not believe that most young people in the twentieth century have been exposed to the true, historical teachings of Christianity. As a result, as Cleage sees it, they have been forced fed a lie they now regurgitate, even to their disadvantage.

There is an unwritten rule in Black Preaching that one ought to not sermonically raise an issue they will not rhetorically resolve in the sermon. Cleage has raised the problem and must provide a reasonable solution. If Cleage's aim is to convince young people that religious ordination is advantageous to them, yet he understands that their perspective on the church makes that less possible, he must rhetorically persuade his congregation to support his premise with hopes that collectively the congregation could gain enough traction to persuade the Black activists to reconsider their relationship with Jesus, the Black Church, and the Christian faith.

Cleage continues to address the problem of perspective by addressing his congregation in ways which suggest his parishioners might misunderstand why young people are so skeptical of organized religion and are reluctant to consider the Christian Church a partner in the struggle for Black Freedom. He describes, "They have rejected [the Christian Church] as it has been presented to them, as they see it in action in the world, as they note its influence, as they try to understand it."[23] To be sure, there were young people involved in the Christian Church. Yet, there was not a unanimous allegiance one way or the other regarding which faith (or nonfaith) offered the best path forward for Black people. As Mark Chapman points out, the assessment of Christianity before and even during the rise of Black Power was ubiquitous at best. Chapman argues, "Black people have always put Christianity on trial. The basic theological dilemma they have continually addressed is whether Christianity is a source of black liberation or oppression."[24]

Cleage concedes the point regarding the Black Church's inefficacy. He expresses that the witness of the Black Church has been inadequate in addressing the needs and desires of many young people connected to the movement. "This is the inescapable fact which makes it very difficult for a Church to offer ordination to these young people, even as a method of continuing their work during the period of crisis."[25] Then, Cleage doubles down on the generational divide and draws lines in the sand at age thirty. "Most of you who are over thirty may find this difficult to understand, and I think that is why young people in today's worlds say that anyone over thirty can't hope to understand them or their outlook on life."[26] It is unclear why the age of thirty was chosen as the threshold. Cleage offers no explanation or evidence to this claim. Nevertheless, he has pointed to a clear divide that was evident in his congregation and in the broader community. The elders who grew up with Jim Crow laws saw the world and the church quite differently than those who were coming up in the age when integrated lunch counters and desegregated schools were not enough to satisfy the thirst for Black Liberation and freedom.

Cleage sees this divide and dismissal cutting both ways. His aim in not simply to redeem the church for the sake of reputation but to use the church as a legitimate foundation to provide even further inspiration and protection to those young people doing movement work. Cleage contends,

> Many young people would rather die in Vietnam or rot in prison than get caught up in what they term "whitey's religious bag." It may be difficult to understand why many of them would be willing to let the Movement which is so important a part of their lives grind slowly to a standstill, as one by one its leaders are immobilized by the draft, rather than sacrifice their principles and cynically embrace a lie, or perhaps even worse from their point of view, rather than

hypocritically, or for reasons of expedience, permit themselves to be embrace by a lie.[27]

The tenor of Cleage's analysis is one of adoration. He observes an ethic of integrity at work in the lives of those so committed to justice they won't tie themselves to a "lie" to achieve it. This ethic also provides a rhetorical opportunity for Cleage to offer them an alternative. The alternative will only be accepted if Cleage can do with young adults' perspective on the church the same thing Cleage sought to do with his parishioners' perspective on the classical hymn—disturb it. If Cleage can embarrass the "lie" and reframe young activists' and Black radicals' perception of Christianity, he thinks he can solve the conundrum. What if Cleage could help "rewrite the song" about Christianity and its relationship to the Black Power Movement?

A BLACKER PATH FORWARD

Not only realizing he's rhetorically reached a point of what some may perceive as oversimplification, but also understanding the nuance necessary to describe the severity of the moment, Cleage confesses,

> I realize that I am not attributing to these gallant young men who make up the front line of leadership of the Movement either sophistication or the selfishness necessary to pretend to be Christian to serve the Movement or even to save the Movement from the cold-blooded and ruthless extermination which it now faces at the hands of the Federal Government, and I say candidly that those I know personally are neither sophisticated nor selfish. They would not use the Church to escape the draft unless they honestly believed in the Church and its teachings.[28]

This statement provides an opportunity for Cleage to offer a path forward. At the same time, it seems clear at this point that Cleage has a person or group in mind. Who is Cleage's primary audience? Who is he trying to reach with this message? Which young Black radicals does he know personally? What exchanges has he had with them that would serve as the impetus for such a presentation? Cleage addresses these inquires explicitly by describing who his intended audience is. Molefi Asante (formerly known as Arthur Smith) describes Black audiences in dichotomous fashion as either religious or secular.[29] These descriptors are challenged in *The Black Messiah* in general and in this sermon more specifically. Cleage is literally conflating the sacred and the secular. This is a rather African or Black conceptuality. It is more akin to what Asante would come to describe as "the Afrocentric method."[30] That is to say, Cleage recognizes the structural limitations of a sacred and secular dichotomy or separation. He leans into an African cosmology that contends that all things are interconnected, all things come from the Divine Being, and thereby all things are sacred. Therefore, he doesn't have to siphon of one part of the Black community as an audience that may not abide by the traditional religious rubric of Black Preaching. Cleage blurs the lines of demarcation by simultaneously addressing those in his immediate congregational audience but also echoing out into a broader societal (or even Perelman's universal[31]) audience.

Cleage states,

> So I address my remarks this morning to you and also to Stokely Carmichael, and to the young men who make up SNICK'S organization throughout the country, and to other young men who work in the Movement in other organizations. I address my remarks to those who believe in the Movement but who do not believe in the Christian Church because they do not understand that the Movement is the Christian Church in the 20th Century and that the Christian Church cannot truly be the church until it also becomes the Movement.[32]

Thus, the title of the sermon.

Cleage is not simply addressing Stokely or the "Stokelies" of the world. Cleage makes sure he informs his congregation that the church and its members or adherents are as much in need of reconstitution as anyone else directly associated with the Black Power or Civil Rights Movement who see the church as anything other than a hub for Black spiritual, social, and political empowerment.

Cleage is now ready to dive into his fundamental premise in the sermon. Cleage full-throatily reconstitutes the identity of his intended audience by saying,

> So then, I would say to you, you are Christian, and the things you believe are the teachings of a Black Messiah named Jesus, and the things you do are the will of a black God called Jehovah; and almost everything you have heard about Christianity is essentially a lie.[33]

This is an intriguing example of rhetorical appropriation. What I mean by rhetorical appropriation is the function of labeling a person or a group with an identification that they have not claimed for themselves. And in this case, it is worth highlighting because the identity being appropriated is, as Cleage has already stated, one with which the young movement leaders have been known to reject. Cleage says, "you are Christian." Customarily, based upon common interpretations of New Testament theology, Christians become Christians by, not only practicing the discipline and teachings of Jesus but, according to the book of Romans, confessing with their [own] mouth that "Jesus is Lord" and believing in their [own] heart that "God raised him from the dead" (Romans 10:9). This recitation is recognized in most Christian circles as the "plan of salvation" which offers the one who makes the confession access to a divine afterlife (thus "salvation" from an eternal damnation). Cleage has subverted this religious rite of passage through rhetorical ingenuity. To be clear, Cleage appropriating the Christian identity and imposing it upon Movement peoples does not make it so. However, it does offer Movement people and his current audience/congregation an opportunity to reconsider their affiliations with both Christianity and the Black Power Movement.

Cleage's rhetorical appropriation is not simply philosophical but also practical. Based upon his observance of and participation with the Black Power Movement, coupled with his understanding of the teaching and practices of Jesus, there is a practical partnership between Christianity and Black Power. Thus, Cleage says, "the things you *believe* are the teachings of a Black Messiah," which is a philosophical claim. And, he says, "the things you *do* are the will of a black God called Jehovah" which is a practical claim. This means, for Cleage, Christianity is as much about (if not more than) what one does as it is about what one believes or proclaims. What Cleage hears Black revolutionaries proclaiming expresses, for him, the essence of what Christianity stands for philosophically/theologically, and what Cleage sees Black revolutionaries doing is, for him, Christianity in practice. It is "preaching-in-action."

Cleage's claim that there is a "black God" that is called "Jehovah" is not a new proclamation. It echoes the claim made by one of Cleage's religious forerunners in Black Theology, Bishop Henry McNeal Turner. Bishop Turner's, *God is a Negro*[34] lays claim to the colorizing of the eternal deity and how it impacts the cosmological and political framework and practices of Black people. As Andre E. Johnson points out, Tuner is engaged in a type of rhetorical theology that intends to construct and situate theological language and ideology "in order to persuade its hearers to a certain position."[35] Cleage's aim is the same. Johnson also, rightfully, contends "all theology is at its core a form of argument," and when theology is presented for public consumption it is a "public theology, which is a rhetorical enterprise" and its primary aim is persuasion "within a specific context."[36] Cleage, like Turner, is exemplifying the art of this enterprise in his claim that God is Black.

NOT THE WHITE MAN'S RELIGION

The claim of God's blackness also opens a portal for Cleage to disturb the conventional conceptuality that has turned so many Black Power adherents and movement affiliates away from the Black Church. Cleage is contending that Christianity is by no means part of "whitey's religious bag." Cleage claims that white Christianity has been a tool of white supremacy to deceive Black Power adherents and movement affiliates away from a vital and viable tool in the toolbox of Black Liberation—Christianity and the (Black) Christian Church. Therefore, Cleage contends, "almost everything you have heard about Christianity is a lie," and his next objective is to reveal the lie and offer an opportunity for reconsideration and reconstitution.

Cleage continues, "You have been misled. Christianity for you has been misinterpreted. That which you believe to be Christianity, the theology and philosophy of history which you reject, is not Christianity."[37] This is an important hermeneutical assessment for Cleage. He does not say, "You have misinterpreted Christianity" but instead, "Christianity has been misinterpreted for you." This claim shifts the onus of responsibility off the movement leaders (and any self-proclaimed Christians who might endorse or adopt a more conventional but ahistorical Christian theology) and places it on those who were responsible for misinterpreting it. Cleage blames the teachers and not the students. The teachers have misinterpreted the essence and origins of Christianity and passed their misinterpretation on to the students. In doing so, they have caused the students to reject the religion instead of rejecting the misinterpretation. Cleage's aim is to offer a history lesson in hopes that highlighting the methodology of misinterpretation would lead his audience to reconsider a more Afrocentric and liberatory version of the faith. He says, "The Christianity we see in the world today was not shaped by Jesus. It was put together by the Apostle Paul who never saw Jesus, and given form and shape during the Middle Ages when most of the hymns were written, the hymns which for the most part enunciate white supremacy."[38] This is obviously a reference to the hymn highlighted at the offset of the sermon which Cleage now lifts specifically, "Fairest Lord Jesus."[39] He continues,

> Most of the famous religious pictures that you see were painted between the fourteenth and the seventeenth centuries by white artists. When Dutch artists painted religious pictures, everything looks just like it all happened in Holland. When French artists painted religious pictures, the biblical characters look French.[40]

Cleage has deconstructed the connections between social and political power and religious symbolism. These audible references to white theological symbols must be understood in contrast to the visual imagery surrounding Cleage in the sanctuary where he's preaching—namely, the Black Madonna and Child. While Cleage is speaking about Eurocentric historiographies and their cultural revisions of Christianity, behind him stands The Shrine of the

Black Madonna and other Afrocentric symbols in the sanctuary of the church. Cleage's parishioners can literally see the contrast in symbols deemed sacred by white theology and those deemed sacred by Black Theology. Cleage has thereby created what Awad El Karim M Ibrahim refers to as a "symbolic system"[41] through which language functions to normalize and constitute a sense of being.

The point here, for Cleage, is the broader historical legitimacy of Black Christianity. He is using this historical journey as a means of disturbing the claims about Christianity which have contributed to its rejection by movement leaders and young radicals, but the indictment is not limited to movement leaders and young radicals. It is also palpable to Cleage's own congregation. The audiences intermingle as Cleage continues,

> But *we* didn't realize this when *we* looked at *our* Sunday School literature as children. When *we* turned the pages and always saw a white Jesus, when *we* saw pictures of a white God pointing down at creation, *we* didn't realize that these were not statements of fact but statements by white men depicting what they wanted *us* to believe was true.[42] (Emphasis mine)

Here, Cleage has finally named the culprit; the "teachers" who are primarily responsible for the proliferation of misinterpretation—"white men." Cleage's claim of misinterpretation does not afford white men an innocent accidentalism. He explains, "I say, what they wanted to believe was true, because essentially they knew that white men did not create Christianity. They borrowed it, more bluntly, they stole it."[43]

RECLAIMING AND RECONSTITUTING CHRISTIANITY

Cleage's historical deconstruction is intended to create space for a new possibility. If Christianity has been stolen from Black people by white people, this might persuade Black people who have rejected Christianity to reconsider it. This is a rhetorical strategy of reconstitution as it reminds Black people of Black bodies that were stolen from African and transported to the Americas by white people. This reorients Christianity as a religion of resistance against white supremacy. To that end, Cleage doubles down on his denouncement of white Christianity (and the colonialism associated with it) by saying, "In fact, of all the peoples on earth, the one people who have never created a religion worthy of the name religion are white people."[44] This is, indeed, a wholesale indictment that might seem overly dismissive. However, when situated in a historical claim of originality and accompanied by the realities of colonialism, this indictment has merit.

Continuing along the theme of religious history (Cleage's philosophical and pastoral wheelhouse), Cleage seeks to discuss the connection between religion and culture in general and situate Christianity within his cultural analysis more specifically. Cleage contends,

> All religions stem from black people. Think of them for a moment. The Muslim religion, the Buddhist religion, the Jewish religion, the Christian religion, they all come from parts of the world dominated by non-white peoples. The white man's religion was the primitive religion of the pagans with a pantheon of gods throwing thunderbolts and cavorting about heaven and earth, filled with lust and violence. To the Romans, religion was the deification of the Emperor. They had no God. They believed that whoever could take power must be God, and they worshipped him. The white man has never created a genuine religion. He has only borrowed religions from non-white peoples.[45]

Cleage presents images of Zeus and other white deities associated with Greece and Rome as a means of drawing a deeper wedge between Eurocentric/White theology and Afrocentric/Black Theology. As George G. M. James points out, "From the conquest of Egypt by Alexander the Great, the Greeks, who were always attracted by the mysterious worship of the Nile-land, began to imitate the Egyptian religion in its entirety; and during the Roman occupation the Egyptian religion spread not only to Italy; but throughout the Roman Empire, including Brittany."[46]

If Cleage is to not only deconstruct and disturb the lie associated with Christianity (and religion in general) but also reconstruct and represent religion as a viable tool in the fight for Black Liberation, he must connect dots between the past and the present. He does so in the next stanza of the sermon which contextualizes and compares the Black Freedom struggle in the twentieth century to that of the ancient Hebrew's in the Old Testament. Cleage argues, "It is important for us to understand [the ancient origins of religion and its association with Black people] because the civilization around us is not ours. We are sojourners in a strange land."[47] This is a reference to the ancient Hebrews (Northeastern Africans) who were liberated from Egyptian slavery but also ended up in other iterations of imperial subjugation. Cleage draws from Psalm 137:4 and recalls for his audience a time when the children of Israel (again, ancient Hebrews) were demanded to sing their religious songs of Zion "in a strange land" (which, in the case of Psalm 137, was Babylon). Cleage continues, "We have been taught what someone else wanted us to know. So what we have been taught about Christianity is not what Christianity is, but what white people wanted us to believe."[48]

Cleage further parallels the African American experience with the ancient Hebrews:

The white man captured the religion of a Black Nation, the revelations of a Black God, the teachings of a Black Messiah, and he has used them to keep black men enslaved. We are the chosen people in a religious sense, in a historic sense, and this I will try to develop for you. The time has come for us to reclaim our God, our prophet, and our power.[49]

These parallels serve to sear in the mind of Cleage's audience the relationship between the historical God of the Bible and the God who affirms Black Power. Cleage places those in current physical, emotional, and psychological bondage with the ancient Hebrews for purposes of self-identification and persuasive appeal. If Black Americans can see themselves within the framework of Hebrew ancestry, then they too would be motivated to embrace the God of Black Power.

CLEAGE'S PROPHETIC RHETORICAL RECONSTRUCTION

Cleage's reclamation project essentializes prophetic rhetoric. Drawing from several scholars such as Cornel West, James Darsey, and Abraham Joshua Heschel, and others, Johnson asserts, "Prophetic rhetoric dedicates itself to the rights of individuals, especially the poor, marginalized, and exploited members of society."[50] I would add to that, the prophetic rhetoric is also dedicated to a deep understanding of what is true about a contextual reality, especially when that truth is unpopular or unconventional. To that end, Cleage is standing in solidarity with those who are oppressed, underprivileged, misinformed, and marginalized. He is evoking common religious rhetorical devices and tropes but simultaneously reconfiguring them in ways that offer new liberatory possibility. In spite of this, we still find Cleage in the thrust of a more conventional sermon which structurally demands a deep engagement with the theme scripture (in this case, Mark 3:27).

To this point, Cleage has not done this. Cleage has not dealt much with the content or historical/literary context of Mark 3:27. Cleage misses an opportunity here to begin weaving together (more seamlessly) where he started, where he is, and where he's headed rhetorically. Instead, Cleage chooses to transition into an extended religious timeline that will more directly connect ancient Hebrews with twentieth-century Black folks. Cleage's aim here is to create a space where he will, later, more directly and explicitly engage with Mark 3:27.

After advancing an argument of disruption and deconstruction, Cleage sets up a transition for reconstruction.

> I would like to outline a few basic facts and you may find it difficult to accept them because essentially they run counter to the things you have been taught. But if you will for a moment realize that many of the things you have been taught have not been for your best interest, and that you have been deliberately taught things which were intended to enslave you, then perhaps you may for a moment try to rethink these basic ideas which you have accepted as unconsciously as the air you breathe.[51]

This appeal seems to be aimed at both those who are current members of the Black Church as well as those who currently stand on the outside of it, conspicuously and dismissively looking in. If Cleage can convince both groups to rethink or reconsider the forthcoming claims regarding Christianity and its origins, it would provide him with a chance to show that Black folks within and outside of the Black Church have more in common than not. In the spirit of commonality, Cleage attempts to use a metaphor that should appeal to all parties involved. He says, "We talk much today about air pollution, but we breathe as if we had no consciousness of the pollution of the air we breathe. We breathe without thinking. The pollution of the air is a part of that which we breath from and there is no escape."[52] Situating himself in the equation, again using more inclusive language, he says, "And so it has been for us. We have accepted the white man's interpretation of our Christian faith because we had no alternative."[53]

What is important here is not simply what Cleage has done, once again intermingling the audiences. What is fascinating is how he has done it. Cleage unifies both groups under the banner of white supremacist and revisionist infections. If Cleage is to continue the trajectory of prophetic rhetoric, he must not only point out the pollution but also offer a path forward. The "pollution" metaphor demands a remedy, and since both Black Church and young Black radical constituents have been infected by white versions of Christianity, they must be willing to revisit and reconsider their affiliation with the faith in order to be cured.

RECONSTITUTION THROUGH HERMENEUTICAL RHETORIC

With sufficient groundwork laid with respect to the illegitimacy of white Christianity and simultaneously alleviating the recipients of such theology of any responsibility related to their miseducation Cleage leans even further into reconstitution and reconstruction. What Cleage incorporates can be called a Black Liberationist hermeneutic. By that I mean, Cleage will exegete the biblical text and the social-political context (both of the ancient and contemporary worlds) to argue for the liberation of Black people as the primary (if not ultimate) will of God.

Cleage proffers, "I ask you to rethink a few of these basic facts. Christianity is essentially and historically a black man's religion. I ask you to go back to the beginning, to where our Christian Bible begins, back to the history of Israel, back to Abraham, the father of Israel."[54] Cleage pinpoints a time frame, "the beginning," but rhetorically conflates this notion of time with a text that is far from historically accurate in its relationship to time. Yes, the Bible is rooted in a historical period; however, it is presumed by most conservative and mainstreamed commentators that the Bible begins at the beginning of human (or recorded) time. This is not the case.[55] Cleage is a religious historian and intellectual. I assume he knows the problematic nature of uncritically historicizing biblical material. At the same time, he is familiar with how biblical literature has been utilized to constitute and orient Black folks' understandings of history. Notice, he says, "back to the beginning, to where our Christian Bible begins." This is not intended to make note of the beginning of human history. It is a rhetorical device Cleage makes use of to (re)introduce the origins of Christianity and the history of Israel. Therefore, Cleage does not start with the creation narratives of Genesis chapters 1 and 2. He instead invites his audience to locate the father of the Hebrew faith—Abraham.

Highlighting Abraham gives Cleage leverage to lean into his primary claim in this section—Christianity is an offspring of the ancient Hebrew faith tradition (which we now refer to as Judaism), and if Christianity is rooted in a Northeastern African geography and Egyptian social and political anthropology, it cannot be a white man's religion. Again, Cleage's intention is to reconnect Christianity with Africa. He contends, "Abraham, the father of Israel was a Chaldean. Look at your map of his part of the world, and you will find that there was very little likelihood that the Chaldeans were white. Abraham went from Chaldea to build for himself and for his family a new way of life"[56] Cleage is not simply highlighting Abraham as a historical figure to promote Afrocentricity but also to promote a certain type of behavior. Cleage wants the audience to connect religion with nation building. But, whereas white Christianity was used to build a nation through subjugation and terror, Cleage sees Black Christianity as a tool to build political independence through liberation and hope.

Cleage continues, "In going out, [Abraham] declared that he had received a revelation from God, and had made a covenant with God, and that God had selected him to build a Nation. This was the beginning of Israel"[57] This further emphasizes Cleage's attempts at reconstitution. The intersections of rhetoric, race, and religion for Cleage are necessary elements in the Black Power struggle that must be employed to advance the divine cause of building a Black nation. You cannot build a Black nation if the nation builders subscribe to a white theological constitution.

Cleage must also make more distinct connections between Abraham's experiences in antiquity and African American's in the twentieth century if he hopes to maximize his persuasive appeal. In that vein, Cleage continues to draw the connections through a rhetorical trajectory that follows the movement of Abraham deeper into Africa and directly into Egypt. He continues, "[Abraham] went out from the Chaldean city of Ur into Africa. He went down into Egypt and dwelt in Egypt among the Egyptians"[58] Situated in Egypt, Cleage associates the religious movement of Abraham with the Blackness of Northeastern Africa. He argues, "Now if there is any question in your mind about where or not the Egyptians were black you only have to look at the Sphinx, the drawings and the inscriptions from Egypt. Recent studies prove that many of the Pharaohs were black or Negroid. Only the American white man tries to pretend that the Egyptians were white."[59]

Cleage has not exhausted the power of his use of Abraham as a rhetorical device for reconstitution. He must continue to build the bridge between the past and present while simultaneously providing his audience with as much material as possible to reorient their interpretation of Christianity and religion. Therefore, the next section is a journey beyond Abraham into some of the most notable narratives and characters in the Old Testament until he can introduce the primary character of the New Testament—Jesus, the Black Messiah.

The method Cleage uses in this section to transport his audience through time and theological reconstitution is what Michael Charles Leff describes as "hermeneutical rhetoric."[60] Similar to how rhetorical studies scholars of the classical and contemporary periods have developed a set of criteria and expectations when engaging certain works/writings, biblical literature has canonized both the scriptures and conventional approaches to it. Leff points out the rigidity in these approaches and how the productive and interpretive exchange is both imminent and inevitable in the rhetorical process. That is to say, how texts get produced and interpreted are part of a broader process which is always subject to (and often need to be) change(d) over time. To that end, as Leff says, Cleage's rhetoric in this section exemplifies a "[focus] upon interpretation as a source of invention and suggests how traditions can be altered without destroying their identity."[61]

Cleage has used a type of hermeneutical rhetoric throughout the sermon, however, that use is most explicit in this section. Cleage will represent biblical stories and characters in a way that entices his audience to reinterpret the stories they are likely familiar with.

> Abraham went into Egypt and he lived with the Egyptians and because his wife was beautiful he was afraid to admit she was his wife for fear that someone

might want her and kill him. So he said, "She is my sister." And so while he lived in Egypt, his wife was taken by the Egyptian King and he made no protest. Obviously, the relationship between the Egyptians and Abraham and his clan was a very close one.[62]

Here Cleage is reinterpreting Genesis 12:10-20. There are some very important observations to make of his presentation. He is undoubtedly using this passage to concretize the connection between Abraham, Israel, and Africa, and Cleage also diverts away from two common interpretations of that passage.

Commonly, interpreters presume Egyptians were so lascivious that they would be willing to do harm to Abraham just to sexually exploit his wife. This interpretation is drawn from Gen. 12:12 which states, "When the Egyptians see you they will say, 'This is his wife.' Then they will kill me but let you live." Cleage, instead, describes an unidentifiable "someone" as the potential culprit. Conventional interpretations paint Egyptians in an unfavorable light, but Cleage re-presents the narrative in a more respectable way in support of the Egyptians.

The second common interpretation comes from an irresponsible read of Genesis 12:13 which states that Abraham says to his wife, "Say you are my sister, so that I will be treated well for your sake and my life will be spared because of you." We do know "someone" says to Pharaoh that Abraham's wife is his sister. The text doesn't say who, and far too many interpreters (scholars, clergy, and lay persons) associate that lie with Abraham's wife. However, Cleage says, "So *he* said, She is my sister," placing the onus and "lie" on Abraham. These two diversions serve as exemplars of how Cleage engages in hermeneutical rhetoric.

There are certainly a lot of moving pieces in this section (and this sermon) rhetorically and philosophically. But Cleage is moving all those pieces in the direction of reconstitution.

Cleage then reemphasizes the timeline and major premise stating, "We are at the beginning. There is no question about Abraham and the beginning of the Nation Israel being very closely related to Africa, to the Egyptians and to Black people. This is the beginning of the nation Israel."[63] Cleage has sufficiently made a claim about "the beginning" and can now move further into describing how Abraham's religion was a catalyst for nation building.

CLEAGE'S POLITICAL THEOLOGY

How do Abraham's experiences in Egypt impact his faith formation and contribute to his conceptuality of nation building?[64] How does this relate to

Black Theology and politics in the United States in the 1960s? Based upon an overly racialized misreading (or maybe just a misapplication) of the First Amendment, most presume there's an innate (and even necessary) "separation of church and state" or, to say it another way, a division between religion and politics. I say overly racialized misreading because this amendment is often interpreted through the lens of white nationalism or the myth that the United States is a "Christian Nation." To be sure, the First Amendment clause is intended to ensure the nation-state cannot establish an official religion and require citizens to adhere to its theological tenants. That does not mean that religion and politics are innately disconnected. Cleage displays the direct connection in this section.

Although Cleage does not state it explicitly, his previous reference to African Americans being the "chosen people" echoes what theologians refer to as covenantal theology.[65] This means that Cleage understands God to have a special and unique partnership and relationship (covenant) with African Americans, and Cleage traces this union back to ancient Africa through Abraham. God's covenant with Abraham is established in Genesis 12:2 which states that God will (among other things) make Abraham "a great nation . . ." Rhetorically this verse ties together theology and politics. God—a religious deity which evokes theological inquiry and engagement—provides a promise (covenant) to Abraham that he would become a nation. Nation is intrinsically a political term. Cleage, drawing from his understandings of scripture and history, sees a divinely mandated merging, not a separation of, religion and politics. Cleage has both a covenantal and political theology.

Building on this connection, Cleage's next section traces Abraham's maneuvering within Egypt and chronicles some important developments which further establish the Hebrew people as an emerging nation.

Cleage notes that "the Egyptians were very good to Abraham."[66] Not only does this provide a counternarrative to the passage that stereotyped Egyptians as sexual predators, but it also projects a positive light into the context of Africa in mid-twentieth-century America. Cleage rhetorically presents Egyptians and Africans as ethically upright and culturally developed. He continues,

> [The Egyptians] gave him cattle and wealth. He came out of Egypt a wealthy man with many black Egyptian servants with him. The Nation Israel (*sic*) is being to develop now as a combination of Abraham, his family and the Egyptians who have been adopted while Abraham was in Egypt.[67]

In other words, had it not been for the expendable resources available and accessible in Egypt, there would likely be no developing nation of Israel. Therefore, Egypt could not be an undeveloped or uncivilized nation. It must have been an epicenter of wealth and culture. Cleage makes this wealth and culture is made evident. "The nature of the relationship [between Egypt and Israel] can be deduced from the fact that [Abraham] himself married Hagar, his Egyptian servant, and had a child by her named Ishmael. We still use the word Hagar. We speak of Hagar's children and you know what that means."[68] That means the child is perceived to be an "illegitimate" child.

Frankly, the sexual politics in Cleage's rhetoric here are quite disturbing. Cleage has minimized the historical realities of rape (as an "Egyptian servant" Hagar would not have the agency or power to "consent") and slavery (which he defines as servitude in the passage above). In fact, Genesis 16 records Hagar being "given" to Abraham by his wife. The passage refers to Hagar as Abraham's wife's "maid" or "servant." Hagar is not "married" to Abraham. She is in fact enslaved by him. Cleage's hermeneutical rhetoric here is helpful insomuch as to redeem the racial misnomers of ancient Israel, but it is also tragically compounding the issue of patriarchy.

This is rather consistent with a lot of Black Power rhetoric and Black Liberation Theology. Quite often, there have been sufficient, redemptive, and revolutionary renderings of race critique and reclamation, but those same analyses have been devoid of or divorced from a more righteous and robust critique of patriarchy, misogyny, and sexism and their connections to racism, white supremacy and violence. Danielle McGuire describes how "analyses of rape and sexualized violence play little or no role in most histories of the civil rights movement, which present it as a struggle between black and white men."[69] Regretfully, Cleage's rhetorical presentation here advances such erasures and minimalizations.

Inadequate gender analysis notwithstanding, Cleage persists in his description of the developments of Israel as a nation. He finally acknowledges Abraham's wife's name and expands the scope of African religious reach when he states,

> Then Sara, his wife, had her own child and got mad and didn't want her son to have to split the inheritance. So she told Abraham to get rid of the child Ismael. So Hagar and Ishmael were driven into the desert and God looked down on Hagar and Ishmael and said, "I will protect them and save them because you, Ishmael, will become the father of a great people." Ishmael is traditionally reputed to be the father of the Arabic Nation. Abraham was very closely identified with the black people of Africa.[70]

Cleage has reiterated the point of connection between Abraham, Africa, and the origins of Christianity. Again, the function of this repetition is to sear in the minds of the audience a new (or renewed) conceptuality through reconstitution, and having substantially chronicled the developments of Abraham,

Cleage shifts to another major character in the Old Testament's nation building project and presentation—Moses.

RELIGIOUS "PURITY" AND BLACK RHETORICAL THEOLOGY

Moses, another figure Cleage wants to ensure, is conceptualized as a historical figure of African ancestry and composition who connects his religious heritage with a political project whose end goal is the establishment of a righteous nation. Cleage states, "Later on, there was Moses, born during Israel's Egyptian bondage. Moses is quite obviously, by the biblical story, part Egyptian."[71] Cleage doesn't rhetorically situate Moses in the direct lineage of Abraham. This may have been a missed opportunity to achieve his goal of a direct trajectory from Abraham to Jesus. But Cleage also has in mind the preeminence of Blackness (or African-ness) in the bloodline of the early Hebrews, and, whereby Cleage used a peculiar term to connect Egyptians to Abraham—adoption—he inverts this connection by claiming that Moses (a Hebrew) is ethnically Egyptian. Cleage has placed a huge stake in affirming a connection between Hebrews, Egyptians, and Black people in general. To further denounce any semblance of a connection between historical Christianity, the Hebrews of the Bible, and white Christianity, Cleage uses more explicitly hermeneutical rhetoric to claim religious purity in Black Theology.

Bible readers should be familiar with the story of Moses and are likely to understand his connection to Egypt to be one of "adoption." Conventional readings of Exodus 2 prescribe the perspective of Moses being taken in by Pharaoh's daughter. This happens because Moses's mother, fearful of the edict issued by the King of Egypt to kill the Hebrew male children at birth (in Exodus 1), puts her baby in a basket and floats him in the Nile River. Pharaoh's daughter is, ironically, bathing in the Nile and sees the baby (Moses) floating along and out of pity takes him in as her own. Cleage isn't buying the historicity of this narrative. He wants to affirm Moses's ethnic and ancestral connection to Egypt more concretely. Therefore, he contends, "[Moses'] adoption by Pharaoh's daughter does not ring true. Moses is at least half-Egyptian and half-Jewish, and to say that he's half-Egyptian and half-Jewish makes him unquestionably all non-white."[72] The use of the term "Jewish" is remarkable. The term "Jew" (root word of Jew-ish) is not found in the Old Testament. Numerous scholars trace the Jews lineage back to the ancient Hebrews.[73] However, Cleage has a broader point to make and appropriating the term Jewish instead of Hebrew here is important. The term "Jew" in the twentieth century has a racialized connotation that Cleage seeks to redress. Moses is not just a rhetorical figure Cleage utilizes to affirm the

Black origins of Christianity but, moreover, a historical figure Cleage lifts to denounce the whiteness associated with Jews in the twentieth century. Cleage asserts, "This is Moses. We're still dealing with the Nation Israel which is always depicted as a white nation. The Nation Israel was not at any time a white nation. Where could they have picked up any white blood, wandering around in Africa? They hadn't even had any contact with white people. Moses married a Midianite, a black woman, and had children."[74]

Simply put, Moses is both Hebrew (Jewish) and Egyptian. Moses is African. Moses' family are Africans. Africans are Black. Jews are Hebrews, and Hebrews are irrevocably Egyptians and, therefore, Africans.[75]

Cleage continues his trajectory of the nation building theological rhetoric. He shifts from Moses individually to the Israelites collectively. It's important to note that Cleage does not make mention of Jacob (grandson of Abraham) who is renamed Israel in Genesis 33:28. The descendants of Jacob are referred to as Israelites (before Israel becomes a "Nation"), and one of the Israelites' most pivotal periods of their existence as a people is their liberation from Egyptian slavery and sojourn through the wilderness to the "promised land." The "promised land" is Canaan. Cleage picks this theme up when he states, "Israel finally fought its way into Canaan and mixed with the people of Canaan."[76]

Cleage's rhetorical angle has slightly shifted. He is still contending that Israel is part of Africa and Israelites (Hebrews) are African (Black) peoples, but he is angling the point that there is no such thing as ethnic purity. This is important because Cleage is not trying to suggest that African American's are direct descendant of the Hebrew-Israelites. Again, his primary contention is that Christianity is an African (Black) religious tradition. Therefore, he uses biblical exegesis and cultural anthropology to describe the broad reach of the ancient Hebrews/Egyptians culturally, politically, and religiously. He continues,

> Those [Canaanites] weren't white people either. "People of the land" they called them. The Israelites looked down on them, after a fashion, but that didn't stop them from sleeping with them. And all throughout the Old Testament you notice every once in a while, a prophet rares (*sic*) up and says, "We have got to maintain our purity." And you know what that means. That means that purity is already gone. There's nothing to maintain.[77]

Cleage, again, draws direct connections between the past and present saying,

> Just as in the South when the white man stands up and talks about maintaining white purity. He wouldn't be talking about it if there was any purity to maintain, and it was exactly the same with the prophets. They looked about and saw that Israel had mixed with the people wherever they went.[78]

Cleage has used a racial and rhetorical analysis when referencing how white people in America have "talk[ed] about maintaining white purity." This analysis is tied directly into the religious ideology of white superiority that Cleage is using the origins of Christianity to refute. He is debunking the myth of racial purity to theologically and rhetorically turn the argument on its head.

The fact is, since race is a social construct, it cannot be maintained with any level of scientific purity, but it can be used as an ideological tool to continue to divide and oppress those viewed in the lower rung or racial caste. And when we attach these racialized theories to theology, we're destined to distort the image of God and damage our relationship with God's creation (human and otherwise). Cleage is displaying how racists' theologies, sociologies, and anthropologies are woven together in ways that complicate the Christian faith. So what he is doing is in this section is using rhetorical theology to dispute the foundation of the claims being used against Black (and African) people and offering a conceptuality of Christianity (and Black Faith more generally) that is viable and compatible with Black Liberation.

BLACK CHRISTIANS AND THE AMERICAN BABYLON

Another pivotal phase of Israel's development was their Babylonian captivity. Cleage sees several parallels between African American's experience in the "strange land" of America and Israel's stint in Babylon. And while some in the Black Power and Freedom Movements were known to advocate for migration back to Africa (Bishop Henry McNeal Turner being one of them), Cleage articulates more of a Jeremiad in that sense that he sees the African American experience in the United States akin to what was attributed to the prophet Jeremiah in the Old Testament. Jeremiah and the Israelites longed for a return to their beloved "promised land." However, their exile was decades long, and a word came to Jeremiah in Jerusalem compelling him to send a letter to those in Babylonian captivity. The letter instructs the Israelites to prepare for long-term stability in Babylon by building houses and settling down (cf. Jeremiah 20:4).

Cleage was a student of Marcus Garvey, the founder of the Universal Negro Improvement Society and ardent progenitor of modern Black Nationalism.[79] Garvey also posited a particular type of religion that Cleage's parents were Garveyites and as such, Cleage promotes a type of Garveyism in his rhetorical theology. Aswad Walker states explicitly, "Cleage gained insight and inspiration from the work of Garvey."[80] Part of this philosophy mandates the maintaining of one's dignity through a connection with their ancestral history even as they adjust to life under social and political oppression, but Cleage is mindful that settling into an indefinite captivity requires offspring. And to Cleage's previous point about intermingling, he must seize an opportunity to lean further into the Israelite/Babylon and African American/U.S. interplay. Jeremiah 20:6 advises Israelites to "Marry and have sons and daughters; find wives for your sons and give your daughters in marriage, so that they too may have sons and daughters. Increase in number [in Babylon]; do not decrease." Cleage appropriates this sentiment and uses it to advance the cause of Black ethnic association. Cleage contends, "When Israel was taken captive into Babylon, they mixed with the people of Babylon, and Babylon was no white nation. They lived with them, intermarried with them, and then the prophets began to write down rules about how God's Chosen People should not mix with other people."[81]

The function of Cleage's hermeneutical rhetoric here is, still, to reclaim the Blackness of Christianity through its origins—reconstitution. His secondary aim is to connect the experiences of biblical Israel to that of African descendants in the Americas for self-identification. He encapsulates this aim in the next stanza saying,

> At this late date, they were trying to build a sense of identity. They petitioned the king to be permitted to return to Israel. But when they finally received permission to go back, most of the Jews wouldn't go. They were happy and content. They were in business. They had friends, relatives, everything. They didn't want to go back. Only a little handful had returned, and when they looked around and saw the Jews who had remained and said, "These Jews have become people of the land. They're like all of the other people. They've intermarried." And the prophet stood up and said, "You've got to separate from the people of the land. We must keep the Jews pure."[82]

This echoes the migration versus integration argument of the early twentieth century following the Emancipation Proclamation. Yet, the mid-twentieth century had found a new contribution to the philosophy of Black Liberation. There was talk of "going back to Africa" and movement around civil rights through integration. There were also voices like Cleage and Malcolm X who began to propose the idea of separation. For Cleage, separation is plausible, at least in part, because African Americans had been far removed enough from Africa and vested enough in the well-being of the United States to organize for their own national independence; an independence Cleage contended would never be fully or tangibly granted by the United States (even if it was granted legislatively). Part of the push for returning to Africa was rooted in an ethnic purity that Cleage believes African Americans no longer possessed. So Cleage intensifies his claim against ethnic purity stating,

> Now how could you keep [the Jews] pure? They had mixed in Babylon, they had mixed in Egypt, they had mixed in Canaan. What was there to keep pure? And yet they tried to issue a pronouncement, "You've got to separate." But it was ridiculous and impossible. It was as impossible to separate the Jew from the people of the land as it was to maintain segregation in the South after nightfall. It could not be done.[83]

To be clear, Cleage does not see separation as an eternal political faux pau. Cleage contextualizes the plausibility of separation within the rhetorical framework of possibility. Israel, at that time, didn't have the economic, militaristic, and geographical capacity to separate and sustain themselves. It was not time, yet. But Cleage was urging his audience to identify with the Israelites, not necessarily urging them to aspire to be Israel. He wants Black Americans to be like Israelites to learn from their missteps and mishaps, but, above all, maintain a sense of dignity and connection with their African ancestry politically and religiously. To that end, Cleage reaffirms the primary purpose of this section stating,

> Israel was a mixed blood, non-white nation. What usually confuses you is the fact that the Jews you see today in America are white. Most of them are the descendants of white Europeans and Asiatics who were converted to Judaism about one thousand years ago. The Jews were scattered all over the world. In Europe and Russia, they converted white people to Judaism. The Jews who stayed in that part of the world where black people are predominant remained black. The conflict between black Jews and white Jews is a problem in Israel today[84]

Having chronicled the ethnic, political, and religious developments of Israel in the Old Testament, Cleage transitions to the primary character of Christianity in the New Testament—Jesus of Nazareth, the Black Messiah.

CLEAGE'S REVOLUTIONARY BLACK CHRISTOLOGY

If Cleage wants to persuade young revolutionaries to endorse or embrace Christianity as a viable vehicle to advance the cause of Black Liberation, this cannot be done if Jesus is viewed as a white man by most of the members of the Black Power Movement. Cleage has traced the origins of Christianity through Abraham, the Hebrews, Egyptians, and emerging nation of Israel. Nevertheless, unless he can connect those dots to that of Jesus's direct ancestry, all would be for naught. Also, there was a plethora of iconography that seared the image of a white Jesus in the minds of so many.[85]

Cleage continues his theme of disruption leading to reconstruction and reconstitution as he hones in on the personhood and humanity of Jesus. He states, "Jesus came to the Black Nation Israel."[86] The term "came" is a riff off more traditional theology that Cleage will quickly divert away from. For Jesus to "come" means he was preexistent in some form and journeyed to or arrived at the location of Israel at some point. Many religious studies scholars interpret this rhetoric through the lens of the Gospel according to John. In John 1, Jesus's birth narrative is extremely cosmological. He is described as the "Word" or "Logos," preexistent in the cosmos, with God, and then, the "Word" became flesh (and blood) and dwelt among human beings. In other words, Jesus "came" to earth from the cosmos, as God, having been "with God."

This theoretical framework is referred to as a "high Christology"[87] that embraces Jesus's divinity and god-ness. It is common among most mainstream Christians who subscribe to the concept of the Trinity (God the Father, God the Son (Jesus), and God the Holy Spirit/Ghost). Three separate entities are seen as One, but Cleage is an equal opportunity disrupter regarding the traditional tenants of Western (white) Christianity. Therefore, he shifts immediately from the cosmological claim into a clarification of who he sees Jesus as and why the Blackness of Jesus is not only historically accurate but also a theological and political necessity. Cleage rebuts,

> We are not talking now about "God the Father." We are concerned here with the actual blood line. Jesus was born to Mary, a Jew of the tribe of Judah, a non-white people; black people in the same sense that the Arabs were black people, in the same sense that the Egyptians were black people. Jesus was a Black Messiah born to a black woman.[88]

Cleage has situated Jesus, not in the cosmological, but in the cultural and concrete human condition. Cleage does not reference Jesus's father (in heaven (God) or on earth (Joseph)). Cleage cites Jesus's matrilineal lineage—through Mary, a Black woman, connecting him to Egypt (cf. Matthew 1:1-17). This opens the door for Cleage to discuss the historical representations and iconographies of Jesus and his mother. Cleage continues,

> The pictures of the Black Madonna which are all over the world did not all turn black through some mysterious accident. Portraits of the Black Madonna are historic, and today in many countries they are afraid to take the ancient pictures of the Black Madonna out of storage so that people can see them. Only this year in Spain they were afraid to parade with the Black Madonna because they feared that it might have political implications. But the Black Madonna is an historical fact, and Jesus as a Black Messiah is an historical fact.[89]

Cleage has leaned into a rhetorical strategy of traditional Aristotelian "logos" to redress the personhood of Jesus. He emphasizes fact over conjecture. The Blackness of Jesus (and Mary) is not a conceptual or rhetorical myth; it's a fact. And if Christianity is a revolutionary faith tradition, and Jesus is the Black Messiah, then it is not possible for this religion (if it is true to its ethnic origins) to be "whitey's religion."

Cleage's next move is a set of rhetorical questions that he hopes to provide substantive answers to. These questions are intended to continue the disturbance of the conventional notions of Christology. For Cleage, the political project he prescribes with Christianity requires him to present a Black Messiah that people can more closely relate to. This cannot be done if Jesus is understood as possessing a degree of divinity unavailable to other humans. Cleage also wants to highlight the Blackness of Jesus and Jesus's connection to the theopolitical promise of God to Abraham (Israel) with God's commitment to Black Liberation and God's solidarity with Black people. Cleage hypothesizes, "We might ask why did God choose to send his son (or to come himself) to the nation Israel? It is a question you should have asked yourself. Why, of all the people on earth did he come to these people? Why?"[90] Then he answers by inferring, "Why not to some little group of white people in Europe who were living in caves and eating raw meat? Why did he pick these people? Why?"[91] He answers more directly thereafter stating,

> Go back for a moment to the Biblical account of creation, "God created man in his own image." We say that all the time, but what does it mean? If God created man in his own image, what must God look like? I know that if you close your eyes, you see a white God. But if God created man in his own image, then we must look at man to see what God looks like[92]

Cleage's aim here is not so much anthropological but theological. He is not trying to describe the development of all humanity. He's trying to redeem the humanity of Black people. He wants Black people to see God as their Creator and representative. Cleage needs Black people to self-identify with a Black God. From there he can move to reconstitute them further toward a liberative political project undergirded by a revolutionary theology. Cleage expands his anthropological appeal: "There are black men, there are yellow men, there are red men, and there are a few, a mighty few, white men in the world. If God created man in his own image, then God must be some combination of this black, red, yellow, and white. In no other way could God have created man in his own image."[93]

Cleage has rhetorically separated Jesus from God and is working diligently to separate both from whiteness, and while he has skimmed the surface of anthropology, he begins to dive more directly into anthropomorphism—attributing human attributes to nonhuman entities. And whereby Cleage spent much time denouncing God's whiteness, he has only skimmed the surface of affirming God as Black. Cleage moves deeper into that agenda stating,

> So if we think of God as a person (and we are taught in the Christian religion to think of God as a person, as a personality capable of love, capable of concern, capable of purpose and of action) then God must be a combination of black, yellow and red with just a little touch of white, and we must think of God as a black God.[94]

At a glance, Cleage has miscalculated the ethnic equation. He does not identify God as an ethno-cultural smorgasbord but as "black?" This can only be understood considering his social and political conditioning. To which, Cleage explains, "In America, one drop of black makes you black. So by American law, God is black, and by any practical interpretation, why would God have made seven-eighths of the world non-white and yet he himself be white? That's not reasonable."[95] By evoking the infamous "one drop rule,"[96] Cleage has not only further distanced God from white supremacy but has also done so using appeals to American legal codes.

The inference here is that God is not only nonwhite but also not an American. Or at the very least, American legal codes rooted in white supremacist ideology are incompatible with the nature or essence of God. All of this is a reemphasis of Cleage's major claim here—God is not white. He continues, "If God were white, he'd have made everybody white. And if he decided to send his son to earth, he would have sent a white son down to some nice white people. He certainly would not have sent him down to a black people like Israel."[97] Cleage breaks with logical consistency here. There is no deductive reason to presume that God's whiteness necessitates the creation of all white humans. If this was the case, the claim that God is Black would demand the creation of all Black humans. Cleage has already conceded this point. What he does rhetorically here is situate white identity in the framework of dominance. Cleage's unstated proposition is that whiteness as an ideology is so pervasive and encompassing that it does not allow room for diversity or difference. Whiteness, or at least white theology manifested in a white God demands full assimilation. But, thankfully, God is not white. God's Blackness, Cleage posits, allows for a broader spectrum of human existence—Black, yellow, red, and even some white.

REJECTING A CORRUPTED (SLAVE) CHRISTIANITY

Early in the sermon, Cleage discussed Black revolutionaries for being misled and being manipulated into misinterpreting the origins and essence of

Christianity. He cited the Apostle Paul as a source of the deception. Now, Cleage is about to revisit the subject while casting a wider net on the impact of the misinformation and specifying a contemporary culprit. He confesses, "We have been misled. We received Christianity as we know it from our slave masters. Most of us didn't have it when we got here. We had lost it. We learned it from our slave masters."[98] Cleage has just severed the relationship between the origins of Christianity and the brand of the faith that landed in the Americas several centuries after its inception. He rhetorically opens the portal of history and points to the effects of the transatlantic slave trade, and since "when [blacks] got here" to the Americas we had already lost Christianity as it was originally constructed, we were subject to a more westernized, Europeanized, and white rendition of Christianity. This distinction is paramount. Thus, he continues,

> The Christianity given to the slaves and used to enslave the continent of African, when the white man sent missionaries back over there with guns and with Bibles, is the white man's distortion and corruption of the black man's historic faith. It is this corruption of Christianity which the black man, and especially black young people, is rejecting today.[99]

At last, Cleage has arrived at the current landscape and sufficiently described the disconnect between the origins of Christianity, it's liberative value for Black people through a righteous connection with nation building, and the developments which led to the disconnection and rejection of the faith by Black radicals who carry out a Black God's initiatives but won't affirm a Christian identity. And Cleage, by conventional rhetorical standards, could conclude here with a simple appeal to reconsideration of the faith. But Black prophetic rhetoric demands more than a mere consideration. It demands liberation, transformation, and hints at the potential for reconciliation.[100] Furthermore, by the conventional standards of Black Preaching, Cleage still has a foundational scripture which he read at the offset that he has not dealt with adequately. More will be said about this momentarily.

Cleage's rhetorical aim is to speak into existence the liberation of Black people, the transformation of the Black Church, and a reconciliation of Black people to the Black Church. The ordination of young Black radicals is a strategy to achieve those ends. Therefore, Cleage cannot conclude until after he has rectified the previously mentioned "rejection." He postulates,

> Let me point out three things which are a part of this rejection. Christianity is essentially and historically concerned with a group, with society, with the community. In the Old Testament and in the Synoptic Gospels, God is concerned with a people, not individuals. Yet, the slave Christianity that you were taught

told us that God is concerned with each individual. And the mast told each slave, "If you are a good slave, God is going to take care of you and you will be saved." He didn't tell them that if all you black people love God and fight together, God is going to help you get free from slavery. The group concept is historic Christianity. Individualism is slave Christianity.[101]

Cleage has further differentiated between the "historic Christianity" and white-washed, corrupted, or "slave Christianity." His inference is that the latter should be rejected wholeheartedly because not only is it ahistorical but it's also counterproductive to the political project of nation building. One cannot build a nation individually. However, Cleage has also highlighted some provocative participles associated with "historic" (read: Black) Christianity. He subtly proposed that under the banner of Black Christianity, a group of people would potentially "love God and fight together," and, because of their unity and effort, God would emancipate them and free them from slavery. (Like God did for the Hebrews in the Old Testament.)

From a rejection on the grounds of individualism, Cleage moves to the next item—moralism. He comments, "The petty personal morality emphasized in the slave Church comes from slave Christianity.[102]" Within the annals of the church in general, and the Black Church in particular, there has been a constant presumption of moral superiority. From this basis has spawned an aspiration for ethical (and even sinless) behavior as well as an earth-shattering encounter with human fallibility. Proponents of the Black Church promote a standard of behavior that is often unattainable and has pushed many a potential parishioner to the margins. The same promotion and standard coupled with the public failures of many pastors and lay people have branded the church with the tattoo of hypocrisy. Morality under this banner is individualistic and based upon the behavior of the person. It is, most often, not concerned with the behaviors or ethics of a system of cultural, political, and theological production. Cleage wants to reposition the church and redefine the standards. Cleage argues, "God is concerned in the Old Testament and Jesus is concerned in the New Testament with social morality, with how a group of people act, how they take care of each other, whether they're concerned about poverty, whether they're concerned about each other."[103]

Cleage has reconfigured the conception of morality from individual to collective, from personal to corporate and institutional. But Cleage is not done with his dismissal of personal morality and its connection to slave Christianity. He continues, "Whence comes, then, this emphasis upon petty personal morality? Do you smoke? Then you're a sinner. Do you drink? Then you're a sinner. This is slave Christianity. Because this was the emphasis that the slave master wanted to make so that he could use religion to control the slaves."[104] Cleage understands that these pious behavioral control regulations have created a rift between the church and the everyday people in the community. For Cleage, Christianity is not intended to simply modify people's individual behaviors and habits. It is purposed to inspire a community to work together toward a common and righteous goal of liberation and nation building. This will not be accomplished by pushing an envelope of exclusion based upon someone's personal habits and vices.

The use of the term "sinner" here provides Cleage with a chance to deal with the church's conventional engagement with "sin" or wrongdoing. The punishment for sin is eternal damnation in another world. But for so many Black radicals and revolutionaries, there was no fire and brimstone or lake of fire that could've been any worse than the pain and persecution of being Black in America in the twentieth century. As a result, for Cleage to recruit the Black radicals into the Shrine and have them consider ordination, he must affirm their rejection of a fear-based theology and invite them to consider an alternative. He does so by saying,

> The other worldly emphasis, where did that come from? That's not in the Old Testament nor in the teachings of Jesus, either. Jesus talked of the kingdom of God on earth. He talked to his followers about building a certain king of world *here*. In the Old Testament the prophets were concerned with building God's kingdom out of the nation Israel. Then when comes this other worldly emphasis? This is slave Christianity. Slave Christianity deliberately emphasized the other world so that we would not be concerned about the everyday problems of this world.[105]

Cleage, again, echoes an affirmation with respect to young radicals' rejection of the tenets of slave (read: white) Christianity, as well as its hyper-moralism connected to a preoccupation with otherworldly emphasis. But Cleage also invites his audience to receive Black Christianity's embrace of communal righteousness through the pursuit of a more just society in the present which comes through nation building offered by Black Christianity.

CLEAGE'S RESPONSE TO PAULINE CHRISTIANITY

After addressing individualism and moralism, Cleage rounds out this section with a rejection of institutionalism. The rejection of institutionalism is also an appeal to recruit Black radicals. Cleage appeal is a righteous strategy. Cleage does not see the Black Church as a generic institution that should be rejected and resisted in the same vein as so many white supremacist institutions. Instead, he sees the Black Church as the potential hub for the Black Power Movement. The Black Church is an independent and autonomous institution that Cleage believes must be leveraged for Black empowerment, uplift, political strategizing, and community organizing. However, he understands that the Black Church has not functioned as such due to white supremacist theology and sentiment infiltrating its ranks. Therefore, Cleage draws back upon the origins of the faith and, again, chronicles more of its important developments. He seeks to contextualize how white supremacy has contaminated the institution and reconstitute the church and community to redeem them both. He teaches,

> The tremendous confusion in Christianity grows out of the fact that after the death of Jesus, the Apostle Paul began to corrupt his teachings with concepts which were essentially the pagan concepts of the Gentile oppressors. From the Greek and Roman world he borrowed philosophical ideas that had nothing to do with anything that Israel had ever believed or anything that Jesus had ever taught.[106]

Cleage's motif here is to further distinguish between modern Christianity and ancient Christianity. The former, according to Cleage, is more Pauline than it is Christian. This is to say that the teachings of Paul as presented in so much of the New Testament has taken precedent over the teachings of Jesus as portrayed in the Gospels. Cleage rhetorically leans into what one may refer to as the Pauline Controversy—the contestation of Paul's authority, apostolic agenda, and legitimate connection to the historical Jesus. Cleage seeks to not only discredit Paul's authority but also, moreover, to scapegoat Paul as the primary cancer and corrupter of Black Liberationist Christianity. Cleage contends,

> The Apostle Paul attempted to break the covenant which the Black Nation Israel had with God. He said, "Circumcision is unimportant, all these little rules and laws are unimportant. We must accept everybody." That is why Paul was in conflict with the real disciples who had walked with Jesus and were still in Jerusalem. They said, "We are a people. We have a covenant with God. We believe in certain things, and when you go out and you try to convert the barbarians you are corrupting our faith." History has proven that they were correct.[107]

Whether one affirms Paul's contribution on the corruption of Christianity or not, Paul's influence on the understanding of the faith cannot be discounted. Cleage is careful to refer to Paul as "The Apostle" which acknowledges Paul's influence on the church as an institution. However, Cleage has also offered a perspective that leads to questioning why Paul has so much influence if his authority has historically been debated. Furthermore, if we consider the canonization process (the method by which ancient writings were canonized into the biblical record), one must consider why Paul's writings (or writings attributed to Paul) have been so prevalent and dominant. Cleage knows these curiosities loom, and needing to claim further space for the rejection of white Christianity in his recruitment of Black radicals, Cleage theorizes on the impact of the Paul's biblical contributions. Cleage states, "The Epistles of Paul are in direct contradiction to the teachings of the Old Testament. Slave Christianity emphasizes these distortions of the Apostle Paul and denies and repudiates the basic teachings of Jesus Christ and the Black Nation Israel."[108]

Cleage's treatment of Paul is both necessary and peculiar. It is necessary if he intends on legitimizing a critique of the white supremacist influences on the Black Church. Because if Jesus is a Black Messiah building a Black nation, one must explain how so much of Paul's work has been embraced by the Black Church as an institution. Remember, Cleage argues that "we have been deceived." To that end, Cleage has situated Paul as a tool of deception. Cleage is not alone in this treatment. His argument aligns with many of the claims made by Robert Eiseman in his book *James the Brother of Jesus*[109] which rejects a great deal of Pauline authenticity and authority. In fact, it goes so far as to discredit Paul as a Roman operative who's function is to deradicalize Christianity and transform it from a revolutionary into an accommodationist movement. But, more provocatively, Cleage's engagement with Paul also harkens back to a treatment of New Testament texts that was given by Howard Thurman's grandmother.

Howard Thurman was a well-known Christian theologian and mystic who served The Church for the Fellowship of All People in San Francisco, California, in the mid-twentieth century. Thurman was regarded as one of the forerunners for racial justice in a congregational context in America. What many do not know is prior to Thurman's arrival at All People's House of Worship, they had two interim pastors—one white, one Black. The Black pastor was Albert Cleage. Cleage recalls his experiences as banal.[110] He was unimpressed with the congregation's cosmetic measures to induce racial reconciliation. Howard Thurman's arrival proved to be beneficial in that Thurman's engagement with the congregation was less aggressive and militant than Cleage's. However, ironically, Cleage's treatment of Paul is peculiar because it echoes that of the story Thurman has told about his grandmother who was emancipated from slavery by the Emancipation Proclamation. According to Thurman, his grandmother could not read but requested that Thurman, a collegiate graduate at the time, read her morning scripture devotion to her each day. Thurman's grandmother gave him a specific directive to not read anything attributed to Paul except the "love" chapter in 1st Corinthians (chapter 13). When Thurman inquired why, she explained,

> During the days of slavery . . . the master's minister would occasionally hold services for the slaves. Old man McGhee was so mean that he would not let a Negro minister preach to his slaves. Always the white minister used as his text something from Paul. At least three or four times a year he used as a text: "Slaves, be obedient to them that are your masters . . . , as unto Christ." Then he would go on to show how it was God's will that we were slaves and how, if we were good and happy slaves, God would bless us.[111]

Grandma Thurman concluded, "I promised my Maker that if I ever learned to read and if freedom ever came, I would not read that part of the Bible."[112] Mrs. Thurman's dismissal of basically all things Paul is along the same vein of what Cleage is promoting with respect to rejecting any white supremacist sentiment found in the scriptures.

Furthermore, Cleage is attempting to draw a line between the functions of the church as an institution and the potential of the Black Power Movement. Cleage wants to align Jesus with Black Power and Paul with white Christianity. To that end he posits, "The Black Messiah Jesus did not build a Church, but a Movement. He gathered together people to follow him and sent them out to change the world. He sent out the seventy two-by-two, and he himself when from place to place. He built a Movement, not a Church."[113] Again, Cleage is situating the Black Church (in its ideal state) as a location for Movement (and Nation) building. He is aligning the activities of the Black radicals and revolutionaries with the Black Messiah to invite them to receive Black Christianity in the affirmative. He further synthesizes the religion with Black radicalism saying, "Like today's young black prophets, [Jesus] rejected the institutionalization of religion. He rejected the Church deliberately because he said, 'It's wrong, it's hypocritical, and it's opposed to the will of God.' He rejected the morality of his time. He rejected the Church of his time. He was a prophet."[114]

Cleage has aligned Jesus and the young Black revolutionaries with the Black Prophetic Tradition.[115] To label these young Black radicals as "prophets" is to affirm a divine inspiration within their ideas and initiatives. Cleage is rhetorically associating movement leaders with a dis-organized or noninstitutionalized religion. He is not simply associating them with a freelance type of spirituality but maneuvering them into a relationship with Black Christianity that exists even when it is not connected to a building or institution. Cleage claims the spirit of the Black Power Movement is prophetic and akin to the same spirit that existed in the Jesus movement.

Cleage then concludes this section tying the movement leaders more strongly to the personality and prophetic nature of Jesus. Cleage says,

[Jesus] was in the same frame of mind as the young black prophets today who reject Christianity as they see it institutionalized in the slave Church. Jesus tried to minister to the every-day needs of his days and he did this within the loose organizational structure of a Movement. He was a dangerous revolutionary.[116]

As paradoxical as Cleage's phraseology is here, it's poignant and true. The Black Christianity Cleage is promoting, offering, and describing for his audience is independent of the institutional Church. It is the spirit of the Movement for Black Liberation which Jesus embodied and lived out. If Black revolutionaries could see themselves as aligned with Jesus's nature, they might reconsider a relationship with the institution that bears Jesus's name—the (Black) Christian church.

(UN)BINDING OUR STRONG MEN

From a homiletical standpoint, Cleage has still left a major pivot point on the table. He has raised a scripture for the purposes of preaching but has not engaged Mark 3:27 much at all. While this is not ideal in the framework of African American preaching, Cleage has maintained the theme of this text in the backdrop throughout the sermon.[117] My concern around this methodology, rhetorically, is that preachers often use a text as a pretext for thought or claim that the text itself does not support. It is clear the text Cleage offered at the offset has not been central to the claims he has made. However, while unorthodox, his claims have been aligned with his broader aim and initiative—the reconstitution of Black Faith toward radical, revolutionary, Black, and historical Christianity. In that vein, Cleage now begins to foreground the Mark 3:27 text in his last transition in the sermon. The theme of Mark 3:27 is the binding of a "strong man." What Cleage does with this text is position Black revolutionaries as "strong men" while simultaneously describe the concern of them being bound by a system and structure of white supremacy. At the same time, Cleage must offer some version of hope that our Black revolutionaries, through an acceptance of the Black Messiah and ordination at the Shrine, can become unbound.

Having sufficiently situated Jesus in the Black Prophetic Tradition and affirmed Christianity as a Black revolutionary religion with hopes of drawing more Black Power activists to the faith, Cleage offers his most direct invitation to the reconstitution of Black Faith and Black Power by angling a few specific supporting passages relating to Jesus's Movement and then, finally, providing the direct impetus for the title of the sermon and for the use of Mark 3:27 at the offset.

Cleage views his foundational text as part of a broader thematic reading which was part of the church's litany that same Sunday. He wants to revisit the earlier theme of misinterpretation and continue to represent Jesus as a Black revolutionary who is cognizant of the social and political needs of his community and prioritizes those needs above any normative conventions. Cleage's broader aim is to, again, affirm the rejection of the white-washed notion of Jesus by Western society and invite Black revolutionaries to reconsider a more militant and historically accurate version and vision of Jesus as the Black Messiah. Cleage purports,

> In our Scripture lesson this morning we read, first, the account of Jesus' first sermon in Nazareth where he described the things that he had come to do. To give sight to the blind, to give food to the hungry, to take the chains off those who were in bondage. These things he had come to do. To minister to the everyday needs of people.[118]

Cleage reminds his audience of the broader mission and methods of Jesus to make him more relatable to those who may be involved in the same initiatives in the current moment. Many Black revolutionaries in the 1960s were involved in organizing efforts to "minister to the everyday needs of people."[119] Cleage is, again, synthesizing the actions of Black radicals with Jesus for self-identification purposes. Cleage continues,

> In another scriptural passage we had the account of Jesus going into the Temple. A man whose arm was withered went up to Jesus, and the Scribes and the Pharisees waited to see whether or not Jesus would help the man on the Sabbath Day. Jesus looked angrily at the Pharisees and the Scribes, and he healed the man right there in the Temple because it was more important to help the man that it was to observe the laws of the Sabbath. At another time he said, "The Sabbath was made for man, not man for the Sabbath."[120]

The latter portion of this section is vital in considering the affirmation of what the broader society would perceive as lawlessness or at least disregard for or breaking the law.

The Detroit riots and other manifestations of Black rebellion were often rebutted with appeals of obedience to laws; even when those laws were deemed unjust by those subjected to them. Cleage situates Jesus in the historical context of his religious and social laws, at odds with religious leaders and legal authorities of his day. Again, Cleage has rhetorically sought to redeem the image of Black revolutionaries who have engaged in "illegal" measures in efforts to assist, empower, and emancipate people who were oppressed. The implication here is, if Jesus was willing to break laws in the name of a greater good, one must not dismiss current "law breakers" who are engaged in similar practices and embrace similar philosophies.

But Cleage is mindful of his audience's appeals to scriptural authority. He therefore addresses, again, biblical interpretation saying, "It's peculiar how we could misread the Bible for so long."[121] This is another return to an earlier theme of misinterpretation. And although Cleage has not yet settled into his foundational scripture he is yet laying the groundwork for an unorthodox conclusion to his sermon and parting the waters heading toward another unconventional interpretation of scripture.

Cleage opened with disturbing the language in a familiar hymn and contesting the efficacy of the theology therein. He has done the same with various scripture passages and is contesting his audience's approach to and understanding of the Bible in general. He returns to the opening in a circular fashion stating, "How could we just keep on singing the same old wrong songs and keep on going through the same old wrong motions when the truth is right here in the book."[122] Notice, Cleage's rhetoric is more indicting and direct here than it was at the offset. This is a rhetorical strategy that denotes an understanding of what is malleable to his audience as well as a commitment to building a platform for prophetic rhetoric to be potentially more persuasive. Cleage offers this explanation to the perils of misinterpretation, "People don't really read the Bible. They listen to what somebody tells them."[123]

Cleage must now transition from deconstruction to reconstitution. He seeks to gain the confidence of his audience to commit to them a better path forward. He states,

> Now, let me tell you, your grandmother and that country preacher down home didn't know all there is to know about Christianity. And if you're going to depend on what they told you, then you're just going to be wrong about almost everything. You've got to go back and look at the Bible itself, read some history books and find out what this Christianity is that you either believe or don't believe. Find out who this Jesus is that you either follow or reject![124]

Cleage is simultaneously indicting, again, the teachers or elders more so than the students or young revolutionaries. He continues to ask them to reconsider or reconstitute their understandings of a faith tradition they "believe" (elders) or "reject" (revolutionaries). This methodology is a synthesis of both *parrhesia* and *nommo*. Cleage's bold and frank speech is intended to both deconstruct or condemn unjust understandings and practices related to their current context. But the same language is also designed to create or bring into being a new (or revised/revisited) sense of being and doing related to Christianity.

Although the African American preaching tradition focuses much on the impact of a highly emotive, image-ridden conclusion also referred to as "celebration,"[125] Cleage's approach in this sermon's close is more cognitive and practical. In Cleage's opening, the primary problem he sought to resolve was the rejection of Christianity by Black radicals and revolutionaries. These are those that Cleage has sought to provide political cover for under the guise of religious liberty. Without this cover, Cleage fears, the young men (and women) who are fighting to obtain Black Power and Freedom would be carted off to war and/or prison. Cleage finally returns to this problem to offer another plea for inclusion. He posits,

> In closing, I take a text from Matthew 7:21, where Jesus says 'Not everyone that says to me Lord, Lord, shall enter the kingdom of Heaven, but he who does the will of my father, who is in Heaven.' Let us try to free ourselves from the 'Lord, Lord' business and try to join those few people in the world today who are trying to do the will of God.[126]

For Cleage, the young revolutionaries are doing the will of God and thereby should be embraced by his congregation. Cleage thereafter, makes a more direct plea to those individuals even calling by name, again, the one who has provided the impetus for the title of the sermon. Cleage pleas, "To Stokely and the young men in SNICK [sic], I would just say briefly that the Christian religion you are rejecting, that you are so opposed to, is a slave Christianity that has no roots in the teachings of the Black Messiah."[127] What is implied here is that Cleage and other adherents to the Black Christianity he seeks to embody also oppose any form of slave Christianity. Hoping to have found solidarity with Stokely Carmichael and the SNICK cohort, Cleage continues with a more formal and direct invitation. He states,

> You could be ordained in this Church as civil rights workers if we could somehow do away with the distinctions which exist in people's minds between what's religious and what's not religious. To ordain civil rights workers for civil rights work would declare that the Christian Church believes that this is what Christianity is all about, that individuals who give their lives in the struggle for human freedom are Christian and that the Movement is not only Christian, but that the Movement is the Church.[128]

In other words, for Cleage, the theology and practice of the Black Church must be consistent with the work being done in the movement to liberate Black people from all forms of oppression. He has aligned this with the biblical and historical practices and philosophies of Jesus and rooted them in a Black Power ethic.

Cleage's ultimate goal is the revitalization and righteous transformation of the Black Church as an institution, and, as conspicuous as it seems, and as much of a homiletical faux pau as it may be, Cleage finally revisits his foundational scripture in the final sentences of the sermon. While there is a thread of theological and ideological consistency within the sermon, I think there have been some missed opportunities to tie this particular text even further into the psychology of theological transformation and reconstitution. Nevertheless, Cleage concludes,

> The Black Church must recapture the loyalty of black youth if it is to be significant in the black revolution, and it must find a way to save its brave young men from death on some distant battlefield. I read from the Gospel of Mark 3:27. "but no one can enter a strong man's house and plunder his goods unless he first binds the strong man. Then indeed he may plunder his house." When they draft all of the cream of our young men, whether they kill them in Vietnam or put them in the penitentiary, they have bound our strong me. Then indeed they may at their will and at their pleasure plunder out house.[129]

The truth of Cleage's words continues to echo into the contemporary moment. The rift between modern Black revolutionaries and the institutional Black Church still exists, and houses in Black communities remain under plunder. Rev. Albert Cleage, Jr. was right.

Having provided a slow-paced and methodical reading of a masterful sermon that highlights the multilayered relationship between Black Theology, Black Power, and African American religious and prophetic rhetoric, the next chapter will substantively add another influential voice to the discussion. I will put Cleage in direct conversation with one of his contemporaries—another forefather of Black Theology—Dr. James Hal Cone. This conversation will further highlight what rhetorical studies offer the field of religious studies and vice versa.

NOTES

1. Cleage, *The Black Messiah*, 35.
2. Womanist Theology is a genre of (Black) Liberation Theology that centers the experiences and spiritual insights of Black Women. See, Delores S. Williams, "Womanist Theology: Black Women's Voices (1986)," *Womanist Reader* (2006): 117–125; Jacquelyn Grant, "White Women's Christ and Black Women's Jesus," *Women's Studies in Religion* (2007) and Stephanie Y. Mitchem, *Introducing Womanist Theology* (Orbis Books, 2014).
3. See Paul A. Minifee, "'I Took Up the Hymn-Book': Rhetoric of Hymnody in Jarena Lee's Call to Preach," *Advances in the History of Rhetoric* 18, no. 1 (2015): 1–28.

4. https://www.hymnal.net/en/hymn/h/175.
5. Delores Carpenter, and Rev Nolan E. Williams, eds. *African American Heritage Hymnal* (GIA Publications, 2001).
6. Cleage, *The Black Messiah*, 35.
7. See Alan D. Desantis, "An Amostic Prophecy: Fredrick Douglass' The Meaning of July Fourth for the Negro," *Journal of Communication & Religion* 22, no. 1 (1999).
8. See William Ronald Jones, *Is God a White Racist?: A Preamble to Black Theology* (Beacon Press, 1973).
9. Cleage, *The Black Messiah*, 35.
10. See Charland, "Constitutive Rhetoric: The Case of the Peuple Quebecois," 133–150; Michael C. Leff, and Ebony A. Utley, "Instrumental and Constitutive Rhetoric in Martin Luther King Jr.'s 'Letter from Birmingham Jail,'" *Rhetoric & Public Affairs* 7, no. 1 (2004): 37–51.
11. Douglas, *The Black Christ*, 54.
12. See Lloyd F. Bitzer, "The Rhetorical Situation," in *Philosophy & Rhetoric* (1992), 1–14.
13. Cleage, *The Black Messiah*, 35
14. Paul Finkelman and Yohuru Williams, *Encyclopedia of African American History: From the Age of Segregation to the Twenty-first Century* (2009), 48–49.
15. Ibid., 48.
16. Ibid., 48.
17. Cleage, *The Black Messiah*, 35.
18. Ibid., 36.
19. Ibid., 36.
20. Ibid., 36.
21. Ibid., 36.
22. Ibid., 36.
23. Ibid., 36.
24. Chapman, *Christianity on Trial*, 3.
25. Cleage, *The Black Messiah*, 36.
26. Ibid., 36.
27. Ibid., 36.
28. Ibid., 36–37.
29. Arthur L. Smith, *Some Characteristics of the Black Religious Audience* (1970), 207.
30. See, Molefi Asante, *Afrocentric Idea Revised* (Temple University Press, 2011), 173.
31. See Antonio Raul De Velasco, "Rethinking Perelman's Universal Audience: Political Dimensions of a Controversial Concept," *Rhetoric Society Quarterly* 35, no. 2 (2005): 47–64.
32. Cleage, *The Black Messiah*, 37.
33. Ibid., 37.
34. Henry McNeal Turner, "God is a Negro," *Voice of Missions* (1898).
35. Andre E. Johnson, "God is a Negro: The (Rhetorical) Black Theology of Bishop Henry McNeal Turner," *Black Theology* 13, no. 1 (2015), 32.
36. Ibid., 32.

37. Cleage, *The Black Messiah*, 37.
38. Ibid., 37.
39. Ibid., 37.
40. Ibid., 37.
41. A. E. K. M. Ibrahim, "Whassup, Homeboy?," in *Joining the African Diaspora: Black English as a Symbolic Site of Identification and Language Learning*, edited by S. Makoni, G. Smitherman, A. F. Ball, & A. K. Spears, *Black Linguistics: Language, Society, and Politics in Africa and the Americas* (2003), 171.
42. Cleage, *The Black Messiah*, 37.
43. Ibid., 37–38.
44. Ibid., 38.
45. Ibid., 38.
46. George G. M. James and Molefi Kete Asante, *Stolen Legacy: Greek Philosophy is Stolen Egyptian Philosophy* (United Brothers Communications Systems), 29.
47. Cleage, *The Black Messiah*, 38.
48. Ibid., 38.
49. Ibid., 38.
50. Johnson, *The Forgotten Prophet*, 7.
51. Cleage, *The Black Messiah*, 38.
52. Ibid., 38–39.
53. Ibid., 39.
54. Ibid., 39
55. See John J. Collins, *The Bible after Babel: Historical Criticism in a Postmodern Age* (Wm. B. Eerdmans Publishing, 2005).
56. Cleage, *The Black Messiah*, 39.
57. Ibid., 39.
58. Ibid., 39.
59. Ibid., 39.
60. Leff, "9 Hermeneutical Rhetoric."
61. Ibid., 203–204.
62. Cleage, *The Black Messiah*, 39.
63. Ibid., 39.
64. For more on Race and Political Theology see, Vincent Lloyd, ed. *Race and Political Theology* (Stanford University Press, 2012).
65. See Ernest W. Nicholson, *God and His People: Covenant and Theology in the Old Testament* (Oxford University Press, 1988).
66. Cleage, *The Black Messiah*, 39.
67. Ibid., 40.
68. Ibid., 40.
69. Danielle L. McGuire, *At the Dark End of the Street: Black Women, Rape, and Resistance—A New History of the Civil Rights Movement from Rosa Parks to the Rise of Black Power* (Vintage), xix.
70. Cleage, *The Black Messiah*, 40.
71. Ibid., 40.

72. Ibid, 40.

73. See José V. Malcioln, *The African Origin of Modern Judaism: From Hebrews to Jews* (Africa World Pr, 1996) and Graham Harvey, "Synagogues of the Hebrews: 'Good Jews' in the Diaspora," (1998): 132–147;

74. Cleage, *The Black Messiah*, 40.

75. See R. C. Bailey, "Is that Any Name for a Nice Hebrew Boy?" *Exodus* 2 (1995): 1–10; "Beyond Identification: The Use of Africans in Old Testament Poetry and Narratives," *Stony the Road We Trod* (1991): 165–186.

76. Cleage, *The Black Messiah*, 40.

77. Ibid., 40.

78. Ibid., 40–41.

79. See, William L. Van Deburg, ed., *Modern Black Nationalism: From Marcus Garvey to Louis Farrakhan* (NYU Press, 1997).

80. Aswad Walker, "Princes Shall Come out of Egypt: A Theological Comparison of Marcus Garvey and Reverend Albert B. Cleage Jr," *Journal of Black Studies* 39, no. 2 (2008): 197.

81. Cleage, *The Black Messiah*, 41.

82. Ibid., 41.

83. Ibid., 41.

84. Ibid., 41.

85. See Blum, and Harvey, *The Color of Christ*.

86. Cleage, *The Black Messiah*, 42.

87. See Edward L. Krasevac, "'Christology From Above and Christology From Below,'" *The Thomist: A Speculative Quarterly Review* 51, no. 2 (1987): 299–306 and Andrew Chester, "High Christology—Whence, When and Why?" *Early Christianity* 2, no. 1 (2011): 22–50.

88. Cleage, *The Black Messiah*, 42.

89. Ibid., 42.

90. Ibid., 42.

91. Ibid., 42.

92. Ibid., 42.

93. Ibid., 42.

94. Ibid., 42–43.

95. Ibid., 43.

96. See Anthony Lemelle, "One Drop Rule," *The Blackwell Encyclopedia of Sociology* (2007).

97. Cleage, *The Black Messiah*, 43.

98. Ibid., 43.

99. Ibid., 43.

100. In his speech at the National Press Club in 2008, Rev. Jeremiah Wright, Jr. gave a lecture about Black Theology. Black Theology is, in some ways, a platform for Black prophetic rhetoric. Rev. Wright describes Black Theology as a theology of liberation, transformation, and reconciliation. See https://www.youtube.com/watch?v=xwSSesNIEU8.

101. Cleage, *The Black Messiah*, 43.

102. Ibid., 43.
103. Ibid., 43–44.
104. Ibid., 44.
105. Ibid., 44.
106. Ibid., 44.
107. Ibid., 44.
108. Ibid., 44.
109. Robert H. Eisenman, *James the Brother of Jesus: The Key to Unlocking the Secrets of Early Christianity and the Dead Sea Scrolls* (Penguin, 1998).
110. Ward, *Prophet of the Black Nation*, 54–56.
111. Howard Thurman, *Jesus and the Disinherited* (Beacon Press), 30–31.
112. Ibid., 31.
113. Cleage, *The Black Messiah*, 44–45.
114. Ibid., 45.
115. See West and Buschendorf, *Black Prophetic Fire* and Darsey, *The Prophetic Tradition and Radical Rhetoric in America*.
116. Cleage, *The Black Messiah*, 45.
117. See Simmons and Thomas, eds. *Preaching with Sacred Fire*, 7–9.
118. Ibid., 45.
119. At least one well-known project was the Black Panther's assistance program to aid women, infants, and children which ultimately became the federal assistance program now referred to as the Special Supplemental Nutrition Program for Woman, Infants and Children (WIC). See https://urbanintellectuals.com/2016/02/10/wic-women-infants-children-program-raise-healthy-children-started-black-panthers-still-operates-today/.
120. Cleage, *The Black Messiah*, 45.
121. Ibid., 45.
122. Ibid., 45.
123. Ibid., 45.
124. Ibid., 45–46.
125. See Frank Anthony Thomas, *They Like to Never Quit Praisin' God: The Role of Celebration in Preaching* (Pilgrim Press, 1997).
126. Cleage, *The Black Messiah*, 46.
127. Ibid., 46.
128. Ibid., 46.
129. Ibid., 46.

Chapter 5

Brother Malcolm, Dr. King, and Black Power

A Close and Complimentary Reading

In chapter 4, I discussed at length Cleage's relationship and engagement with the Black Power Movement and Black revolutionaries through the personality of Stokely Carmichael. Cleage's *An Epistle to Stokely* is one concrete example of a Black, socially conscious pastor, committed to the empowerment and liberation of Black people, sermonizing in ways that take into account the social and political landscape in light of biblical literary content. This was not a one-off for Cleage. There are two more sermons within *The Black Messiah* that very poignantly build upon this rhetorical strategy. These sermons, in tandem with *An Epistle to Stokely*, grant us a fuller understanding of how underrepresented forms of Black Faith praxis offer a more comprehensive resistance to white supremacy than some of the more notable or conventional personalities associated with Christianity and even Black Theology have provided. Those two sermons, *Brother Malcolm*, and *Dr. King and Black Power*, look at two more notable personalities (people who Cleage had direct relationship and numerous encounters with) who were pivotal in the 1960s (and into the present). These two sermons are dealt with at length in this chapter.

For decades, Dr. King and Malcolm X have been joined at the hip in the psyche of those interested in civil rights, Black Power, Black Preaching, and Black Faith. Some have surmised that Malcolm and Martin were opposites. Others contend they are two sides of the same coin. Considering their rhetoric and theology, one of the more responsible engagements with their works, ideas, and public speeches comes from one of their contemporaries, Dr. James Hal Cone. In his book, *Martin & Malcolm & America* (MMA), Cone theorizes the relationship and impact of Malcolm's nationalism and Martin's integrationism from formation to maturation (as much as can be captured in the brief lives shared by both).

Cleage is one of Cone's contemporaries and also shares some significant views on Malcolm and Martin's contribution to the Black Freedom and Liberation movements, for better or worse. In Cleage's sermons entitled, *Brother Malcolm* and *Dr. King and Black Power*, respectively, we see themes emerge that shed light on a more militant engagement with the themes of civil rights, Black Power, Black Preaching, and Black Faith than Cone was willing or able to provide.

I have previously mentioned the relationship between Cleage and Cone in the introduction and subsequent chapters of this book. I expressed how shocked I was to discover Cone's seminal work, *Black Theology and Black Power*, only provided one line of reference to Cleage and no substantial engagement with his theological or political contribution. This is especially troubling when we consider Cleage's function in the foundations of Black Liberation Theology (not just in theory but also in practice). By joining together, the themes of Cleage's two sermons with the substance in Cone's MMA (which builds on many themes Cone introduced in *Black Theology and Black Power*), we can offer a more well-rounded example of the rhetorical, theological, sociological, and ideological complexities that made the prophets of the 1960s so riveting and our reviews of them so nostalgic. We must do more than consider what they said/wrote and the impact it had on the community, country, and culture. We must analyze how they said what they said. We must delve into the communicative strategies they employed and what those strategies teach us about the rhetoric of social change, and we must reconsider why some figures are revered, while others are reviled.

CONE'S RHETORICAL SEQUENCING

According to Cone, "Although the media portrayed them as adversaries, Martin and Malcolm were actually fond of each other."[1] One cannot definitively assess whether Cone's claim of them being "actually fond of each other" is historically accurate. It is deeply subjective, and a modest perusal of speeches from Martin and Malcolm where one references the other would provide enough substance for dispute. And while Cone describes their personal fondness of one another, he also details Martin and Malcolm's philosophical and political adversarial positions—integrationism and nationalism.

Cone approaches this endeavor with a perspective that is made evident in the structure and substance of his presentation. It is important to note the sequential order by which Cone engages these figures and their ideologies because it illuminates possibilities for us to understand who and what Cone sees as priority and preeminent.

For instance, Malcolm was older than Martin (born in 1925 and 1929, respectively). Malcolm emerges on a national public radar a year prior to King (Malcolm in 1953 as lead minister of Boston Mosque, Temple 11, and Martin as Pastor of Dexter Avenue Baptist Church in Montgomery in 1954). Nevertheless, Cone still presents Martin and integrationism as the sequential standard bearer of analytical engagement. Rhetorically speaking, for the reader, Martin and integrationism are seared into the mind of the reader prior to any in-depth discussion of Malcolm and his nationalist philosophies and rhetorical strategies and dispositions. Any consideration of Malcolm and nationalism will thereafter be compared to what Cone sets as the standard—Martin and integrationism.

Rhetorical structures and sequences say a lot about the perspectives and values of the orator. Fredrik Sunnmeark describes a rhetorical "ladder of signification" by which sequential order and rhetorical structures communicate how a speaker "orders and understands the world" through a "hierarchy of values."[2] In other words, how and where a speaker situates and sequences people, places, and things when they are being compared can instruct us on who or what the speaker thinks is standard and who or what is supportive. What we can surmise is, Cone has made a rhetorical decision reflective of his epistemology. This is much like what Cleage did in his introduction to *The Black Messiah* when he "permitted" white people to "listen to a black man talking to black people."[3] Both of them write with an audience in mind. And if Cone intends to persuade his audience to reconsider the efficacy of Malcolm's contributions to Civil Rights, Black Power, and religious thought, Cone sees it as advantageous to offer what many whites consider the more palatable approach to racial justice—integrationism. Grappling with the "dilemma that slavery and segregation created for Africans in the United States" through the lens of W. E. B. DuBois and offering responses to DuBois's question of whether one can existentially be American and Negro, Cone posits that integrationists like Martin believe that answer is "Yes." Cone describes his understanding this way:

> The integrationist thought goes something like this: If whites really believe their political and religious documents, then they know that black people should not be enslaved and segregated but rather integrated into the mainstream of the society. After all blacks are Americans, having arrived even before the Pilgrims. They have worked the land, obeyed the laws, paid their taxes, and defended America in every war. They built the nation as much as white people did. Therefore, the integrationists argue, it is the task of African-American leaders to prick the conscience of whites, showing contradictions between their professed values and their actual treatment of blacks. Then whites will be embarrassed

by their hypocrisy and will grant blacks the same freedom that they themselves enjoy.[4]

Cone has described this philosophy without directly denouncing it. This description centers heavily on white psychology (appeals to conscience), white emotions (such as embarrassment), and charity (granting blacks freedom). These elements all echo an approach that prioritizes a white (or at least white-centered) audience and epistemology.

PHILOSOPHICAL UNDERPINNINGS OF CONE'S RHETORICAL ENGAGEMENT

With his audience centered, Cone transitions in a way that re-emphasizes Martin and integrationism as the standard. Cone writes, "On the other hand, nationalist thinkers have rejected the American side of their identity and affirmed the African side, saying, 'No we can't be both.'"[5] And while Cone's reflections on integrationism were centered on white psychology, emotions, and charity, his reflections on nationalism are quite different. His tone is much more aggressive than his description for integrationism. He contends, "The nationalists argue that blacks don't belong with whites, that whites are killing blacks, generation after generation. Blacks should, therefore, separate from America, either by returning to Africa or by going to some other place where they can create sociopolitical structures that are derived from their own history and culture."[6]

In many ways, these sentiments echo a rather mainstream understanding of Martin and Malcolm's difference of perspective and philosophy. And even though both can be viewed as complementary and under the banner of what Cone cites as being "shaped by what Vincent Harding has called the 'Great Tradition of Black Protest,'"[7] there are other ways to engage and analyze what Malcolm and Martin offer to the Black Freedom Movement theologically, philosophically, rhetorically, and politically.

CLEAGE'S COMPLIMENTARY READING OF MALCOLM AND MARTIN

Cleage's sermonic material in *The Black Messiah* offers an alternative and complementary perspective to Cone's reading of Malcolm and Martin. When read in tandem they provide a holistic and well-rounded engagement with basic questions about Black Power, rhetoric, and identity.

That said, I believe Cleage's reflections are, in some ways, weightier than Cone's. This is not to minimize Cone's analysis or suggest that Cleage's is better. I am suggesting that Cleage's commentary should be privileged because Cleage had direct experiences and a personal relationship with both Malcolm and Martin. Cleage has shared historical platforms with and organized events that featured them both. Cleage spoke on program before King at the March to Freedom at Cobo Arena in Detroit. Cleage also spoke on program before Malcolm's infamous "Message to the Grassroots" speech at the Northern Grassroots Leadership Conference, as well as the well-referenced "Ballot or the Bullet" speech. Therefore, Cleage's reflections come from firsthand experience and not simply a righteously academic read of tapes and speeches. Cleage's words are primary source material. Cleage has aligned himself more closely with Malcolm philosophically and ideologically, and while he is associated more with Martin religiously, the lines of demarcation in their understanding of Christianity are remarkable. This might possibly explain Cleage's sequencing of his reflections on Malcolm and Martin.

CLEAGE'S RHETORICAL SEQUENCING

Cleage's sermon "Brother Malcolm" sequentially and chronologically precedes his sermon "Dr. King and Black Power" in TBM. This (re)ordering shifts the standardizing and prioritizing of comparative material for the reader of TBM. It also echoes a difference in the intended audience. Cleage is not constructing his sermonic material under a white gaze. Cleage's parishioners are primarily black, and Cleage states explicitly in his introduction,

> The sermons included in [TBM] were preached to black people. They are published in the hope that they may help other black people find their way back to the historic Black Messiah, and at the request of many black preachers who are earnestly seeking ways to make their preaching relevant to the complex and urgent needs of the black community.[8]

These distinctions are instructive because they provide a significant window of interpretation into the content of the materials found in Cone's book and Cleage's sermons. Furthermore, Cleage identifies himself as a nationalist (not to be confused with a separatist—a distinction Cleage makes in his sermonic materials), and Cleage's nationalistic expressions do not neatly align with the presentations made by Cone. Nevertheless, both Cleage and Cone offer something significant to the understanding of Black Faith, Black Power, and Black Preaching. Cleage's book is a rhetorical artifact that opens a portal of experiential articulation into the Black Power Movement of the mid-/late 1960s. Cone offers a religious and rhetorical analysis of what Martin and Malcolm meant to the Black Power and the Civil Rights Movements socially, politically, and religiously.

CLEAGE'S BLACK CHRISTIAN NATIONALISM

Cone suggests that Martin and Malcolm were rooted in "a tradition that comprised many variations of nationalism and integrationism."[9] However, Malcolm and Martin are from what are traditionally seen as two separate religious communities. Martin is a Protestant Christian with liberal sensibilities. Malcolm is a Muslim in the Nation of Islam which is customarily associated with a religious conservatism, and it is within the religious affiliations and associations that Cleage's presentation of Malcolm provides a distinct shift in insight and perspective. Cleage's political and religious ideology is Black Christian Nationalism.[10] On its face, this reads like a mixture of Martin and Malcolm, but Cleage's take on Malcolm's contribution to Black Empowerment and Black Faith troubles the waters of conventional reads related to a Christian and Muslim dichotomy.

Cleage's early reflections on Malcolm (posthumously) situate Malcolm squarely in the same religious and political tradition of Jesus of Nazareth—the Black Messiah. Since Jesus is understood as the founder of Christianity, directly comparing and associating Malcolm with Jesus disrupts conventional understandings of both figures and their regularly assigned religious traditions. But Cleage does just that. Cleage states, "I cannot resist the temptation to compare Brother Malcolm to Jesus, the Jesus whom we worship."[11] Referring to this comparison as a "temptation" suggests that Cleage understands some will view his reflection as a transgression to the common and systematic understandings of the Abrahamic religions. However, Cleage's centerpiece in examining religion (and politics) is Black Liberation. To that end, Cleage describes his understanding of Malcolm not through strict definitions of religion but by motive and method of political engagement. Cleage argues,

> The conditions which both faced in many ways were similar. The conditions faced by Jesus in trying to bring into being a Black Nation two thousand years ago were in many ways similar to those faced by Brother Malcolm just a few years ago. Both tried to bring black people together, tried to give them a sense of purpose, and to build a Black Nation.[12]

Cleage fuses together the sociopolitical realities of two seemingly distant religious figures. Whereby Cone situated Malcolm in a nationalism of separatism, pronged by its relationship to white society, Cleage presents Malcolm as a Black nationalist who is seeking to "bring black people together" as opposed to simply separate themselves from white people. Furthermore, Cleage's understanding of Christianity is in association with the Black Power Movement. It is not centered on a strict set of religious dogma and doctrines. This provides a space for Cleage to include Malcolm in the litany of followers of Jesus of whom in the mid-twentieth century would be identified as Christians. This follow-ship is contingent upon actions and not verbal confessions or written covenants. For Cleage, Malcolm and Jesus are in the same (Black prophetic) tradition because their theological understandings and political practices are both rooted in a divine desire for Black Liberation.

CONE'S REORIENTATION OF MALCOLM

Cone thoroughly chronicles the American (and Canadian and European) misunderstanding and dismissal of Malcolm in their public imagination listing numerous publications that described him as a "messiah of hate," "demagogue," "petty punk," "Black vigilante," "Black extremist," and even "mentally depraved."[13] And while there is no explicit denouncement of Malcolm's Muslim faith in these exact phrases, it can be implied through these ad hominem attacks. To that end, Cone seeks to reorient the public to a more respectable version of Malcolm in memoriam. Cone writes, "The negative assessment of Malcolm is not as widely promoted among African-Americans today.... He is now being quoted by mainstream black leaders who once despised him. Some have compared him to Nelson Mandela of South African and Martin King, saying that Malcolm's image embodies the best in both."[14] Yet, Cone is not willing to merge Malcolm into the religious ranks with King (or Jesus). Cone posits, "Like Martin, Malcolm was a minister, a 'man of the cloth,' to use a phrase often heard in the black community. But Malcolm was a minister of the religion of Islam, initially as defined by Elijah Muhammad and later according to the teachings of the worldwide Sunni Islamic community." And, in stark contrast to the presentation made by Cleage, Cone clarifies, "Although there were many similarities between Martin King's and Malcolm's social, religious, and educational development, their *dissimilarities* stand out the most (Emphasis mine)."[15] This seems to suggest that, for Cone, Malcolm is like Martin, Martin is like Jesus, but Malcolm is not like Jesus.

CLEAGE'S RECEPTION HISTORY OF MALCOLM

When Cleage presents a reception history of Malcolm, like that offered by Cone, Cleage also describes public dismissal. Yet, the grounds for dismissal are rooted not in a religious dissimilarity but in a sociopolitical ignorance. Cleage contrasts a Black community awaiting a messiah with a Black community longing for integration. Cleage states,

> At the time Jesus was born, men were expecting a savior. The Nation Israel realized that it was fragmented, that its people were despised, that they looked down on each other and upon themselves. They realized their oppression, and even though they betrayed each other to the oppressor, even though they did what the white man wanted them to, they knew that they needed someone to save them from this kind of degeneration and make them a Nation. . . . They did not receive him only because they wanted a different kind of Messiah.[16]

Cleage continues,

> How different it was for Brother Malcolm! The same fragmentation of black people, divided, exploited, oppressed; the same white Gentiles with their system of oppression; the same degeneration of a people who had lost pride in themselves—who fought against each other, who had no sense of dignity or of their future as a people. The Nation Israel waited for a Messiah that they might again become a Nation. But Brother Malcolm came to a people who waited that they might disappear as a people, a people who prayed every night that God would make them cease to be a people. . . . No, Brother Malcolm didn't come to a people who were waiting for a Messiah. He came to a people who were tired of being a separate people.[17]

One important note of rhetorical analysis here is, Cleage has described those who Malcolm has come to as those "tired of being a separate people." This implies that Cone's understanding of nationalism is different from Cleage's. Cleage is suggesting that Black people are already "a separate people." This means his perception of nationalism cannot be one which calls people into separatism, but, at the very least, admonishes them to accept, understand, embrace, and potentially leverage that separatism. Malcolm is not calling people to separate. He is calling them to acknowledge the social and political exclusion they already exist in. He is recommending that denial of that disenfranchisement leads to more exclusion. Cleage is promoting a resurgence of independent pride and dignity. He is contending that nationalism, for both Malcolm and Jesus, is calling and cultivating people to develop a stronger sense of self-determination because the conditions demand it.

It is within nuances of the philosophical understanding of nationalism and separatism that Malcolm's religious affiliation becomes dissimilar from Cone's understanding of King's religious affiliation. Cone situates King within a Christian tradition centered on (racial) reconciliation. This echoes what Cleage would consider to be white Christianity. But Cleage situates Jesus within an Afrocentric (Hebrew/Israelite/Northeastern African) religious tradition centered on Black Liberation. Therefore, Cleage can format Malcolm within the Black Christian religious tradition because of his interpretation of Malcolm's allegiance to Black Liberation. Cone's rendition of Christianity appeals to Martin's ideals of racial inclusion and equality but stops short of a demand for Black Liberation "by any means necessary."

CONE, CLEAGE, AND MALCOLM'S RELIGIOUS ILLEGIBILITY

Cone enhances his dissimilarities with Malcolm and Christianity. Describing Malcolm's conversion to Islam in 1948, Cone contests,

> The religion of transformation had to be one derived from the world in which he lived. It had to be a religion of the black ghetto experience. The public images of Christianity were both middle-class and white—including those of God, Jesus, and all the angels—so no preacher of Christianity, be he ever so black, had a chance with Malcolm.[18]

According to Cone, Malcolm could not be Christian no matter how you slice, source, or interpret the faith. The world Malcolm came from would not allow it because the symbolism and rhetorical presentations of Christianity were not black or ghetto enough.

Cleage would beg to differ. Cleage had a chance. And Cleage's Black Messiah seemed to resonate with Malcolm, not in terms of conversion, but with respect to the capacity to inspire Black people to fight for their own liberation. In fact, Malcolm is on public record affirming Cleage's ministerial presentation. At least twice in Malcolm's riveting "Message to the Grassroots" Speech[19] he echoed and ratified Cleage's words and theological witness. At one point, while discussing the tenants of what makes a revolution and delineating between a "Negro revolution" and a "Black revolution," Malcolm states, "Whoever heard of a revolution where they lock arms, as Reverend Cleage was pointing out beautifully, singing 'We Shall Overcome'? Just tell me. You don't do that in a revolution. You don't do any singing; you're too busy swinging." At another point, Malcolm was distinguishing between the "house Negro" and the "field Negro." His rhetorical strategy in this section of the speech was to distinguish moderate ministers like King who, according to Malcolm, was being used by white liberals as a numbing agent (Novocaine) teaching Black people to "suffer—peacefully," contrasted with more militant ministers like himself and Cleage. Malcolm argues,

> The white man does the same thing to you in the street, when he want [*sic*] to put knots on your head and take advantage of you and don't have to be afraid of your fighting back. To keep you from fighting back, he gets these old religious Uncle Toms to teach you and me, just like [Novocaine], suffer peacefully. Don't stop suffering—just suffer peacefully. As Reverend Cleage pointed out, "Let your blood flow in the streets." This is a shame. And you know he's a Christian preacher. If it's a shame to him, you know what it is to me.[20]

Malcolm has not disassociated himself with Cleage's brand of Christianity in the least bit. Malcolm does not deny that Cleage is a "Christian preacher." He has, in fact, recapitulated Cleage's religious presentation as one that is salutatory to Malcolm's theological sensibilities. And although Cone will later offer a healthy analysis of Malcolm's speech, he never fully redresses how Black Christianity played a significant and positive role in the shaping of Malcolm's presentation.

Cone mentions Cleage's involvement in orchestrating the "nationalist meeting" which "was hastily called in Detroit by the Reverend Albert B. Cleage, Jr., pastor of the Shrine of the Black Madonna." But, Cone also dichotomizes Black Theology and Black Nationalism in his analyses of the speech. Cone contends, "Message to the Grass Roots" was the most "political" talk Malcolm had given" until that time.[21] The concern here is that the dichotomy between a political talk and a theological speech (especially when coming from a religious figure speaking in public and addressing spiritual matters) harkens back to an unhealthy separation that could further drive a wedge between Malcolm and Christianity that does more harm than good. Cone will also cite a few other ministers who "supported Malcolm and appeared on the platform with him"[22] such as Cleage, Nelson C. Duke, and Adam Clayton Powell. Nevertheless, Cone does not reconcile Malcolm's theology with any substantive form of Christianity. Each of these ministers is placed in association with Malcolm, only insofar as they represent a fringe that is only understood in relation to them not being more like Martin. What this means, primarily, is that Malcolm and Cleage both embrace an unconventional, maladjusted type of theological and religious stance. And when this stance is presented to the public, it is illegible. It can hardly be understood by the masses and is usually misassociated or reduced to fit into frames that are inconsiderate of the necessary nuances.

Illegibility and the misconsceptualizing of Black radical and revolutionary rhetoric is not unfamiliar to rhetorical studies. As prominent as the African

American Jeremiad[23] has become, it is most often insufficient when attempting to understand and grapple with the complexities of Black prophetic rhetoric. How can a Jeremiadic presentation be centered in African American discourse when, religiously speaking, the biblical prophet Jeremiah is rendered a place of biblical privilege. The prophet's words are couched within a rhetorical document (the bible) that affirms Jeremiah's existence and theological claims as primary. However, when Black prophets speak in America it is from outside of the space of privilege. They speak from a place devoid of political and structural value and infringe upon cultural hegemony. The prophet's words and theology are not only revelatory—revealing God's will for the world—but also revolutionary. Their words and theology literally call forth a new vision of existence.

To that end, Malcolm and Cleage's theology and discourse are about much more than *parrhesia* (frank speech). They offer far more than the conventional appeals of justice and reconciliation. They are rooted in a Black sovereign expression that decenters white gazes. They embody a type of hush harbor rhetoric[24] that results in the demonization of the speaker by those within and without conventional faith circles.

Cone goes on to summarize Malcolm's philosophy, resulting from Elijah Muhammad's teachings, as "two ideas—the utter rejection of white values and the embracing of black history and culture."[25] If these ideas are foundational, and Cone sees Malcolm's theological framework as inconsistent or incompatible with Martin's Christianity (or Cone's understanding of Christianity in general) this reveals something deeper. The dominant projection of Christianity, according to Cone, has no room for the unapologetic rejection of white values and/or the unashamed embracing of Black history, agency, and culture. This is hard to conceive or rationalize knowing Cone spent a great deal of his academic career denouncing white supremacist histories and aversions of western (white) Christianity.

More so, what does this say about Cleage's version of Christianity which exacts an utter rejection of white values and embrace of African history and culture? Or maybe Cone's rendition of Malcolm's theology is insufficient because Cone's privileging of white Christianity will not make room for Malcolm (or Cleage's) militancy within the Christological framework. Maybe Cone's Black Theology is still a theology of integration with white repentance as a prerequisite?

CONE, CLEAGE, AND WHITE CHRISTIANITY

Cone has two wonderful sections of Martin and Malcolm's faith and theologies in his chapters entitled, "We Must Love Our White Brothers" and "White Man's Heaven Is A Black Man's Hell," respectively. These two chapters are separated in the book by a series of photos of both Martin and Malcolm in action and in repose. The section designated to Martin will be mentioned later. But the section on Malcolm's faith and theology clarifies the type of Christianity Cone most often centers and privileges.

It is this brand of Christianity which Cone sees as incompatible with Malcolm's experience and desire for Black Liberation. What Cone highlights as Malcolm's "alienation from Christianity" is explicitly white Christianity. This type of faith expression and doctrinal belief is most pervasive, even within many Black Churches. Add to that, "[Malcolm's] experiences of violence and humiliation from 'the good Christian white people' of Omaha, Nebraska, and Lansing, Michigan" could easily legitimize Malcolm's dismissal of Christianity altogether. Cone contends, "Malcolm's rejection of Christianity did not arise so much from intellectual doubt as from his personal experience of being treated as less than human by white Christians."[26] What Cone does not do is describe (or give any possible consideration to) the potential impact of Malcolm having a robust encounter with a more militant, Afrocentric, Black Christianity prior to his conversion to Islam, and what that could have meant for his formation. I am not suggesting that such an encounter would have resulted in Malcolm's Christianization. The point I am pressing is that Cone's rhetorical framework for Malcolm's faith formation is limited to two simple (and equally dogmatic) options—a white Christianity or the (blacker) Nation of Islam.

The above sentiment is codified in Cone's analysis:

> the nation of Islam was created for the specific needs of blacks, Euro-American Christianity was designed for the particular needs of whites who perceived themselves and their culture as the standard by which all others were to be judged. Therefore, God, Jesus, the angels, and all the heroic biblical characters were portrayed as white, and the devil and sin, of course, were often pictured as black. Malcolm remembered his parents and other black Christians singing, "Wash me and I'll be whiter than snow." With Christian churches and their theologians and preachers defining everything good in this life and the next as *white* and defining everything bad in this world and the next as *black*, how was it possible for that religion to bestow self-worth upon the *black* personhood of a prisoner like Malcolm? It seems that, in Malcolm's case, it was not possible. Only a *black* religion, a black God, could "resurrect" a person like Malcolm from the "dead," from the "grave of ignorance and shame," and stand him on his feet as a human being, prepared to die in the defense of the humanity of his people.[27]

Cone separates Christianity from Islam in terms of racial affiliation and theo-rhetorical construction.[28] Christianity is white. Islam is black. This dichotomy highlights the disruptive intervention Cleage is making in his claim that Jesus is the Black messiah.

In contrast to Cone, Cleage is intentional about offering the exact type of Black Christianity Cone excludes from his formula of Malcolm's faith formation. Cleage provides a Black Christianity that is compatible with Malcolm's theology and presents Malcolm's life and death in direct association to Jesus of Nazareth—the Black Messiah. Cleage consistently uses hermeneutical rhetoric to provide his audience with an opportunity to reconsider and reconstitute their affiliation with Malcolm, Black Power, and Black (militant) Christianity.

Cleage offers a section in his sermon that compliments Cone's reading of Malcolm's preaching and ideology but is simultaneously adding a theological twist. Cleage contends,

> They said, "He's preaching hate against the white man; he's telling us to hate the white man." They thought there was something wrong with that. It just shows you how far down we were. We were even ashamed to hate a people who had hated, oppressed, and exploited us for almost four hundred years, who had brought us to America in slave ships, sold us on slave blocks, raped our women and lynched our men! Not to hate people like that was a sign of mental illness.[29]

Here, Cleage centralizes the historical pain and plight of Black people in America in Malcolm's preaching presentation. It echoes Cone's assessments that Malcolm's ideology (and his theology by proxy) wedded a rejection of white values with the affirmation of Black history and culture. By not shying away from Malcolm's claims but providing a theological justification for them, Cleage expands the reach of Black Christianity. Cleage is a Black Christian preacher synthesizing the substance of Malcolm's preaching with the social realities of the Black Messiah in Rome the first century and Black people in America in the twentieth century.

Cleage continues,

> He's preaching separation, the white folks said, and black folks started echoing, "Oh, he's preaching separation." And they had been separated all their lives by the white man. You were born separate, you will live separate, you will die separate, and you'll be buried separate. Malcolm didn't have to preach separation. All he had to do was say, "Look around you, fool. You run around talking about integration. Everything you've got is separate." And that's what we did—we began to look around.[30]

What Cleage has offered is a different window of interpretation into the theorhetorical method of Malcolm's preaching. What is underneath Cleage's claims is the idea that Malcolm's message and personality had been distorted and deserved to be beautified in service of a Black liberatory project.

CLEAGE'S THEORETICAL MERGER OF MALCOLM AND JESUS

What must happen, if Cleage's audience will fully associate Malcolm with Jesus (as he has rhetorically and theologically intended), is a direct correlation to Jesus's preaching and politics not simply his social and political context. In other words, Cleage must rhetorically present a platform whereby Jesus can be considered as advocating for separation or at least affirming that his Hebrew community was, indeed, separate. And one way for Cleage to present Jesus in the same light as Malcolm would be to talk about Jesus's formation like Cone talked about Malcolm and Martin's formations. Cone concluded his chapter, "The Making of a 'Bad Nigger'" by stating,

> The great dissimilarity in [Martin and Malcolm's] social and intellectual development certainly provides a clue to their different views regarding America and the black struggle for freedom in it. . . . Almost everything that separated them in their later lives, including their speaking styles and the content of their message, is traceable to their early lives.[31]

Following this pattern of logic, Cleage should present Jesus from his childhood, being born in a manger, to a black-teenage-single-parent mother with questionable sexual proclivities. Cleage could contextualize what Jesus's life was like growing up and having to escape to Egypt to avoid a potential execution based upon federal legislation issued by King Herod. However, Cleage is already in the middle of his sermonic tribute to Malcolm. He has already referenced "the night that Jesus was born" earlier in his sermon to emphasize the community that was anxious for the arrival of a Black Messiah. Instead, what Cleage does is compare the distortions of Malcolm's message after his death and aligns them with what happened to the legacy of Jesus:

> Jesus was distorted by the institution that was set up in his name. Jesus didn't organize anything except a few people who believed in him, some revolutionaries who followed him in a nationalistic movement. Jesus didn't organize any kind of Church. He brought together people who believed in doing what was necessary to create change. That's what Jesus did.[32]

Notice, Cleage has already laid groundwork for those who desire to reconsider Jesus as a Black nationalist. Furthermore, Cleage is presenting this revolutionary Jesus in the same way he presented Malcolm, as one willing to "do what was necessary to create change." He continues,

> But after Jesus was killed, they organized a Church in his name. The Apostle Paul, who was really a great organizer, set up Churches everywhere and said, "This is Christianity. All of you who follow after Jesus, come right on in here." And then he changed the whole thing around. No longer was it about building a Nation, it was tearing down a Nation. It was leading people right back to the same old individualistic kind of thing which Jesus had fought against all of his life. In the name of Jesus they created a new kind of individualism. "Come into the Church, be washed of the blood of the lamb and you will become white as snow."

Cleage has done a lot rhetorically in this passage. He evokes the tragic death of a Black nationalist Jesus knowing full well that his audience will recognize a similar fate happening to Malcolm. Cleage also eludes to the "Uncle Tom" syndrome of those he viewed as more moderate ministers like King with that of the Apostle Paul who deradicalizes Jesus in the name of Christian individualism—a very common theme in Cleage's work. Lastly, Cleage returns to the racial identities of Christianity and its associations with the sacrificial atonement theory, stating that the new (read: white) Jesus only wants people to attend Church, accept Jesus's sacrificial atonement for sin through his bloody death on the cross, and the blood becomes the cleansing agent which "washed" people (especially Black folks) "white as snow."

Aware that this individualistic type of theology is inadequate for Black Liberation and inconsistent with Cleage's views of the message of Jesus and Malcolm, Cleage immediately denounces this rendition of Christianity. Cleage states,

> We did all that. We came in here and were washed in the blood of the lamb. But we stayed black, and the white man kept us in black Churches. That old individual thing had us. You said to yourself, "Well, I'm white on the inside, even if I am black on the outside." And no kind of washing seemed to make any real difference.[33]

This next section is critical,

> *That is what they did to Jesus and to his teachings about the Black Nation.* The teachings of Jesus were destroyed. The Church which carried his name went back to individualism, telling people, "You can find escape from your problems in heaven, after death."[34] (Emphasis mine)

And Cleage concretely joins together Malcolm and Jesus stating,

This was true during the lifetime of Jesus; it was also true during the lifetime of Brother Malcolm. Two saviors came to a black people. The people were different in each instance, but both saw the oppression that black people suffered and each saw the power of their oppressors—and they saw that there was no one to comfort those who are oppressed. So today as we remember Malcolm, and as we remember our weaknesses and how far we have come, let us remember the basic things that Brother Malcolm taught that are so important for us. Because we too can forget, we too can distort Malcolm's teachings as the Apostle Paul distorted the teachings of Jesus. We can make something else out of them to suit our purposes if we forget what Brother Malcolm actually taught.[35]

The previous five block quotes all function in unison as a section where Cleage has wielded together what Cone and others might find as irreconcilable. Cleage draws a direct parallel from the life and teachings of Jesus to the life and teachings of Malcolm. Two seemingly incompatible religious ideologies—Christian and Muslim. Nevertheless, when Black Christianity is centered and privileged as Cleage does, it not only becomes compatible with Islam but also readily accessible as a tool for nation building and Black empowerment. In other words, while Cone has contended that no Christianity would be black enough for Malcolm, Cleage has provided one that Malcolm himself adorns and in substance is directly aligned with.

CLEAGE, CONE, AND THE SYMBOL OF MARTIN LUTHER KING, JR.

Cleage and Cone's takes on Martin are equally interesting and rather disjointed. Cone has a fascination with Martin's oratory, fervor, and commitment to the cause of integration. Cone situates Martin in the tradition of Black Faith leaders like Frederick Douglas and Richard Allen, Martin's contemporaries Adam Clayton Powell, Sr., William Holmes Borders, Vernon Johns, Reverdy C. Ransom, and Martin's mentor, Benjamin E. Mays.[36] Cone is so fond of Martin he describes him as "the symbol not only of the civil rights movement but of America itself: a symbol of a land of freedom where people of all races, creeds, and nationalities could live together in beloved community."[37] This framework further essentializes Martin as the rhetorical, symbolic, and substantive standard of engagement relative to Black Freedom and Liberation. Martin is pedestalized as the standard every American (including Malcolm) ought to aspire to. And if Martin is the epitome of the American democratic project (or at least the racial liberalism[38] associated with such project), Malcolm will inevitable be considered in relationship to Martin. But, if Martin is the quintessential American, Malcolm could be politically, psychologically and religiously "good" but still "not Martin." This explains Cone's sequential placement in his works—again, Martin comes first with Malcolm to follow.

We must further interpret Cone's analysis of Martin and Malcolm considering this epitomizing framework. What Cone's dramatizing of America through the symbolizing of Martin has done is shrink the space of accessibility for more radical actors at the intersection of rhetoric, race, and religion in the country. Although Malcolm is being given more than a fair read (or access) by Cone, we can see a pattern of theological marginalization in Cone's work. Martin is the synecdoche for American, liberal, integrationist Christianity. Malcolm is the Black nationalist, militant, and separatist Islamic. But Cleage stands in the center of these two figures. Cleage is an American, Black nationalist, militant, Christian, and Cleage's engagement with Martin is reflected that way.

In Cleage's sermon, "Dr. King and Black Power," rendered days after the assassination of Martin, we find a respectful, but much less-deified presentation of King, still within a Christian-centered framework. Cleage's foundational scripture is Luke 19:39-40 which is commonly referred to as the triumphal entry of Jesus into Jerusalem, and Cleage introduces Martin, like he previously introduced Malcolm, in association with the Black Messiah. However, Cleage offers a different type of affirmation for Martin than he did for Malcolm. Cleage states, "We have come together to commemorate the triumphal entry of the Black Messiah into Jerusalem two thousand years ago, and to pay tribute to Dr. Martin Luther King, a black leader." This coarse reference to Martin's blackness and leadership is not nearly as nostalgic as the symbolism rendered by Cone. This coarseness seems to reflect a dismissiveness and boarders on disrespect of Martin's life and work if not quantified and clarified in Cleage's following statements. Cleage continues,

> It is a profound tribute to Dr. King that so many of us have come here this morning, since few of us really agreed with his position. We respected him for his sincerity, for the dedication which he brought to the task of leadership, and for the things which he accomplished. And so we have come together to pay him tribute. A mighty oak has been felled in the forest, and there is an empty space against the sky.[39]

These words bear witness to the complex nature of Black Theology in relationship to Black Power, Black Preaching, and the racial liberalism which seemed to reach a point of contestation in the late 1960s. Cleage is honoring King, yet not fully endorsing or embracing him as a champion for Black Power or Black Theology.

CLEAGE'S RHETORICAL ASSAULT ON MLK'S NONVIOLENCE

A primary source of tension between moderates like King and militants like Cleage and Malcolm was the philosophy of nonviolence and its efficacy to the Black Freedom Movement. As Cone offers "an investigation of [Martin's] social, educational, and religious development"[40] which led him to embrace nonviolence as "the only practical and moral course"[41] to freedom through integration, the philosophy itself is juxtaposed in Cleage's preaching platform to King's brutal assassination. Cleage describes the juxtaposition this way:

> Early last Thursday evening, Dr. King was murdered by a white man in Memphis, Tennessee. I suspect that many of you have forgotten by this time that he was murdered by a white man. That simple fact has been obscured by the copious crocodile tears which are being shed everywhere. . . . Since that time, we have been constantly reminded by radio, television and every branch of the mass communications media, that Dr. King believed in non-violence. You would think they were afraid we didn't know that.[42]

Cleage is setting the stage for a rhetorical encounter with the philosophy of nonviolence that uses Martin's assassination as the prima facie evidence that nonviolence (alone) does not work in the quest for Black Freedom. This is a conclusion that Cone reaches and expresses when reflecting on the legacies of Martin and Malcolm. Cone argues, "Both nonviolent direct action and self-defense needed to be accented, the former in public demonstrations and the latter as a human right. There was not and is not today a need to choose between them."[43]

More theologically aggressive, Cleage is going to mandate a more militant form of theology and politics as necessary to be Christian and to pursue Black Liberation in America. Cleage continues,

> All right, Dr. King believed in non-violence. But then they add something to it, "Dr. King believed in non-violence, and any retaliation for his murder would desecrate his memory." They say Dr. King would not want us to be violent. How do we know this? Because white folks have been telling us every day, all day, ever since white folks murdered him. Dr. King died to prove that non-violence can work. Now that's an absurd statement if I ever heard one. White folks killed Dr. King because he was black, and then they come right back at us, saying that Dr. King died to prove that non-violence can work.[44]

Cleage is challenging the fundamental logic of nonviolence by associating it with white manipulation; as a rhetorical tool of white people to promote pacifism and describing the inevitable result of nonviolence as Black death. Furthering this line of reasoning Cleage argues,

> There's no kind of logic in that statement, no kind of way. If Dr. King's death proved anything beyond the shadow of a doubt, it proved that non-violence will never work in a violent white racist society. I have a feeling they are very much afraid that we will see this is what has been proven conclusively by his brutal murder. They are afraid we will now see that this is the real meaning of his life. He tried in every way possible to be non-violent. He took no steps to protect his life. He believed in the power of non-violence. He hoped, and he prayed, that the black man's non-violence could somehow redeem white people. He believed it. And you know what white people did to him? They killed him!

Cleage is not only disrupting the philosophy of nonviolence and its woeful potential to achieve Black Freedom, but he is also pushing back against the idea the Jesus demands nonviolence. This is imperative to Cleage's hermeneutical rhetoric. Part of what made Martin's philosophy so palatable and persuasive in Black sacred spaces is the fundamental presumption that Jesus of Nazareth (the Black Messiah) was, indeed, nonviolent.

CONE AND CLEAGE CONTRASTING NONVIOLENCE

Cone powerfully describes Martin's theological associations of nonviolence and Christianity. In one of the most instructive passages in MMA, Cone details the connections and convictions Martin shared theologically and philosophically and how "King's theological views about suffering and nonviolence separated him not only from white Christians; they also separated him from many blacks in the freedom movement, especially Malcolm X."[45] Cone clearly and concisely depicts Martin's theological foundation for nonviolence as evidenced in Jesus this way,

> For King, the cross was the essence of the Christian faith, emphasizing that suffering was an inherent part of the Christian life in the struggle for freedom.
>
> King's theological claim about the cross and the suffering of Jesus was the source of his absolute commitment to nonviolence. Many persons have misunderstood his commitment to nonviolence because they separated it from his faith in God.[46]

Cone tethers nonviolence to Martin's faith and understanding of Jesus. Rhetorically, Cone has also situated Christianity at the intersection of the nonviolent and sacrificial atonement theories. In the nonviolent atonement theory[47] framework, the suffering and death of Jesus are used to express Jesus's commitment to nonviolence. That is to say, despite Jesus having the capacity to use divine and lethal means of defending himself (which is debatable), he submits himself to the violence on the cross to exemplify and exude the transformative and redeeming power of love and nonviolence. This framework is coupled with the most traditional reference to the execution of Jesus on the cross as a sacrifice. In this regard, Jesus is viewed as the sacrificial lamb who has been slain to redeem the sins of the world[48].

Cleage, both theologically and rhetorically, is pushing against these notions. He weaves together a reconstitution of Martin's last speech, King's evolving philosophy, and Jesus's revolutionary politics. Using the Luke 19 text as the foundation, Cleage surmises,

> The night before he was murdered, Dr. King said, "I've been to the mountain top and I have seen the promised land, I don't expect to enter in, but I know that my people will enter in." You know, on that last night he sounded like he belonged to the [Black] Nation. "I believe that my people will enter in."[49]

CLEAGE'S RHETORICAL HERMENEUTICS

Cleage is adjusting the lens by which his hearers and readers interpret the life and death of Martin Luther King, Jr. and Jesus of Nazareth. Cleage aligns Martin more closely with the militant philosophies of Black nationalism. This is quite contrary to Cone's dichotomous rendition of Martin the integrationist and Malcolm the nationalist. Cleage also (re)presents the Black Messiah as a nationalist who, during the triumphal entry, is making a trek into an impending execution (read: assassination). Cleage is inviting his audience to revisit their understanding of Jesus's revolutionary politics,[50] Martin's evolving nationalist philosophies, and the social and political ethos which leads to the killing of both Jesus and Martin. Cleage transitions,

> Today our Scripture has to do with the Black Messiah entering Jerusalem. A lot of his followers were there because it was a political thing, this entrance into Jerusalem. And they were screaming and yelling "Blessed be the king who comes in the name of the Lord!" because they expected him to take power. They were with him. They were supporting him. A multitude of his followers had come together, and there was loud rejoicing.[51]

The way Cleage contextualizes this passage allows for a neat comparison with the reception giving to Martin ("the king") by the masses and the cheers being bellowed out as Jesus makes his triumphal entry. It is important to note that many interpreters have neglected to consider this entry to be, as Cleage has deemed it, a "political thing." The processional by which Jesus engages is seen as an endorsement of a political campaign which would be a direct affront against the governmental order of the Roman Empire. In many of the same ways Martin's direct actions were affronts to the American government, Cleage highlights the political nature of the religious leaders' actions. He continues,

> Seeing this, the Pharisees, or the Toms, came over and whispered to Jesus, "Don't you think you ought to rebuke your disciples? The things they are saying are going to make the Gentiles mad. In other words, white folks don't like a Black Messiah coming into Jerusalem with his disciples screaming about taking over. Jesus looked at these Uncle Toms, much as I believe Dr. King would look at these Uncle Toms who are around supposedly representing him now, and answered simply, "I tell you, if these were silent, the very stone would cry out."[52]

This section is powerfully redemptive for Cleage's perception of King. In part, Cleage describes King (one who Cleage formerly referred to as an Uncle Tom) as someone who would reject any attempt by those dismissive of aggressive responses to King's murder. At the same time, Cleage is opening a portal of reconstitution for those within the Black Power Movement to see King in a more radical and revolutionary light.

CLEAGE'S DIVINE AND SERMONIC MILITANCY

It is important to note that immediately following Martin's assassination, uprisings broke out in many cities across the United States. In the wake of these militant and violent ordeals, there had been a call for peace and a denouncement of violence by moderate Black leaders. Cleage previously described this setting earlier in his sermon. He accused Roy Wilkins, Sammy Davis, Jr., and Reverend Wyatt T. Walker of being far too dismissive of the young revolutionaries who were responding to Martin's assassination. Cleage responded to the moderate Black leader's claims by inquiring, "Even if you feel that they shouldn't have carried on like this, is it possible that Black people in America could have let this dastardly deed pass without some retaliatory measures? Even as you sit in your home scared, aren't you glad that somebody did something about it?"[53] And in the quote above, Cleage has aligned moderate Black leaders denouncing violent responses to Martin's assassination with Pharisees and Uncle Toms who did not honor the legacy of King and would not have affirmed the revolutionary politics of the Black

Messiah. The point Cleage is pressing above is that moderate influences are often resistant of militant maneuvers. Nevertheless, militancy is efficacious. Furthermore, that Martin (much like Malcolm and Jesus) was necessarily militant and the events unfolding in response to King's assassination were righteous responses endorsed by God.

Cleage explains,

> There are some things that cannot be silenced. If these people shut up, the very stones would cry out. This thing is in the very heart and nature of the universe. It is the will of God that black people should be free.
>
> This is true right here today. You know that if black people hadn't done something to retaliate for the murder of Dr. King, the very stones would have cried out, because some things strike at the very meaning of the universe. If black people are men, created in the image of God, then in a situation like this, they could not but strike back. This is what Jesus meant. If these were silenced, the very stone would cry out.[54]

What Cleage has done here is render Martin much more militant and dangerous than the white media had been presenting him after his assassination. This is another instance of insightful hermeneutical rhetoric. In this rhetorical maneuver, Cleage uses a bible passage where the revolutionary politics of Jesus are on full display. Cleage makes radical behavior divine—consistent with God's will for the world—when it is performed in the service of Black Freedom because "It is the will of God that black people should be free." That sentence cannot be accented enough. It speaks directly to the theological (divine) disposition Cleage has toward Black Theology and Black Power. To that end, Cleage interprets Jesus as engaged in and endorsing of militant and overtly political actions. He presents Jesus's triumphal entry as part of a broader liberatory project which calls for more confrontation and less rebuke of radicalism. Cleage says,

> So Holy Week is a series of confrontations that Jesus set up. He was making clear that some things just have to be done. They can't be avoided, no matter how afraid you are. Someone must do them because they must be done. And so Jesus refused to rebuke his disciples. If they were silenced, the very stones would cry out.[55]

While Cleage reclaims a radical Jesus, we must also ask, how did Cleage reach such a militant impression of Martin? Cone situates Martin as the standard and Malcolm as the compliment, Cleage has presented Jesus as the prototype and found a way to align Malcolm and Martin—both practically and theologically—with the Black Messiah.

CLEAGE'S RECLAMATION OF MARTIN'S MILITANCY

From a nationalist framework, as Cone points out, conventional reads of most of Martin's life wouldn't pass the smell test. Cone describes Malcolm as becoming more moderate after his break with the Nation of Islam. Cone contends, "As Malcolm moved out of the Nation of Islam and began to plot his own course, he consciously moved toward the politics of Martin King and the civil rights movement." Further, Cone describes Malcolm as willing to alter his image for "participation in the civil rights movement, of which Martin King was the most visible symbol."[56]

Cone's description of Martin's evolution is not as sharp.[57] According to Cone, Martin evolves into a more militant stance (of Black Power, not Black Nationalism) after a series of disappointing and disturbing events (especially the quest for voting rights which lead to several deaths and subsequent uprisings in Watts and other cities around the country). Cone has a specific section describing Malcolm's "Movement Towards Martin,"[58] but, on the other hand, when describing Martin's move, the movement is not explicitly toward Malcolm, but instead a "Movement Towards Separatism."[59]

Cleage does not move Malcolm or Martin toward each other. He moves them both toward the Black Messiah. From a militant standpoint, this seemed like a logical move for Cleage to make regarding Malcolm. But for Cleage to authentically acknowledge and pay tribute to a more militant Martin, he must address any prior disconnections and further elaborate on his earlier statement, "since few of us really agreed with his position." This calls for a confession of sorts from Cleage.

Cleage admits, "I was not a follower of Dr. Martin Luther King. I respected him, but very early in his ministry I differed with him in his approach to the problems of black people. He was not my leader in that sense, and yet I respected him for his position."[60] This claim of respect despite differing approaches and perspectives give Cleage some rhetorical leverage. He thereafter lays out examples of their disagreements and struggles against each other's initiatives. King worked against Cleage's organizing of the Freedom Now Party. Cleage perceived Martin erred in his philosophy of nonviolence and his theology of redemptive suffering. Then Cleage synthesizes their differences under the umbrella of Black Power. Discussing the impact of the Montgomery Bus Boycott Cleage reflects,

> Think back to Montgomery, thirteen years ago, how disunited we were, how fearful we were, how without courage we were—when that little bunch of black people in Montgomery came together and said, "We're not going to sit in the back of the bus anymore." Dr. King was willing to take leadership of that little movement that seemed to have no chance of success. He led it non-violently, but

140   *Chapter 5*

> black folks stood face to face with white folks and said what they were going to do, and what they were not going to do. And they did what they said they were going to do, and did not do what they said they were not going to do. And black folks won. . . . That was success."[61]

Cleage highlights this victory, not in terms of nonviolence or redemptive suffering but, moreover, in terms of Black Power through Black courage. He describes the connection while denouncing the theology:

> Now I suppose we can say that he was engaged in redemptive suffering. You're suffering when you walk all the way across Montgomery, after working all day. You're suffering, and your suffering redeems white folks. But it wasn't really redemptive suffering. It was black courage. Black folks were learning that they had power, and they were willing to do the things that were necessary to use it. And they won.[62]

Here, this explicit connection with the political demonstrations (boycotts) and sacrificial expressions of Black folks have been centered in Cleage's analysis. It is, again, this centering of the Black experience that makes Cleage's approach disparate to Cone's. Therefore, when Cleage reaches a point of direct comparison between Malcolm and Martin, his claim is not that Malcolm complimented Martin, but vice versa. Cone has clearly described Malcolm as politically and practically moving toward Martin. However, Cleage sees them both as parallel figures which shed light on how to best interpret the theological and political actions of the Black Messiah. Furthermore, when the blackness and revolutionary politics of Jesus are at the center, the interpretation of Malcolm and Martin's complementarity read differently from Cone but are equally insightful. As Cleage points out,

> White folks remember what [Martin] said, his words. But we remember where we were thirteen years ago, and where we are today. Not that he did it by himself, but he created the confrontation situations in which we could learn, in which we could work, and which Brother Malcom could interpret. Everything was working together. The white people couldn't see it because they thought that they had two antagonistic elements here, splitting the black community, Malcolm X on one side and Dr. King on the other. So they gave all their money to Dr. King to keep his voice speaking, but he was at the same time creating the very situations which Brother Malcom could interpret.[63]

Notice how Cleage re-emphasizes that Malcolm has a more righteous analysis of the social conditions than Martin. He affirms Martin's practices but rejects his nonviolent philosophy. He continues,

We needed both of them. It wasn't enough to say, "We've got our enemy. We've got to fight." No one would have listened to Brother Malcolm until Dr. King had created the confrontation situations in which we began to learn, step by step, that black people can unite, black people can fight, black people can die for the things they believe in.[64]

Cleage concludes his section on how he embraces King's actions but not his philosophy and how they both align with Malcolm and the Black Messiah saying, "This is the kind of thing that Dr. King actually accomplished. I criticized the things he said, but I have only admiration for the things he did. We learned from the struggle and conflict which he made possible."[65]

In other words, Cleage has bought some rhetorical real estate by complimenting King in a way that does not harm or neuter Black Power. And he uses that real estate to draw those who are fond of King closer to the Black Liberation Theology and political revolutionary praxis (a la Malcolm and Jesus).

CLEAGE'S HOMILETICAL AND RHETORICAL STRATEGIES REVISITED

From a sermonic standpoint, Cleage's homiletic and rhetorical strategy might leave us wanting. It seems his use of the Lukan text at the offset is more of a functional text than a foundational tool. Cleage uses the text as a contextual device that offers his audience an opportunity to see where the contemporary realities of King's assassination and emergent militancy, coupled with Malcolm's nationalistic philosophy and Black Power analysis align with Jesus's revolutionary politics from a theological standpoint. To be sure, much of what Cleage accomplishes here rhetorically is advanced by his use of Luke 19 but not necessarily dependent upon the text itself. The text is used to advance Cleage's ethos and creditability but is not essential to the overarching claims he intends to make. However, if hermeneutical rhetoric is the foundational premise and if Cleage is primarily seeking to reorient his audience's understanding of the bible and the Black Messiah, then his mission has been accomplished.

Cleage provides an equivalent to what Cone presents Malcolm as demanding in Malcolm's infamous "The Ballot or the Bullet" speech. This is a speech, Cone argues, which describes Malcolm's movement toward Martin. Within the speech, Cone analyzes Malcolm's comparison of his own Black Nationalism with "Billy Graham's preaching of Christianity, which [Malcolm] called "white nationalism." According to Cone, Malcolm was promoting a freedom to "join any organization where [black nationalism] was preached." But Cone never mentions Cleage's church as an epicenter for such preaching.

Nevertheless, as we can see in this sermon, Cleage offers a Black Nationalist (or Black Power) interpretation to a well-known scripture. I believe it is the type of theological presentation that Malcolm affirms and endorses. Cleage has simultaneously honored the life of a freedom fighter with which he had known disagreements, while still standing firm in his affirmation of Black Power and Black Nationalism as the governing principles of his theology. What he displays here is the efficacy of hermeneutical rhetoric as a homiletical strategy. In the field of homiletics, exegesis is a common method used for uncovering biblical truths and revelatory insight. However, much of the exegetical methodology reinforces traditional, conventional, and mostly conservative readings of bible passages. What Cleage does here, in concert with what Cone does in his rhetorical analysis of Martin and Malcolm's formation and speeches, is further wed together the connections of rhetoric, race, and religion in the righteous service of Black Liberation.

NOTES

1. Ibid., 2.
2. Fredrik Sunnemark, *Ring Out Freedom!: The Voice of Martin Luther King, Jr. and the Making of the Civil Rights Movement* (Indiana University Press, 2003), 14.
3. Cleage, *The Black Messiah*, 9.
4. Grant, "White Women's Christ and Black Women's Jesus," 4.
5. Ibid., 4.
6. Ibid., 4.
7. Ibid., 16.
8. TBM, 9.
9. Cone, *Said I Wasn't Gonna Tell Nobody*, 16.
10. See, Albert B. Cleage Jr, *Black Christian Nationalism* (originally published in 1972).
11. TBM, 186.
12. Ibid., 186.
13. Cone, *Said I Wasn't Gonna Tell Nobody*, 39–40.
14. Ibid., 40.
15. Ibid., 42.
16. TBM, 187.
17. Ibid., 187.
18. Cone, *Said I Wasn't Gonna Tell Nobody*, 51.
19. This speech was given at the Northern Grass Roots Leadership Meeting, an event heavily orchestrated by Cleage and the Group on Advanced Leadership (GOAL). See Cone, *Said I Wasn't Gonna Tell Nobody*, 114 and Peniel E. Joseph, *Waiting 'Til the Midnight Hour: A Narrative History of Black Power in America* (Macmillan, 2007), 88–92.
20. http://teachingamericanhistory.org/library/document/message-to-grassroots/

21. Cone, *Said I Wasn't Gonna Tell Nobody*, 114.
22. Ibid., 202–204.
23. See, David Howard-Pitney, and David Howard-Pitney, *The African American Jeremiad: Appeals for Justice in America* (Philadelphia: Temple University Press, 2005), *UofM Libraries*, EBSCO*host* (accessed July 5, 2018).
24. See, Vorris L. Nunley, *Keepin'it Hushed: The Barbershop and African American Hush Harbor Rhetoric* (Wayne State University Press, 2011).
25. Cone, *Said I Wasn't Gonna Tell Nobody*, 152.
26. Ibid., 153.
27. Ibid., 153.
28. What I mean by theorhetorical construction is the way religious language is used to describe and develop our understanding of God and the iconography, images, and ideas associated with it. Broader and more rhetorically and theologically intentional than anthropomorphism, theorhetorical construction seeks to build an understanding, a rhetorical exchange, between a speaker and their audience which intends to establish a set of values that are projected onto a deity or deities and the people who worship, affirm, and embrace that deity or deities.
29. TBM, 190.
30. Ibid., 190.
31. Cone, *Said I Wasn't Gonna Tell Nobody*, 57.
32. TBM., 192.
33. Ibid., 192.
34. Ibid., 192.
35. Ibid, 193.
36. Cone, *Said I Wasn't Gonna Tell Nobody*, 5–7.
37. Ibid., 19.
38. See, Charles W. Mills, *Black Rights/White Wrongs: The Critique of Racial Liberalism* (Oxford University Press, 2017).
39. TBM, 201.
40. Cone, *Said I Wasn't Gonna Tell Nobody*, 20.
41. Ibid., 78.
42. TBM, 201–202.
43. Cone, *Said I Wasn't Gonna Tell Nobody*, 303.
44. Ibid., 202.
45. Cone, *Said I Wasn't Gonna Tell Nobody*, 129.
46. Ibid., 128.
47. See J. Denny Weaver, *The Nonviolent Atonement* (Wm. B. Eerdmans Publishing, 2011).
48. See Stephen Finlan, *Problems With Atonement: The Origins of, and Controversy About, the Atonement Doctrine* (Liturgical Press, 2005).
49. TBM, 205.
50. See, Obery Hendricks, *The Politics of Jesus: Rediscovering the True Revolutionary Nature of Jesus' Teachings and How They Have Been Corrupted* (Image, 2006).
51. TBM., 205.

52. Ibid., 205.
53. Ibid., 203.
54. Ibid., 205–206.
55. Ibid., 206.
56. Cone, *Said I Wasn't Gonna Tell Nobody*, 193.
57. Echoing an earlier point made regarding sequencing, it is worth nothing that while initial presentations were structured with Martin proceeding Malcolm, when Cone engages in discussion of their transitions into a more relatable or aligned posture, Cone presents Malcolm first, then Martin. This inversion furthers my assessment that, for Cone, Martin is the standard by which Malcolm is supposed measured and not vice versa. Yes, Cone sees them as complimentary and necessary to the Black Freedom struggle. That said, Malcolm is presented as directly identifying with and moving toward Martin, almost immersed into Martin's philosophy. However, Martin is presented as reluctantly embracing parts of Malcolm's message and moving toward separatism, but never fully melding into Malcolm's nationalism. Malcolm's influence on King is associated primarily with the rise of Black Power (and not the philosophy of Black Nationalism, per se). Here, Cone couples Malcolm with other figures like Stokely Carmichael when describing the elements that lead to Martin's militancy. Yet, Martin stands heads and shoulders above the rest as the primary (if not the sole) influence in Malcolm's choice to join the fight for civil rights.
58. Cone, *Said I Wasn't Gonna Tell Nobody*, 192.
59. Ibid., 225.
60. TBM, 206.
61. Ibid., 208.
62. Ibid., 208.
63. Ibid., 209–210.
64. Ibid., 210.
65. Ibid., 210.

Chapter 6

Conclusions
Building on and Beyond The Black Messiah

In the earlier chapters, we have displayed the prophetic persona of Albert Cleage. Chapter 1 describes the "who" of Cleage and lays the foundation for understanding the personality and provocation of what gave rise to *The Black Messiah* as a sermonic project and subsequent publication. The book itself received noteworthy reviews and engagement early on. But as the decades waned and the broader concern or curiosity about Black Theology and more militant expressions of Black Church life gave way to the perception of upward mobility among Black people, religious respectability politics and prosperity gospels pushed figures like Cleage even further to the margins and situated him in the shadows of James Cone, Dr. King, and other Black religious figures who are far more legible to the mainstream of a white evangelical Christianity and white liberal-leaning academy.

The second chapter interrogated the gatekeeping impulses of both religious studies and communication as academic disciplines. It describes some of the developments that have allowed rhetoric to claim a peculiar type of rehabilitation while still, currently, underappreciating the role and function of Black religious rhetoric. It argues for a deeper reflection and consideration of what books like *The Black Messiah* and other sermonic materials provide to the field. It decenters white gazes that are so prevalent and paralyzing to scholars and practitioners alike. It recommends a reclamation of a more Afrocentric and liberationist approach to rhetoric and religion and proposes Albert Cleage Jr. and *The Black Messiah* as significant and substantial case studies.

Chapter 3 begins to explicate and expand upon the rhetorical themes, strategies, and structures of *The Black Messiah*. It begins to bring Cleage's rhetoric and theology to life and displays its relevance in modern times. It previews some of the deeper rhetorical analysis of the specific sermons that will follow in chapters 4 and 5. But it also lays bare how Cleage's desire to reorient Christianity as a religion of resistance against white supremacy is not only simply a theological project but also a rhetorical and political one. The chapter presents Cleage's rhetorical situation and the reception history of the Black Messiah as a bridge into the sermonic materials that follow.

Chapters 4 and 5 are the weightiest chapters because they display how rhetorical criticism coupled with a Black liberationist religious reflection give us a window into the past and a roadmap into the future. Cleage's *Epistle to Stokely* is a revolutionary attempt to reclaim Christianity and deploy it as a weapon against white supremacy. It interrogates and examines a Black preacher's relationship with sacred text, a marginalized community, radical and accommodationist leadership, all under the umbrella of a complicated religious history. It is a Black revolutionary religious leader—a pastor and a prophet—in a pulpit positing liberatory possibility through sermonic militancy. It takes chapters 1, 2, and 3 to fully appreciate what Cleage is not just *saying*, but what he is *doing* with what he's saying sermonically.

In the same vein, chapter 5 reintroduces Cleage in conversation with James Cone—another person with whom Cleage shares a complicated relationship with. It lays bare some of what Cleage does as a theologian through his sermonic presentations. This chapter widens the lens on Black Liberation Theology. It's about how a pastor integrates Black Theology within a congregational context at some of the most pivotal times in the life of a church—when we experience the loss of sacred figures; figures Cleage will claim as Black Messiahs in their own right. Cleage shows himself to be a missing, misrepresented, or undervalued voice in the chorus of the Black religious community over the past fifty years. Despite helping to lay the foundation for the field, too much Black Theology is discussed and digested without Cleage's practical and prophetic perspective.

While these chapters don't cover the entirety of what *The Black Messiah* has to offer, they are a healthy start. This book serves as a stable runway by which I intend to launch much more rhetorical and religious engagement with Cleage's persona and public proclamations in all its complicated splendor.

REVIEWING CLEAGE'S ROLE AND *THE BLACK MESSIAH'S* BLIND SPOTS

The now venerable elder an ancestor, Dr. Gayraud S. Wilmore wrote a critical text on the interpretation of religious history of African Americans, *Black Religion and Black Radicalism*.[1] In the second chapter of this seminal book, he describes the evolution of "The Religion of the Slave" and muses on where race, religion, and politics encounter each other within the context of Africa itself. In this particular section of that chapter, Wilmore mentions some "quasi-religious groups that sponsor African culture" within urban centers but only lists one person in particular—Albert Cleage. Wilmore states that Cleage (and other unnamed ministers like him) serve as a reminder that "black religion is a complex concatenation of archaic, modern, and continually shifting belief systems, mythologies, and symbols, none of which can be claimed as the exclusive property of any one religious tradition—yet sharing a common core related to Africa and racial oppression."[2]

The role Cleage plays in the development and emergence of Black Liberation Theology added with the model he presents for pastoral militancy and radicality has yet to be fully accounted for. This book is one of the developing efforts to include Cleage, righteously and rightfully, within the canonized list of forerunners in Black Theology in particular and Black Church Studies in general. Cleage's rhetoric, theology, and theopolitical witness are codified within the sermonic material in *The Black Messiah*.

While, for better or worse, people like Rev. C. L. Franklin have received significant attention for their contribution to the preaching, pastoral, and political landscape (especially in Detroit), Cleage's offerings remain in the shadows. However, even in the most notable book on the life of Franklin, *Singing In A Strange Land*, Nick Salvatore deemed it necessary to give ample space to Cleage's impact as one of the "New Voices" and someone who gave "black Detroit yet another alternative to voices of the community's traditional leaders."[3] In the following chapter entitled, *A Rising Wind*, Salvatore goes on to discuss Cleage and Franklin's complicated relationship in ways I hope to document and discuss in a future project with emerging scholar Rev. R. Janae Pitts-Murdock.[4] While Cleage only mentions Franklin directly in *The Black Messiah*,[5] it is clear that their relationship and Cleage's role in Detroit and throughout the country was significant enough to be discussed more poignantly than it has heretofore. Cleage had a lot to say sermonically about figures ranging from Roy Wilkins, Adam Clayton Powell, H. Rap Brown, Marcus Garvey, Booker T. Washington, W. E. B. Dubois, A, Phillip Randolph, Whitney Young, Elijah Muhammad, Walter Reuther, Sammy Davis Jr., Reverend Wyatt T. Walker, and other notable figures during the Civil Rights and Black Power era. Cleage notably misses opportunity to highlight and engage (more explicitly) the role prominent Black women played in the era in *The Black Messiah*. He deserves significant critique for that. I would hope that a Black womanist theologian and/or Black woman rhetorical studies scholar would dig into that oversight and add the necessary nuance while putting Cleage in conversation with is sister-counterparts. And while I deal with his sermonic offerings relative to Stokely Carmichael (chapter 4), Malcolm X, and Dr. King (chapter 5), it's clear that other sermons deserve more attention than I have provided in this book. I plan to deal with the other sermons across a broader span of time and a wider array of topics. These crucial assessments and interventions make *The Black Messiah* a necessary text in the research of the intersections of rhetoric, race, and religion.

CLEAGE AND COINTELPRO'S "BLACK MESSIAH": ANOTHER OPPORTUNITY

Cleage's sermonic depictions of the dichotomy between white and Black Christianity are nuanced. They are not new. They offer us an opportunity to more deeply engage and interrogate the parameters and possibilities of Black Prophetic Rhetoric and Black Theology. When read closely, Cleage's sermonic militancy builds upon distinctions laid bare by Frederick Douglas in the appendix of his autobiography. Douglas writes,

> What I have said respecting and against religion, I mean strictly to apply to the *slave-holding religion* of this land, and with no possible reference to Christianity proper; for, between the Christianity of this land, and the Christianity of Christ, I recognize the widest possible difference—so wide, that to receive the one as good, pure, and holy, is of necessity to reject the other as bad, corrupt, and wicked. To be the friend of the one, is of necessity to be the enemy of the other. I love the pure, peaceable, and impartial Christianity of Christ: I therefore hate the corrupt, slaveholding, women-whipping, cradle-plundering, partial and hypocritical Christianity of this land.[6]

Cleage's interventions and excursions are and theological and rhetorical, religious and political. In chapter 4, I briefly discussed the COINTELPRO Papers.[7] These documents validate the hysterical nature of a governmental entity so deeply invested in its racialized and colonial oppression of people of color that they infiltrated Black radical spaces and even executed Black revolutionary figures. J. Edgar Hoover's fear was that someone would inspire Black people to effectively organize and resist their oppression resulting in the lost power and social control for those in the U.S. government. That individual (really several individuals) was considered to be a Black messiah. Cleage makes no explicit mention of COINTELPRO in his book, and the COINTELPRO papers do not become public knowledge until several years after the dismantling of the Black Power movement. This means it is unlikely that Cleage was seeking to rhetorically undermine or usurp the efforts of the federal government through his branding of Jesus as the Black Messiah. At the same time, Cleage's phraseology, rooted in his historical and theological analysis, landed exactly where the pulse of the Black Community and Black Church was beating. Cleage was demanding a reconstitution and reclamation of Black Identity in a way that remains relevant today.

Tragically, the conditions that gave necessity to the sermons and situations that add such flavor to *The Black Messiah* still exist. On November 15, 2017, the *New York Times* published an article by Khaled A. Beydoun and Justin Hansford linking the unjust infiltration and surveillance tactics (and eerily similar axe-grinding elected officials) of the late 1960s to the present. They write,

> An F.B.I. report leaked in October and scrutinized during an oversight hearing of the House Judiciary Committee on Tuesday warns of an emergent domestic terror threat sweeping the nation and threatening the lives of law enforcement officers: the "Black Identity Extremist" ("B.I.E.") movement. This designation, just recently invented by the F.B.I., is as frightening and dangerous as the bureau's infamous COINTELPRO program of the 1960s and 1970s, under which J. Edgar Hoover set out to disrupt and destroy virtually any group with the word "black" in its name. Today, entirely nonviolent black activists face violations of their civil liberties and even violence if they're deemed part of B.I.E.

The term "black messiah" is not stated explicitly. However,

> The 12-page report, prepared by the F.B.I. Domestic Terrorism Analysis Unit ... both announces the existence of the "Black Identity Extremist" movement and deems it a violent threat, asserting that black activists' grievances about racialized police violence and inequities in the criminal justice system have spurred retaliatory violence against law enforcement officers.[8]

In other words, past is prologue. And the words rendered by Cleage in the late 1960s are still instructive for those of us living in and responding to the social, political, and religious conditions before us in 2018.

MOVING THE FIELD(S) FORWARD: BROADER HORIZONS

A close reading of *The Black Messiah* opens the portal of engagement with Contemporary Rhetorical Theory, African American Religious/Prophetic Rhetoric, and Black Power Studies. It adds value to each field. It exemplifies what religious rhetoric adds to the rhetorical landscape as part of rhetoric's rehabilitation. It draws the lines of theory beyond the Jeremiadic conventions of African American religious rhetoric and reaches beyond parrhesia into nommo through reconstitutive and hermeneutical rhetoric. It also reformulates the theology of Black Power beyond the Coneian norms of Black Theology for a primarily academic audience. These sermons are the real-time manifestation of Black Theology, Black Rhetoric, and Black radical/political praxis rooted in sacred performance during one of the most critical periods in our nation's history.

Both rhetorical and religious studies need a more intentional and robust engagement with Black radical and militant rhetoric. Much of what has made its way into the academic mainstream is far too cautious and politically convenient to do justice to the fields. What is clear is that without the more radical and militant rhetoric, the more recognizable forms of discourse will not be as effective. And without a more formal and direct engagement with Black militant and prophetic rhetoric, both rhetorical and religious studies will continue to produce short-sighted scholarship that erases and marginalizes some of the most necessary expressions of social, political, and theological empowerment.

The Black Messiah is not an anomaly in the sense that there are no other figures or texts that offer an equally significant contribution to the intersections of rhetoric, race, and religion. Robert Scott's essay, "Justifying Violence—The Rhetoric of Militant Black Power,"[9] and his subsequent book, *The Rhetoric of Black Power*,[10] were groundbreaking and set forth a course for more direct engagement with rhetorical (and theological) presentations that were not relegated to the mainstreamed associations of Dr. King and Malcolm X. Lisa Corrigan's dissertation challenges us to reimagine Black Power rhetorically.[11] Andre Johnson's work on Bishop Henry McNeal Turner[12] is helpful in restructuring our understanding of and engagement with Black prophetic rhetoric and the Black Prophetic Tradition. Kimberly Pimblott's work, *Faith In Black Power*,[13] highlights the Black Power Movement within faith communities in Cairo is essential. Peniel Joseph's contribution to Black Power Studies[14] is significant but lacks the rhetorical and religious analysis needed to impact fields outside of history. To that end, this book is necessary. It models a type of engagement that fills the gaps and builds upon the research presented by others within and outside of the field.

The idea undergirding "radicalism" itself is troubling. When looked at through the lens of the oppressed, exploited, and potentially exterminated (which is the case for many people of color) what one group deems "radical" is what another group appropriates as rational. In other words, it simply makes sense for people who are in danger to employ every righteous measure (rhetorical, ideological, political, and practical) to ensure their survival and position themselves for progress. Yet, most academicians have marginalized or minimized figures like Nat Turner, Denmark Vessey, Gabriel Prosser, Henry Garnett, and underappreciated the contributions of Ida B. Wells, Harriet Tubman, Sojourner Truth, and other men and women of color who embraced militant postures in their fight for freedom.

David W. Houck and David E. Dixon's *Rhetoric, Religion, and the Civil Rights Movement*[15] takes a great stab at capturing underrepresented voices of the movement between 1954 and 1965. And even as the time period echoes the insufficient categorizing, regionalism, and moderation renders Houck and Dixon unable or unwilling to deal with figures like Cleage (and even Malcolm X). Neither is mentioned in their several hundred pages. To be sure, I am not suggesting that historians have not embraced or engaged any of these figures (some much more intently than others). What is true is, the fields of rhetoric and religion have not done enough analysis of the speeches and public discourse of the most militant figures. I have not found work on the theology and rhetoric of Stokely Carmichael (Kwame Ture), Huey P. Newton, Angela Davis, or Assata Shakur. These figures, just like Cleage, have a priceless perspective and something unique to offer the academy, the church, and the community writ large.

It is also important to consider research on native Africans and other revolutionaries whose theology and religious identities served as the foundation of their revolutionary work. They too live at the intersection of rhetoric, race, and religion with the added nuances of the African continental experience. Some of the figures who come to mind are John Chilembwe, Nelson Mandela, Queen Nzinga, Simon Kimbangu, and Alice Auma to name a few. They deserve some research attention as well.

This book is intended, in part, to broaden the trajectory of our research pallet in rhetorical and religious studies. I hope to whet the appetite of scholars who are hopeful to find shadowed figures who deserve more direct engagement. Someone should read this project, find my blind spots, and fill the gaps. I do not intend to neglect Cleage's contributions to patriarchal presentations of divine figures. The Shrine of the Black Madonna as a mural does good in terms of embracing a more righteous posture for race in religion but is not as beneficial for a rhetorical and theological engagement with constrictive gender norms. Cleage's rhetoric is not as inclusive as it should be (even when his pastoral and theological praxis is progressive for its time period). Cleage's Afrocentricity privileges Northeastern Africa (with no robust explanation as to why—which we can presuppose is a by-product of the influence of the Abrahamic faith traditions across the centuries) over and above West African faith traditions such as Ifa, Bantu, Yoruba, and Vodun (Vodoo). These are missteps in Cleage's theology and rhetoric which deserves severe critique and consideration. My hope is that scholars would pick up on these gaps and venture into them from a rhetorical and theological perspective much further than I have here.

Furthermore, the academic landscape is longing for a thorough, theorhetorical analysis of womanish[16] figures such as Fannie Lou Hamer,[17] Ella Baker,[18]

Pauli Murray, Rosa Parks, and those of that ilk. The field is wide open. People have done good rhetorical analysis of some of these figures. However, in revisiting the point, I made in chapter 1 about rhetoric's "rehabilitation" and the need for a more intentional engagement with the theorhetorical analysis of these figures is still incomplete. We cannot sufficiently appreciate their rhetorical contributions while simultaneously neglecting the racial and religious aspects that help shape them. Also, as I pointed out in chapter 2, even when rhetorical analyses have been offered, they are often too deeply vested in the Jeremiadic structures and sentiment to provide rhetoricians, theologians, and practitioners with what they need for adequate understanding.

Finally, again, *The Black Messiah* has several more sermons that I intend to engage over the next few years but are beyond the scope of this project. Nevertheless, with the content presented in these pages, I stand firm in my belief that when it comes to Black Freedom and the measures and methods of faith, Black activism, and Black radical practice, Albert Cleage Jr. was right. Jesus is Black. Militancy is divine and necessary when fighting for the freedom of the oppressed. And I look forward to offering more of Cleage's work in the near and distant future—if the Black Messiah says the same.

NOTES

1. Gayraud S. Wilmore, *Black Religion and Black Radicalism: An Interpretation of the Religious History of African Americans* (Orbis Books, 1998).
2. Wilmore, *Black Religion and Black Radicalism*, 24.
3. Nick Salvatore, *Singing in a Strange Land: CL Franklin, the Black Church, and the Transformation of America* (Little, Brown, 2007), 216.
4. Rev. R. Janae Pitts-Murdock is the Senior Pastor of Light of the World Christian Church (DOC) in Indianapolis, Indiana, and a PhD Candidate in the African American Preaching program at Christian Theological Seminary. Her dissertation topic looks at "The Theo-Rhetorical Artistry of Rev. C. L. Franklin."
5. Cleage, *The Black Messiah*, 147.
6. Frederick Douglass, *Autobiographies* (1994), 97.
7. Ward Churchill and Jim Vander Wall, *The Cointelpro Papers: Documents from the FBI's Secret Wars Against Dissent in the United States*. Vol. 8 (Cambridge, MA: South End Press, 2002).
8. https://www.nytimes.com/2017/11/15/opinion/black-identity-extremism-fbi-trump.html
9. Robert L. Scott, "Justifying Violence-The Rhetoric of Militant Black Power," *Communication Studies* 19, no. 2 (1968): 96–104.
10. Robert Lee Scott and Wayne Brockriede, eds. *The Rhetoric of Black Power* (Harper & Row, 1969).

11. Lisa Marie Corrigan, "Reimagining Black Power: Prison Manifestos and the Strategies of Regeneration in the Rewriting of Black Identity, 1969–2002." PhD diss., 2006.

12. Johnson, *The Forgotten Prophet*.

13. Pimblott, *Faith in Black Power*.

14. Joseph, *Waiting'til the Midnight Hour*.

15. Davis W. Houck and David E. Dixon, eds. *Rhetoric, Religion and the Civil Rights Movement, 1954–1965*. Vol. 1 (Baylor University Press, 2006).

16. Kimberly Johnson has done good foundational work on womanist rhetoric that should be built upon by more scholars of rhetoric and religion—see Kimberly Johnson, *The Womanist Preacher: Proclaiming Womanist Rhetoric from the Pulpit* (Lexington Books, 2017).

17. Megan Parker Brooks has recently published a wonderful rhetorical engagement with the speeches of Fannie Lou Hamer that are ripe for more theorhetorical analysis—see Megan Parker Brooks, *A Voice That Could Stir an Army: Fannie Lou Hamer and the Rhetoric of the Black Freedom Movement* (University Press of Mississippi, 2014).

18. Mittie K. Carey has offered a preliminary reading of the rhetorics of Ella Baker that I hope will be expanded—see Mittie K. Carey, "The Parallel Rhetorics of Ella Baker," *Southern Communication Journal* 79, no. 1 (2014): 27–40.

Bibliography

Bailey, Randall C. "Beyond Identification: The Use of Africans in Old Testament Poetry and Narratives." *Stony the Road We Trod* (1991): 165–186.
———. "Is That Any Name for a Nice Hebrew Boy?" *Exodus* 2 (1995): 1–10.
Bitzer, Lloyd. "The Rhetorical Situation." In *Contemporary Rhetorical Theory: A Reader*, edited by John Louis Lucaites, Celeste Michelle Condit, and Sally Caudill, 217–231. New York: The Guilford Press, 1999.
Blake, Cecil. *The African Origins of Rhetoric*. Routledge, 2010.
Blum, Edward J., and Paul Harvey. *The Color of Christ: The Son of God and the Saga of Race in America*. UNC Press Books, 2012.
Boesak, Allan Aubrey. *Farewell to Innocence: A Socio-Ethical Study on Black Theology and Black Power*. Wipf and Stock Publishers, 2015.
Brooks, Maegan Parker. *A Voice that Could Stir an Army: Fannie Lou Hamer and the Rhetoric of the Black Freedom Movement*. Univ. Press of Mississippi, 2014.
Brueggemann, Walter. *Prophetic Imagination: Revised Edition*. Fortress Press, 1978.
Carey, John J. "Black Theology: An Appraisal of the Internal and External Issues." *Theological Studies* 33, no. 4 (1972): 684–697.
Carey, Mittie K. "The Parallel Rhetorics of Ella Baker." *Southern Communication Journal* 79, no. 1 (2014): 27–40.
Carpenter, Delores, and Rev Nolan E. Williams, eds. *African American Heritage Hymnal*. GIA Publications, 2001.
Chapman, Mark L. *Christianity on Trial: African-American Religious thought before and after Black Power*. Wipf and Stock Publishers, 2006.
Charland, Maurice. "Constitutive Rhetoric: The Case of the Peuple Quebecois." *Quarterly Journal of Speech* 73, no. 2 (1987): 133–150.
Chester, Andrew. "High Christology–Whence, When and Why?" *Early Christianity* 2, no. 1 (2011): 22–50.
Clark, Jawanza, Albert Cleage Jr. *The Black Madonna and Child*. Palgrave MacMillan. 2016.
Cleage, Albert B. *The Black Messiah*. New York: Sheed and Ward, 1969.

———. *Black Christian Nationalism: New Directions for the Black Church.* Luxor Publishers of the Pan-African Orthodox Christian Church, 1987.
Collins, John J. *The Bible after Babel: Historical Criticism in a Postmodern Age.* Wm. B. Eerdmans Publishing, 2005.
Cone, James H. *Martin and Malcolm and America: A Dream or a Nightmare.* Orbis Books, 1993.
———. *Black Theology and Black Power.* Orbis Books, 1997.
———. *Said I Wasn't Gonna Tell Nobody: The Making of a Black Theologian.* Orbis Books, 2018.
Corrigan, Lisa Marie. "Reimagining Black Power: Prison Manifestos and the Strategies of Regeneration in the Rewriting of Black Identity, 1969–2002." PhD diss., 2006.
Darsey, James. *The Prophetic Tradition and Radical Rhetoric in America.* NYU Press, 1999.
DeSantis, Alan D. "An Amostic Prophecy: Fredrick Douglass' The Meaning of July Fourth for the Negro." *Journal of Communication & Religion* 22, no. 1 (1999): 65–92.
De Velasco, Antonio Raul. "Rethinking Perelman's Universal Audience: Political Dimensions of a Controversial Concept." *Rhetoric Society Quarterly* 35, no. 2 (2005): 47–64.
Dillard, Angela D. *Faith in the City: Preaching Radical Social Change in Detroit.* University of Michigan Press, 2007.
Douglass, Frederick. *Autobiographies.* Vol. 68. Library of America, 1994.
Douglas, Kelly Brown. *The Black Christ.* Vol. 9. Orbis Books, 1994.
Ellis, Carl F. *Beyond Liberation: The Gospel in the Black American Experience.* InterVarsity Press, 1983.
Finkelman, Paul, ed. *Encyclopedia of African American History: 5-Volume Set.* Vol. 1. OUP USA, 2009.
Finlan, Stephen. *Problems with Atonement: The Origins of, and Controversy About, the Atonement Doctrine.* Liturgical Press, 2005.
George, G. M. *Stolen Legacy: Greek Philosophy is Stolen Egyptian Philosophy.* African World Press, 1993.
Gutierrez, Gustavo. *On Job: God-Talk and the Suffering of the Innocent.* Maryknoll, NY: Orbis Books, 1987.
Harvey, Graham. "Synagogues of the Hebrews: 'Good Jews' in the Diaspora." In: Jones, Sian and Pearce, Sarah eds. *Jewish Local Patriotism and Self-Identification in the Graeco-Roman Period. Library of Second Temple Studies (31)*, edited by Sian Jones and Sarah Pearce, 132–147. Sheffield: Sheffield Academic Press, 1998.
Hendricks, Obery. *The Politics of Jesus: Rediscovering the True Revolutionary Nature of Jesus' Teachings and How They Have Been Corrupted.* Image, 2006.
Houck, Davis W., and David E. Dixon, eds. *Rhetoric, Religion and the Civil Rights Movement, 1954–1965.* Vol. 1. Baylor University Press, 2006.
Howard-Pitney, David. *African American Jeremiad Rev: Appeals For Justice In America.* Temple University Press, 2009.

Ibrahim, Awad El Karim M. "'Whassup, Homeboy?' Joining the African Diaspora: Black English as a Symbolic Site of Identification and Language Learning." In *Black Linguistics: Language, Society and Politics in Africa and the Americas*, edited by Arnetha Ball, Sinfree Makoni, Geneva Smitherman, and Arthur K. Spears, 181–197. Routledge, 2005.

Johnson, Andre E. *The Forgotten Prophet: Bishop Henry McNeal Turner and the African American Prophetic Tradition*, Lexington Books, 2012.

———. "God is a Negro: The (Rhetorical) Black Theology of Bishop Henry McNeal Turner." *Black Theology* 13, no. 1 (2015): 29–40.

Johnson, Kimberly. *The Womanist Preacher: Proclaiming Womanist Rhetoric from the Pulpit*. Lexington Books. 2017.

Jones, William R. *Is God a White Racist?: A Preamble to Black Theology*. Beacon Press, MA, 1997.

Joseph, Peniel E. *Waiting'til the Midnight Hour: A Narrative History of Black Power in America*. Macmillan, 2007.

Krasevac, Edward L. "'Christology From Above'And'Christology From Below'." *The Thomist: A Speculative Quarterly Review* 51, no. 2 (1987): 299–306.

Leff, Michael. "Words the Most Like Things: Iconicity and the Rhetorical Text." *Western Journal of Communication (includes Communication Reports)* 54, no. 3 (1990): 252–273.

———. "Hermeneutical Rhetoric." *Rhetoric and Hermeneutics in Our Time: A Reader* (1997): 196–214.

Leff, Michael, and Andrew Sachs. "Words the Most Like Things: Iconicity and the Rhetorical Text." *Western Journal of Communication (includes Communication Reports)* 54, no. 3 (1990): 252–273.

Leff, Michael C., and Ebony A. Utley. "Instrumental and Constitutive Rhetoric in Martin Luther King Jr.'s" Letter from Birmingham Jail"." *Rhetoric & Public Affairs* 7, no. 1 (2004): 37–51.

Lemelle, Anthony. "One Drop Rule." In *The Blackwell Encyclopedia of Sociology*, edited by G. Ritzer. 2007, https://doi.org/10.1002/9781405165518.wbeoso011.

Lewis, Myran E. "Cleage: A Rhetorical Study of Black Religious Nationalism." Ph.D. diss., The Ohio State University, 1974.

Lloyd, Vincent, ed. *Race and Political Theology*. Stanford University Press, 2012.

Malcioln, José V. *The African Origin of Modern Judaism: From Hebrews to Jews*. Africa World Pr, 1996.

McGuire, Danielle L. *At the Dark End of the Street: Black Women, Rape, and Resistance—A New History of the Civil Rights Movement from Rosa Parks to the Rise of Black Power*. Vintage, 2010.

McWilliams, Weldon IV. *The Kingdom At Hand: Black Theology, The Pan African Orthodox Christian Church and their Implications on the Black Church*. Denver, CO: Outskirts Press, 2017.

Mills, Charles W. *Black Rights/White Wrongs: The Critique of Racial Liberalism*. Oxford University Press, 2017.

Minifee, Paul A. ""I Took Up the Hymn-Book": Rhetoric of Hymnody in Jarena Lee's Call to Preach." *Advances in the History of Rhetoric* 18, no. 1 (2015): 1–28.

Nicholson, Ernest W. *God and His People: Covenant and Theology in the Old Testament*. Oxford University Press, 1988.

Nunley, Vorris L., and Vorris Nunley. *Keepin' it Hushed: The Barbershop and African American Hush Harbor Rhetoric*. Wayne State University Press, 2011.

Pimblott, Kerry. *Faith in Black Power: Religion, Race, and Resistance in Cairo, Illinois*. University Press of Kentucky, 2017.

Raboteau, Albert J. *Slave Religion: The" Invisible Institution" in the Antebellum South*. Oxford University Press, 2004.

Roberts, James Deotis. *Liberation and Reconciliation: A Black Theology*. Westminster John Knox Press, 2005.

Salvatore, Nick. *Singing in a Strange Land: CL Franklin, the Black Church, and the Transformation of America*. Little, Brown, 2007.

Scott, Robert L. "Justifying Violence-the Rhetoric of Militant Black Power." *Communication Studies* 19, no. 2 (1968): 96–104.

Scott, Robert Lee, and Wayne Brockriede, eds. *The Rhetoric of Black Power*. Harper & Row, 1969.

Simmons, Martha. *Preaching with Sacred Fire: An Anthology of African American Sermons, 1750 to the Present*. WW Norton & Company, 2010.

Sleeper, Charles Freeman. *Black Power and Christian Responsibility: Some Biblical Foundations for Social Ethics*. Abingdon Press, 1968.

Smith, Arthur L. "Some Characteristics of the Black Religious Audience." *Communication Monographs* 37 (1970): 207–210.

———. "Markings of an African Concept of Rhetoric." *Communication Quarterly* 19, no. 2 (1971): 13–18.

Sunnemark, Fredrik. *Ring Out Freedom!: The Voice of Martin Luther King, Jr. and the Making of the Civil Rights Movement*. Indiana University Press, 2003.

Thomas, Frank A. *They Like to Never Quit Praisin' God: The Role of Celebration in Preaching (Revised, Updated)*. The Pilgrim Press, 2013.

———. *Introduction to the Practice of African American Preaching*. Abingdon Press, 2016.

Thurman, Howard. *Jesus and the Disinherited*. Beacon Press, 1996.

Turner, Henry McNeal. "God is a Negro." *Voice of Missions* 1 (1898): 154–155.

Walker, Aswad. "Princes Shall Come out of Egypt: A Theological Comparison of Marcus Garvey and Reverend Albert B. Cleage Jr." *Journal of Black Studies* 39, no. 2 (2008): 194–251.

Ward, Churchill, and Van der Wall, J. *The COINTELPRO Papers: Documents from the FBI's Secret Wars against Domestic Dissent*. Boston: South End Press, 1990.

Ward, Hiley H. *Prophet of the Black Nation*. Pilgrim Press, 1969.

Warnock, Raphael G. *Divided Mind of the Black Church: Theology, Piety, and Public Witness*. Vol. 9. NYU Press, 2013.

Washington, Joseph R. *The Politics of God*. Vol. 326. Beacon Press, 1969.

Weaver, J. Denny. *The Nonviolent Atonement*. Wm. B. Eerdmans Publishing, 2011.

West, Cornel, and Christa Buschendorf. *Black Prophetic Fire*. Beacon Press, 2015.

White, James Boyd. *When Words Lose Their Meaning: Constitutions and Reconstitutions of Language, Character, and Community*. University of Chicago Press, 2012.

Wilmore, Gayraud S. *Black Religion and Black Radicalism: An Interpretation of the Religious History of African Americans*. Maryknoll, NY: Orbis Books, 1998.

Wilmore, Gayraud S., and James H. Cone, eds. *Black Theology: A Documentary History, 1966–1979*. Vol. 1. Orbis Books, 1979.

Woodson, Carter G. *The Mis-Education of the Negro*. Book Tree, 2006.

Index

African American (Black) Preaching, 18, 28, 32, 68–69, 76, 108, 111
African American Heritage Hymnal, 76
Afrocentricity, 40, 89, 151
Aldridge, J. William, 64
Allen, Richard, 132
Aristotle, 39; Aristotelian, 4, 8, 34, 100; neo-Aristotelian, 11, 31, 34
Asante, Molefi, 5, 28, 31, 38, 81
Aslan, Reza, 64
Augustine of Hippo, 61–62, 64
Auma, Alice, 151

Baker, Ella, 151
Ball, Arnetha F., 46
Ballot or the Bullet (Speech), 121, 141
Bitzer, Lloyd, 30
Black Christian Nationalism, 2, 19, 53, 71, 122–23
Black Freedom Movement (Struggle), 9, 14, 20, 54–57, 80, 96, 111, 118, 120, 132–35
Black Hebrew-Israelites, 34, 38–39
Black Liberationist Rhetoric, 54, 62
Black (Liberation) Theology, 1–8, 10, 12–16, 18–22, 38, 58–63, 65, 71, 77, 85–86, 92, 94, 112, 117, 126–27, 133, 138, 141, 145–50
Black Linguistics, 46–47

Black Muslims, 19, 64
Black Panther Party, 58
Black Power Movement, 2, 8–14, 21–22, 33–34, 54–58, 60, 64, 75, 78, 81–84, 96, 98, 104, 107–8, 117, 122–23, 137, 148–50
Black Power Studies, 21–22, 149–50
Black Prophetic Tradition, 6, 9, 23, 46–48, 61, 68, 71, 107–8, 123, 150
Black Social Gospel, 6–7
Blum, Edward, 60
Borders, William Holmes, 132
Boston Mosque (Temple 11), 119
Brown, H. Rap, 66, 147
Brown-Douglas, Kelly, 5, 19, 77
Brueggemann, Walter, 60
Buschendorf, Christa, 46–47

Carey, John J., 62–63
Carmichael, Stokely, 56–58, 70, 82, 111, 117, 144, 147, 151
Chapman, Mark, 7, 55, 80
Charland, Maurice, 17, 28–42, 46–48
Chilembwe, John, 151
Christology, 15, 98–100
Chui, Mbiyu, 4
Church for the Fellowship of All People, 106
Cicero, 31

civil rights movement, 2, 9–10, 12–14, 54–55, 57–58, 78, 82, 93, 122, 132, 139, 151
Clark, Jawanza Eric, 5, 14–16, 19–20
Cobb, Charles E., 54, 65
COINTELPRO, 78, 148–49
Committee for Racial Justice Now, 54, 65
Cone, James Hal, 4, 10, 13, 18–19, 21, 61–64, 112, 117–30, 132–36, 138–46, 149
contemporary rhetorical theory, 8, 21–23, 27–28, 36, 47, 49, 149
Corrigan, Lisa, 150

Darsey, James, 4, 6, 41–42, 47, 70, 87
Davis, Angela, 78, 151
Davis, Sammy, Jr., 137, 147
Delaney, Martin, 53
De Pass, Stephen C., 65
Dexter Avenue Baptist Church, 119
Dillard, Angela, 5, 20
Dixon, David E., 151
Douglas, Frederick, 46, 132, 148
DuBois, W. E. B., 119, 147
Duke, Nelson C., 126

Eagleton, Terry, 29, 37
Einstein, Albert, 31
Ellis, Carl F., 55–56

Fanon, Frantz, 41
Foucault, Michael, 42–45
Franklin, C. L., 147
Freedom Now Party, 139

Gardiner, James J., 62
Garnett, Henry Highland, 150
Garnett, Marcus, 3, 70, 96, 147
Gehrke, Pat J., 43–44
Gorgianic, 34. *See also* Sophistic

Hamer, Fannie Lou, 151
Hampton, Fred, 78
Hare, Julia, 45

Harvey, Paul, 60
Henry, Milton, 57
Heschel, Abraham Joshua, 87
Hill, Kamasi, 5
Hobson, Christopher, 68
Holmes, Barbara, 31
Hoover, J. Edgar, 78, 148–49
Hopkins, Dwight, 13
Houck, David W., 151

James, George G. M., 86
Jarratt, Susan C., 43–44
Johns, Vernon, 132
Johnson, Andre, 4, 31, 48, 68, 83, 87, 150
Jones, Major, 62
Jones, William, 13, 19
Joseph, Peniel, 56–57, 150
Judy, Marvin T., 66

Kimbangu, Simon, 151
King, Martin Luther, Jr., 10, 56, 58, 117–19, 121, 123, 125–27, 130, 132–42

ladder of signification, 119
Lee, Rev. Jarena, 76
Leff, Michael Charles, 5–6, 17, 28, 31–32, 34–35, 42, 58, 90
Lewis, Myran Elizabeth, 4–5, 8, 20
Lucas, Lawrence, 21

Maat/Mayet, 39
Makoni, Sinfree, 46
Malcolm X, 3, 10, 13, 33, 46, 56, 66, 70–71, 97, 117–44, 147, 150–51
Mandela, Nelson, 123, 151Marshall, Calvin, 21
Mass Communication, 29, 134
Mays, Benjamin E., 132
McGuire, Danielle, 99
McWilliams, Weldon, 9, 19–20
Message to the Grassroots (Speech), 121, 125
Minifee, Paula A., 76

Montgomery Bus Boycott, 57, 139
Muhammad, Elijah, 55, 123, 127, 147

Nation of Islam, 121, 128, 139
Nelson, (Bishop) Kimathi, 10
Newton, Huey P., 151
nommo, 9, 58, 75, 110, 149
nonviolent atonement theory, 135–36
Northern Grassroots Leadership Conference, 121
Nunley, Vorris, 28, 44–45, 47

Pan-African Orthodox Christian Church (PAOCC), 3
Parks, Rosa, 57, 152
parrhesia, 9, 28, 37, 40, 42–48, 50, 58, 70, 75, 127, 149
Paul, the Apostle (of Tarsus), 3, 8, 39, 43, 58, 65–66, 84, 102, 131–32; Pauline Christianity, 64, 104–8
Pimblott, Kerry, 7, 55, 150
Pitts-Murdock, R. Janae, 147
Plato (Platonic), 39, 42, 46
political theology, 19, 91–94
Powell, Adam Clayton, 126, 132, 147
Prosser, Gabriel, 150
Ptah-hotep, 39

Queen Nzinga, 151
Quintilian, 36

radicalism, 35, 37, 41–42, 45, 47–48, 138, 150; Black radicalism, 63, 77, 107, 146; democratic radicalism, 44–46
Randolph, A. Phillip, 147
Ransom, Reverdy C., 132
Reuther, Walter, 147
rhetoric: African American (Black) Religious, 4–6, 21–22, 28, 32, 44–49; classical, 5, 27–28, 34–36, 42, 48; constitutive, 9, 16, 18, 37, 39–41, 75, 149; habitation of, 31; hermeneutical, 17–18, 71, 88, 90–91, 93; prophetic, 4–6, 9, 13, 18, 20–22, 33–34, 40–43, 46–48, 58, 60–61, 66, 68, 71, 76–77, 87–88, 102, 110, 112, 127, 148–50
rhetorical appropriation, 82–83
rhetorical culture, 40–41
rhetorical pedagogy, 33–34
rhetorical philosophy, 33
rhetorical reconstruction, 87–88
rhetorical sequencing, 118–22
rhetorical situation, 1, 12, 28, 30, 36, 47, 58–61, 77, 146
rhetorical theology, 83, 94–96
rhetorical theory, 8, 21–24, 27–30, 32, 34–38, 40, 47–49
Roberts, J. Deotis, 13, 62

Sachs, Andrew, 5–6
Salvatore, Nick, 147
sermonic militancy, 1, 13–14, 19, 137–38, 148
Shakur, Assata, 151
Shrine of the Black Madonna, 2, 5, 20, 53, 55, 57, 65, 84–85, 126, 151
Simmons, Martha, 69
Sleeper, C. Freeman, 62
Smitherman, Geneva, 46
Socrates, 39, 45–46
Sophistic, 34. *See also* Gorgianic
Spears, Arthur K., 46
student non-violent coordinating committee (SNCC), 57–58
Sunnemark, Fredrik, 119

Temme, Jon M., 61–62, 67
Terrill, Robert, 46
Thomas, Frank, 18, 25, 28, 31–32, 69
Thurman, Howard, 106–7
Truth, Sojourner, 150
Tubman, Harriet, 150
Turner, Bishop Henry McNeal, 53, 64, 83, 96, 150
Turner, Nat, 46

United Church Herald Journal, 66
Universal Audience, 82

Universal Negro Improvement Society, 96

Veblen, Thorstein, 35
Vessey, Denmark, 150
Vivian, Bradford, 43–44

Walker, Aswad, 3, 96
Walker, David, 46, 53
Walker, Wyatt T., 137, 147
Walzer, Arthur, 42–44

Ward, H. H., 4, 11–12, 53
Washington, Booker T., 147
Wells, Ida B., 150
West, Cornel, 45–47, 87
Wilkins, Roy, 137, 147
Wilmore, Gayraud, 21, 146–47
Womanist Theology, 62, 76, 147
Woodson, Carter G., 2
Wright, Jr., Jeremiah, 18

Young, Whitney, 147

About the Author

Rev. Earle J. Fisher, PhD, is a native of Benton Harbor, Michigan, and a resident of Memphis, Tennessee since 1999. Pastor Earle is the senior pastor of Abyssinian Baptist Church and an adjunct instructor of Religion, Communication, and African American Studies at several local colleges and universities. Dr. Fisher is married to Denise Lloyd-Fisher and has one son, Jalen Fisher.

www.ingramcontent.com/pod-product-compliance
Lightning Source LLC
Chambersburg PA
CBHW020124010526
44115CB00008B/957